Reaching an Understanding

Innovations in How We View Reading Assessment

John P. Sabatini, Tenaha O'Reilly,
and Elizabeth R. Albro

ROWMAN & LITTLEFIELD EDUCATION

A division of
ROWMAN & LITTLEFIELD PUBLISHERS, INC.
Lanham • New York • Toronto • Plymouth, UK

Published by Rowman & Littlefield Education
A division of Rowman & Littlefield Publishers, Inc.
A wholly owned subsidiary of The Rowman & Littlefield Publishing Group, Inc.
4501 Forbes Boulevard, Suite 200, Lanham, Maryland 20706
www.rowman.com

10 Thornbury Road, Plymouth PL6 7PP, United Kingdom

British Library Cataloguing in Publication Information Available

Library of Congress Cataloging-in-Publication Data

Reaching an understanding : innovations in how we view reading assessment /
edited by John P. Sabatini, Tenaha O'Reilly, and Elizabeth R. Albro.
p. cm.
ISBN 978-1-4758-0100-2 (cloth : alk. paper) -- ISBN 978-1-4758-0101-9
(pbk. : alk. paper) -- ISBN 978-1-4758-0102-6 (electronic)
1. Reading--Ability testing. 2. Reading--Remedial teaching. I. Sabatini,
John P. II. O'Reilly, Tenaha. III. Albro, Elizabeth, 1966-
LB1050.46.R37 2012
372.48--dc23

2012021771

∞™ The paper used in this publication meets the minimum requirements of American National Standard for Information Sciences—Permanence of Paper for Printed Library Materials, ANSI/NISO Z39.48-1992.

Printed in the United States of America

Literacy represents both a national aspiration and a set of human practices anchored in space and time. From this dual existence literacy has acquired both a sociopolitical dimension, associated with its role within society and the ways in which it is deployed for political, cultural, and economic ends; and a psychological dimension, associated with cognitive and affective properties that lead to greater or lesser individual motivation for and competence with writing and print.

Richard L. Venezky, 1991, p. 46

Contents

List of Figures

List of Tables

Preface

Assessment Technology and Culture in the Twenty-first Century

Humans are tool and technology inventors and users. It is the foundation of our culture and society. In my own past, I learned the trade of shoe repairing from my uncle. I learned how to use the tools of the craft, just as surgeons use the tools of their profession. There are commonalities and differences in the tools of the two professions. The types of knives used by a cobbler versus those used by a surgeon represent one of the differences, though in both domains, the blades are crafted and tooled to the situation and purpose of their use. One commonality that transcends the domains is that it is more dangerous to use a dull blade than a sharp one.

But simple tools and craft knowledge eventually yield to more advanced technologies and systems, which themselves are embedded in more sophisticated contexts of knowledge of practice. The surgeon's scalpel is sometimes replaced by the advanced technology of laser surgery. The stitching of small wounds with sutures, however, continues to be performed by hand, and still largely resembles hand sewing, while in shoe repair the stitching of soles is carried out by a complexly machined stitching device.

These are small illustrations of how tools and technologies advance across time, transforming and evolving with the systems from which they stem. Eventually, technologies reach a level of maturity where they become inseparable from the culture in which they are embedded. Modern-day medicine is one of many domains in which such integration of technology and the culture of practice are seamlessly intertwined.

In editing this volume, we had hoped to report on a new sophistication of the tools and technologies of assessment as applied to the issue of reading comprehension, i.e., to provide a slick "product catalog" of such techniques as might be proffered by a surgical supply representative to doctors of advanced, modern-day medicine. But we are not there yet. The contributors to this volume are the pioneers innovating and inventing a new field. They stem from interdisciplinary, scientific craft trades—education, psychology, linguistics, neuroscience, psychometrics, statistics—learning to work together to build new tools and technologies to address a larger social purpose—measuring and helping to promote high levels of reading proficiency across our school-age populace.

Like the dawn of the industrial or digital revolutions, one can see the inevitability of a new age on the horizon, but one cannot see the shape or nature yet—the Internet or iPad of assessment technologies is still waiting to be invented. There are likely a few steam engines described in this volume, stepping-stones to a jet-engine future. You will read stories of trials, some successful, some still struggling to ensure that the promise and potential of the capability fits the context of its educational use, whether it aims to serve the individual student, the classroom teacher, the school administrator, or the policy maker.

There should be, however, no doubt about the trajectory of this enterprise. We will not raise achievement levels in the next generation without embracing new ways of learning and assessment. The wisdom of past educational practice may be the foundation of the future, but it must be enhanced with new tools of assessment to provide feedback for the entire system to improve.

In this era of the Common Core Standards, Race to the Top, and the Reading for Understanding initiative, the craft of assessment as it exists today must yield to more advanced technologies of measurement. The stakes are higher, and blunt instruments will not suffice. Local craft solutions, though still imbued with the wisdom of practice, are proving insufficient to address the low educational outcomes that are epidemic in our children, youth, and adults, limiting their potential and our society's long-term stability (Kirsch, Braun, Yamamoto, & Sum, 2007).

The large-scale state consortium assessment systems under development are anticipated engines of intervention and reform; they will have impact. Whether that impact is on the whole positive or negative is in large part a function of whether these new, more advanced tools and technologies are embraced and shaped by the professionals that are destined to use them—the policy makers and practitioners that comprise the educational industry. In these volumes, we make one step toward preparing for these eventualities, introducing some ideas and innovations that will impact the future.

—John Sabatini

REFERENCES

Kirsch, I., Braun, H., Yamamoto, K., & Sum, A. (2007). *America's perfect storm: Three forces changing our nation's future.* Princeton, NJ: Educational Testing Service.

Venezky, R. L. (1991). The development of literacy in the industrialized nations of the West. In R. Barr, M L. Kamil, P. B. Mosenthal, & P. D. Pearson)Eds.), *Handbook of Reading Research*, (Vol. 2, pp. 46–67). New York: Longman.

Acknowledgments

This volume was preceded by a conference on Assessing Reading in the Twenty-first Century, held in Philadelphia in April 2008. We are extremely grateful to the Institute of Education Sciences and Educational Testing Service for sponsoring and supporting this conference. We would also like to thank the many individuals who organized, presented, and served as discussants and as a rapt audience at the conference. We are grateful to the chapter reviewers for their dedication to the field, and to those who provided invaluable feedback along the way, and to Jennifer Lentini, for her work in coordinating, reviewing, and editing this volume. Finally, we would like to thank the authors who contributed chapters to this volume. Without the innovative work they have conducted in the areas of reading comprehension, reading assessment, and technology, this volume would not have been possible.

Introduction

This book concludes a two-volume series on reading comprehension and assessment. The impetus for these volumes emerged from a joint IES and ETS conference that gathered experts from a wide range of disciplines to rethink the construct of reading comprehension and how it is measured in the twenty-first century. The chapters contained in volume I of this series, *Measuring Up: Advances in How We Assess Reading Ability*, are focused on developing coherence in the construct of reading comprehension and exploring ways to advance the science of assessment and the proficient reader. The perspectives represented in volume I are largely theoretical in nature; they help define the scope of the problem and they propose alternative solutions for moving the field forward.

In contrast, volume II represents some early attempts to apply theory to help guide the development of new assessments and measurement models. Volume II is divided into two sections: Section I is titled "Assessment, Learning, and Instruction: Connecting Text, Task, and Reader/Learner," and section II is titled "How to Build for the Future." These sections are further contextualized in the discussion below.

OVERVIEW OF VOLUME II: SECTIONS I AND II

Section I: Assessment, Learning, and Instruction: Connecting Text, Task, and Reader/Learner

The advent of information technologies such as the Internet has dramatically increased access to information from multiple sources. In turn, the skills needed to reconcile and synthesize different sources have increased given the wide variation in source quality. Despite this trend, many existing reading comprehension assessments only measure a student's ability to comprehend a single text in isolation. Addressing this limitation, Lawless, Goldman, Gomez, Manning, and Braasch have designed a reading comprehension assessment that focuses on students' ability to comprehend and integrate information from multiple text sources. While multiple text comprehension undoubtedly draws on similar skills involved in comprehending single texts, there are also differences.

Lawless and colleagues have used an evidence-centered design process to create an assessment architecture for multiple text comprehension. Their model of multiple text comprehension includes a constellation of skills related to interpreting tasks, followed by gathering, sourcing, analyzing, synthesizing, integrating, and applying information. Empirical examinations of the model indicate it is able to distinguish key differences between skilled and less skilled readers that might be overlooked by some traditional measures of reading comprehension.

Reading is a purpose-driven activity that helps readers identify what is and what is not important to attend to. Despite the well-known influence of reader purpose on text comprehension, very few reading assessments incorporate authentic purposes for reading into the design. In many traditional reading assessments the purpose for reading is simply to answer reading comprehension questions. Realizing these and other limitations, Sheehan and O'Reilly have proposed the development of a cognitively based assessment of reading that measures comprehension under various purposes for reading.

Sheehan and O'Reilly present a scenario-based reading comprehension assessment that was based on a review of the research in the learning sciences. The skills cover the fundamental reading abilities (e.g., decoding) up to higher-level critical thinking skills. By incorporating empirically supported reading strategies and scaffolding techniques into the design, the assessment has the potential to have indirect, positive influences on instruction. Early data suggests the approach seems promising in this regard.

Traditionally, reading comprehension is assessed after the student has read a passage or document. While this test format is invaluable for measuring the *end product* of reading comprehension, it does not take advantage of opportunities for measuring the processes that occur *while* a student reads. Gaining more insight into the process of reading is potentially fruitful not only for understanding how students form a mental representation of text, but it may also be potentially diagnostic and revealing of particular reading subskill weaknesses, misconceptions, gaps, or fundamental errors in understanding.

Building on these issues, Millis and Magliano have conceptualized and built a tool for assessing reading comprehension while it unfolds. Their system, called RSAT, is an automated program that presents a text one sentence at a time and periodically asks the student questions based on their understanding up to that point. Questions are sometimes general in nature to probe the student's current thinking, while other questions are more specific and focus on key events or causes in the text. These responses can be very revealing (and instructionally relevant), as they may provide indications of whether the student is linking what they just read to earlier parts of the text and of whether they are connecting the text to their existing knowledge—two key pieces of evidence for deep reading. Empirical examinations of the algorithms seem promising.

Vocabulary is a critical component of reading comprehension, so it is no surprise that some off-the-shelf reading comprehension assessments include a separate test of vocabulary as a part of the battery. While traditional measures of vocabulary are useful for estimating the size of a particular student's vocabulary, it grossly underestimates the intricate complexity of vocabulary knowledge. Deane argues that vocabulary acquisition is not an "all-or-none" process—the intricate meanings of words are learned over time and to varying degrees. At lower levels of vocabulary knowledge, a student may be able to correctly identify whether a word is grammatical given a particular context, but they may not even know what topic it belongs to. Similarly, a student may know that a particular word belongs to some topic, but they do not know what its function is.

Given these issues, Deane is building assessments based on a more fine-grained model of vocabulary knowledge and acquisition that elaborates on the basic notions of breadth and depth constructs. Several models have observed that students can vary in how many words they know (breadth) and at what level they know them (depth). These models assume that words can be learned to varying degrees, so that the student can have partial word knowledge. This partial knowledge is, however, complicated by the fact that words co-occur and are organized within topics. Understanding the meaning of a particular word is related to the topic and domain from which it is selected. Following on this line of reasoning and employing natural language processing approaches, Deane and his colleagues are creating automated tools that may prove useful for identifying what words are likely to be learned together.

Identifying children who are struggling to read is a critical function of assessment. If identified appropriately (and early), students can be given more intensive and focused instruction targeted to their particular weaknesses. Compton, Elleman, and Catts describe the documented success of current measures at identifying children at high risk of developing early word reading difficulties, and the need for measures to identify students with "late-emerging" reading disabilities. For many readers, these late-emerging disabilities are correlated with reading comprehension problems.

The chapter by Compton, Elleman, and Catts provides evidence for the existence of three subgroups of "late-emerging" reading disabilities, and as in the Cain and Oakhill chapter (volume I), the authors evaluate which subskills (or subprocesses in their terms) uniquely predict membership in the different subgroups. The authors explore candidate subskills at both the word reading and comprehension levels, including subword orthographic-phonological connections and a set of executive function skills. Many of these subskills are not currently measured in diagnostic assessments used with young readers, and there is a need for additional research to develop appropriate measures so that students at risk for late-emerging comprehension difficulties can be identified early and supported with targeted instruction.

Connor, Morrison, Fishman, and Schatschneider illustrate how current assessments are being used to inform instruction. A challenge confronted by most teachers is how to digest the knowledge that can be gleaned from current assessments and used to provide individually targeted assessment. Building on a line of research that identifies both the types and amount of instruction needed to support readers with different profiles of reading skills and vocabulary knowledge, this team has built a software system that groups students according to their instructional needs and indexes teachers' current curricular materials to these needs. Using this system to guide instruction over the course of a full school year leads to improved reading achievement for students. This chapter explores whether differential uses of the system by teachers is associated with different patterns of student achievement.

Understanding the reasons why students struggle to comprehend text, and describing the heterogeneity of those reasons, is the focus of the Cutting and Scarborough chapter. As is true of many of the chapters in this volume, the authors frame their discussion as an expansion of the Simple View of Reading. While the two-factor explanation offered by this theoretical model has many benefits as well as empirical support, the authors argue that the listening comprehension factor of this model is multidimensional and deserves systematic and close attention.

In addition, Cutting and Scarborough assert that the cognitive skills often labeled as "executive function" contribute to reading comprehension deficits and provide descriptive data of the prevalence of different profiles. As in the Keenan chapter (volume I), Cutting and Scarborough also describe how different reading comprehension assessments provide different classifications of readers, such that an individual identified as a poor comprehender on one assessment is identified as a good comprehender on another assessment.

Trying to understand the sources of these discrepancies in the characteristics of the assessments and the readers improves our theoretical explanations for comprehension failures. At the same time, the Cutting and Scarborough chapter raises important considerations for current users of assessments and cautions the diagnostician to use multiple measures of reading comprehension skill when making decisions about the presence or absence of a reading disability.

Section II: How to Build for the Future

Most measures of reading comprehension serve the purpose of describing where individual learners fall on a predetermined scale. That is, students are understood to be reading at a certain level as compared to their peers, whether that be defined as advanced, proficient, basic, or below basic, or on a numerical continuum. Wilson and Moore argue, however, that new psychometric models can be used to broaden our understanding of what properties of the item or individual contribute to responses to items.

Calling this model explanatory, Wilson and Moore describe how features of an individual, such as gender or English learner status, can be used to predict how an individual might perform on a test. Using the explanatory approach also allows psychometricians to examine whether characteristics of the items themselves, such as genre or reading task, predict performance. This chapter walks the reader through an application of these two explanatory approaches and illustrates how these approaches may add value in some instances, but may not in others. This discussion of novel approaches to conceptualizing psychometric analysis fits well with theoretical understandings of the complexity of factors that contribute to reading comprehension.

As noted throughout this volume, assessments can serve critical diagnostic functions. At the same time, current measures of reading comprehension are not well designed to serve as diagnostic tools. Gorin and Svetina discuss a novel approach to test construction, *cognitive psychometric models* (CPM), in which items and responses are designed to identify why students are performing poorly. This model has been used successfully in designing mathematics and science assessments, but using these techniques to design comprehension assessments is relatively new. This chapter sees this as one promising new technique that may allow the emerging consensus around subskills contributing to reading comprehension to be measured systematically and in ways that are diagnostically sensitive.

Section I

ASSESSMENT, LEARNING, AND INSTRUCTION: CONNECTING TEXT, TASK, AND READER/LEARNER

Chapter One

Assessing Multiple Source Comprehension through Evidence-Centered Design

Kimberly A. Lawless, Susan R. Goldman,
Kimberly Gomez, Flori Manning, and Jason Braasch

INTRODUCTION

For the past four years, we have engaged in a broad scope of work focused on garnering a better understanding of where adolescent readers struggle when presented with tasks that require the comprehension and application of information from multiple sources in the disciplines of science and social studies.

Our main thrust has been to develop an in-depth theory of inquiry-based, multiple source comprehension. To support this theoretical development, we have designed a battery of assessments that is sensitive to the skills required for the successful comprehension of multiple text sources, identifies areas of struggle for individual readers, and provides information that is instructionally useful for teachers.

In this chapter, we first present the background literature and problem of practice that provided the impetus for our research. We then discuss the assessment approach used to build the tools necessary to collect evidence of multiple source comprehension. To illustrate this approach, we provide an elaborated example of how we developed assessment tasks for one of the more simple components of multiple source comprehension as we have defined it. We conclude by reflecting on some of the persistent and difficult challenges of this work.

BACKGROUND AND RATIONALE

Research on reading suggests that moving from basic to advanced levels of comprehension requires flexible application of a variety of knowledge and skills.

3

The research shows that successful readers rely on multiple types of knowledge (e.g., of words, concepts, sentence structures, text structures, genres) as they try to interpret print. They monitor their success at this process and use a range of strategies in response to failures to understand what they are reading (Palincsar & Brown, 1984; Pearson & Fielding, 1991; Pressley, 2000; RAND, 2002; Tierney & Cunningham, 1984).

To achieve deep comprehension, successful readers connect ideas within a text to each other and with relevant prior knowledge; explain the ideas and connections; and actively engage with the text to construct coherent representations (Chi, Bassok, Lewis, Reimann, & Glaser, 1989; Coté & Goldman, 1999; Goldman & Saul, 1990; Magliano & Millis, 2003; van den Broek, Risden, & Husebye-Hartman, 1995).

In contrast, when less successful readers make connections among ideas, they tend to make surface-level connections. Rather than explaining ideas in a text, less successful readers tend to paraphrase or restate verbatim the information presented in the text (Coté, Goldman, & Saul, 1998; Magliano & Millis, 2003; O'Reilly & McNamara, 2007). Although we have fairly comprehensive characterizations of the differences between more and less successful readers for single-text comprehension, we know little about sources of difficulty for readers engaged in multiple source comprehension.

But understanding multiple sources is a major literacy demand of the twenty-first century. If we limit work on instruction and assessment to single texts, we will not be adequately preparing students for the realities they will face in their twenty-first-century lives.

The twenty-first-century knowledge society brings increases in the availability of, and access to, different kinds of information resources. Considering the Internet alone, recent estimates indicate that the amount of information available to the average consumer has increased more than 60,000percent in the last 10 years alone (Gulli and Signorini, 2005; Lawless & Schrader, 2008). Moreover, well over 1 billion people worldwide report active participation in online activities (Miniwatts Marketing Group, 2006).

This amount of information and use is unfathomable and only constitutes a small portion of what individuals have available to them. Meanwhile sources like books, newspapers, magazine/journals, and television have not gone away. In order to grapple with this information glut, readers need additional literacy skills, specifically those associated with locating, synthesizing, integrating, and evaluating the quality of sources and the information within them (Goldman, 2004; Hartman, 1993; Orr, 1986).

These literacy skills enable critical analysis of information and constitute the cognitive activities of critical reading in today's society. They make it possible for individuals to take a critical stance toward information with which they are constantly bombarded (Goldman & Bisanz, 2002; VanSled right, 2002a, 2002b). They make clear that reading comprehension today needs to become a more explicitly intertextual practice, in that understanding a set of texts or sources means understanding the relations across texts at basic meaning and advanced interpretive levels (Goldman & Bloome, 2005; Orr, 1986).

However, we simply do not have sufficient knowledge of readers' skills and strategies for successful learning in multiple text situations to draw conclusions about the skills needed to comprehend multiple sources of information or about where readers struggle with multiple source inquiry tasks. Preliminary evidence suggests that for single and multiple source situations there are both overlapping and nonoverlapping skills and strategies.

For example, Wiley et al. (2009) indicate that in a multiple text situation, both more and less successful learners explain parts of individual texts. However, among these college students, the more successful learners differentially allocated their explaining and connection-making across texts, while less successful learners did not. Specifically, more successful readers explained and connected across texts significantly more often if the texts were reliable and relevant to the task for which they were reading.

In contrast, less successful learners were just as likely to explain and connect reliable and unreliable, relevant and irrelevant texts when formulating a response. Although the same strategy—explaining—is important in both single and multiple text situations, the conditions of use are not the same. An unanswered yet important question is whether readers who are successful with explaining single texts continue to be successful in multitext situations or if they struggle.

Multiple texts also introduce a number of complexities that are frequently absent in single text comprehension and learning situations. For example, while single texts can include conflicting information, different perspectives, and alternative points of view—features that are commonly found in critical reviews or news articles—a single source is still written by an individual author(s), for a specific purpose, at a single point in time and published within a particular venue.

This is not the case, however with multiple text situations. In multiple text situations, texts each have their own authors (and related voice and structural elements), are published for different purposes and audiences, and constitute different contexts in terms of the time and place when they were published. So in addition to comprehending the content and purpose of a single text, readers in multiple text situations must also resolve differences across texts along these and other dimensions in order to create a unified structure and coherence for the information space they are creating.

Furthermore, multitext situations provide more opportunities for connections and explanations, and readers may need to exercise more critical selection strategies to decide what to connect and explain both within and across texts. Indeed, Lawless and Kulikowich (1996; 1998) found that linking related text segments can be difficult for readers with low domain knowledge, interest, or motivation, thereby hindering the identification of appropriate sources as well as the comprehension and integration of information across multiple sources.

APPROACH TO ASSESSMENT DESIGN

According to the National Research Council (NRC) report *Knowing What Students Know: The Science and Design of Educational Assessment* (KWSK; Pellegrino, Chudowsky, & Glaser, 2001), quality assessments of student learning require three major components.

They must (1) include a model of how students represent knowledge and the skills they need to appropriate to develop competence; (2) use tasks that provide evidence regarding student performance; and (3) delineate a process for the interpretation of this evidence. Further, although the manner in which each of these elements is used varies, no assessment can function properly without careful consideration of their interdependence.

To develop assessments consistent with the KWSK model, we relied on the work of Mislevy, Steinberg, and Almond (2003). They proposed a principled, evidence-centered model for the design of assessments that specifically addresses the vertices of the assessment triangle. In addition, the guidelines set forth by the model are sensitive to the individual nature of the domains and situations for which the assessment is being constructed. Because of its flexibility, the manner in which the principles of evidence-centered design (ECD) are enacted across varying contexts is unique.

ECD describes assessment as a process of reasoning from evidence that includes three critical and interconnected components: a student model, a task model, and an evidence or interpretation model. The student model refers to detailed conceptual and empirical analyses of the skills and knowledge that define domain competence and should be assessed; the task model refers to a clear sense of how the tasks to be used would elicit the target skills and knowledge; and the interpretive model concerns how to appropriately "fit" the student model and the observations together.

This evidentiary reasoning logic, and the ECD approach that it gives rise to, provided conceptual guidance to our process of defining what needs to be assessed, how to assess it, and how to make sense of it.

STUDENT MODEL OF MULTIPLE SOURCE COMPREHENSION

Our model was informed by the extant but limited research base on online and multiple source comprehension skills (e.g., Goldman, 2004; Goldman & Bloome, 2005; Rouet, 2006; VanSledright, 2002a, b; Wiley et al., 2009) and a series of descriptive microethnographic studies that we conducted to document students' intertextual activity as they carried out classroom research assignments within their social studies or science project–based work.

It is important to note that our definition of multiple source comprehension is couched under the context of inquiry-based activities. This in no way presumes that this is the only time that multiple source comprehension is necessary. It merely reflects our understanding for how to best embed these types of activities into the effective classroom practices espoused by our perspective on how people learn (Bransford, Brown, & Cocking, 1999).

Using the literature base and our findings from the microethnographies, we specified a preliminary model of multiple source comprehension. This model, presented in figure 1.1, consisted of five major components:

1. *Interpreting the Task,* understanding objectives, limitations, and boundaries;
2. *Gathering* information, engaging in search strategies;
3. *Sourcing,* evaluating information for relevance and reliability;
4. *Analyzing, Synthesizing, and Integrating* information within sources and across multiple sources;
5. *Applying* information to accomplish the task.

In addition to the five primary components of the model, our work further delineated an overarching metacomponent: *evaluating.* Evaluation has dual functionality within our model of multiple source comprehension. First, it is an enabling skill required of each of the original components of the model. For example, within sourcing, a learner must be able to critically evaluate the qualifications of an author to determine source usefulness.

In addition, evaluation serves an executive function, mediating the movement among model components during multiple source comprehension. For instance, as readers engage with analyzing or synthesizing, their knowledge base grows, causing them to reevaluate their information needs (*gathering*) or the usefulness of particular sources (*sourcing*) in answering a given target inquiry question. In this way, evaluation serves as a sort of "air traffic controller" as a learner engages in multiple source comprehension, directing students to elicit components in a dynamic back-and-forth process.

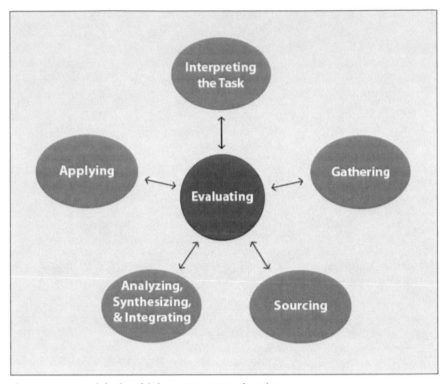

Figure 1.1. Model of multiple source comprehension

The identification of the main components of the model was the first step in the ECD design process. In order to begin to build a system of assessments to capture multiple source comprehension, we had to "unpack" the meaning of each of the components to ascertain a concrete set of knowledge, skills, and abilities (KSAs) required for competent multiple source comprehension. This step in the ECD process yields a model of the domain.

To accomplish this, we asked the same kind of question about each of the five components in our model. For example, "What is meant by evaluating information for accuracy and reliability?" This process resulted in a set of claims about what readers must know and be able to do and a parallel set of evidence statements that indicate what kind of performances could be taken as support for inferences about the presence of the KSAs.

This unpacking process yielded the student model of competencies against which we began to compare student performance. Table 1.1 provides examples taken from our student model for the sourcing component—the claims and evidence statements that define sourcing. The full student model is not provided due to space constraints. We have done a similar unpacking process

Table 1.1.   Exemplar claim and evidence statements for sourcing component.

Subcomponent	Claim Statement Stem: The student makes use of...	Evidence Statement Stem: The work includes information ...
Relevance	content information during the sourcing process	about the relevance of the content for answering the inquiry question
Author	author information in the sourcing process	about the credibility of the author or efforts to determine credibility of the author
Venue	publishing location in the sourcing process	about the credibility of the publication location or efforts to determine where something was published and its credibility
Currency	publication relative to the content of the task in the sourcing process.	indicating attention to date of publication in relation to task
Type	differences among kinds of resources (e.g., primary vs. secondary; fiction vs. nonfiction; opinion piece/ editorial vs news story) relative to their utility for completing the task.	about differences among kinds of resources and their appropriateness for the task.

for the analysis, synthesis, and integration component, discussed elsewhere (Goldman et al., 2010, in press).

TASK MODEL FOR SOURCING

The task model describes the situations and tasks that could be used to elicit observable student work that can provide evidence for a corresponding claim. Selected tasks differ by the kinds of evidence that are required to support inferences of understanding. For example, a simple multiple-choice item could provide evidence of declarative content knowledge, but it might not provide evidence that students could gather data over time in multiple contexts or reason with data to construct a scientific argument.

A good task model is basically a template that isolates various attributes that can be manipulated to create multiple functionally equivalent tasks. Based on the sourcing component of the student model and various versions of the sourcing task we piloted, we constructed a task model that outlines a blueprint for designing specific tasks with which to assess sourcing.

The task model for sourcing aligns with the student model and represents the structure and features of sourcing tasks in terms of the characteristics of (1) source; (2) work product; (3) context; (4) medium; (5) scaffolding; and (6) instructions.

The source parameter defines the specific attributes of the texts that need to be specified when designing a sourcing task (e.g., relevance of content, author information, venue of publication, type of publication, etc.). The source parameter also delineates some additional considerations that must be taken into account, such as the total number of sources that must be examined.

The work product parameter represents the type of work product students must produce such as Likert rating, forced-choice yes/no response, essay, and so on. The context parameter indicates the type and amount of contextualization present for a given task and includes attributes such as the presence/absence of cover story in the task. The medium parameter denotes the medium on which a task is performed (e.g., computer or paper and pencil). The scaffolding parameter characterizes the type and degrees of scaffolding provided in the task. Finally, the instruction parameter designates the specific attributes of the instructions provided to students (e.g., where they appear, how much detail is provided, and how explicit they are).

In this way, the task model makes the process of assessment task design transparent, because all the attributes of an assessment task are explicitly specified or explicitly marked as unspecified. This process, in turn, constrains the interpretation of the data the assessment task yields.

This task model was then used to generate a set of three activities that constitute the source usefulness assessment: Relevance Judgments, Trustworthiness Judgments, and Usefulness Ranking. Each activity taps a different aspect of sourcing as defined within the student model.

The students were introduced to the inquiry question "Why did Chicago become a big city?"—the cover story in the task model—and were told they were going to decide which of eight sources help them answer this question. The first activity—Relevance Judgment—was designed to assess whether students could effectively discriminate relevant from irrelevant sources of information based on the content summary and title of each source.

Using a 3-point Likert scale (1 = highly relevant, 2 = somewhat relevant, 3 = not relevant), students judged the relevance of the content of eight sources of information in relation to the Chicago inquiry question. According to expert judges, two of the eight sources included are not relevant, three are highly relevant, and three are somewhat relevant. Sources that a student rates as "highly relevant" or "somewhat relevant" are retained for further examination in the second selection activity. Students make no additional judgments about sources that are rated "not relevant."

In the second activity the students are asked to rate the trustworthiness of any source they judged relevant by considering and rating four source attributes (author, type, publication date, and publication source). Hence this task requires students to think about things such as the credibility of the author, the reliability of the information, and its currency. Students need to carefully attend to the source attributes in the context of the content and the inquiry question.

For example, a geese migration expert may be highly credible in his or her field but does not have any apparent expertise in historical trends in human population growth. Using their ratings for individual source attributes for trustworthiness, students are then asked to provide a holistic rating of the trustworthiness of each source. Again, the rating is a 3-point, Likert-type scale indicating highly trustworthy, somewhat trustworthy, and not trustworthy. Only sources rated as "highly trustworthy" or "somewhat trustworthy" move forward to the Usefulness rating activity.

In the Usefulness rating activity, students are asked to rank order the sources they rated as relevant and trustworthy in terms of overall usefulness in answering the inquiry question, "Why did Chicago became a big city?" This task is accomplished by assigning a first-place "award ribbon" to the source they think is most useful. The students continue to award lower-order ribbons to sources until they have assigned a ribbon to each of their relevant and trustworthy sources.

The sourcing task was programmed in Flash and delivered via the Internet. As such, it is possible to administer the task to multiple students on multiple computers simultaneously without need to install any proprietary software.

A computer-based log records students' ratings and rankings across sourcing task activities. In addition, the log records keystrokes, sequencing and navigation of screens, and time spent completing various subcomponents of the selection task. From these data, it is possible to reconstruct how students approached and actually executed the decision process at each key point of the task. A fully functional version of the sourcing task described here is available online at http://www.lsri.uic.edu/diglit/chicago/new.html.

Through the use of the task model template, we have been able to develop parallel tasks in both science and social studies broaching different questions of inquiry. In total, we now have four sourcing tasks across two domains: science and social studies.

INTERPRETIVE MODEL OF SOURCING

Data gathered through the sourcing task provides a means to test the fit between our assessment and the knowledge, skills, and abilities outlined in our student model of multiple source comprehension.

To accomplish this, we first developed a "gold standard" response for each of the three steps: content relevance, trustworthiness, and final usefulness rankings. The gold standard for each set of activities became the benchmarks against which students' data were compared and constitute the interpretations model for the sourcing component of multiple source comprehension. The "gold standard" essentially captures what expert performance across activities would look like.

To establish the fit between the task model and the interpretations it generated, a sample of 64 fifth-grade students were asked to independently complete the sourcing task. Students were recruited through their computer teacher from three classrooms in an inner-city neighborhood within a large midwestern U.S. city.

The activity was conducted in a computer lab setting as a whole-class session. Each student had his or her own computer, and students worked at their own pace to complete the various steps of the task. The computer captured each student's responses, including the sequence and timing of their ratings, in a separate web log. All procedures were completed within an average class session of approximately 45 minutes.

Student data at each of the three steps was converted into numerical scores for relevance, trustworthiness, and final usefulness performance. For example, student-generated evaluations for content relevance were converted to relevance scores in the following way. On the four sources that were deemed highly useful in the "gold standard," students were given a score of 1 if they rated the source as Highly Relevant, 2 points if they rated the source to be Somewhat Relevant, and 3 points if they rated the source as Not Relevant.

The same process was done on sources that experts deemed not useful; however a reverse scoring procedure was used. If students rated a source that was actually not useful as Highly Relevant, they received a score of 3. Conversely, if they rated the Not Useful source as Not Relevant (an accurate judgment), they received a 1. As such, better performance results in a lower numerical score. Average relevance scores were computed using their relevance scores across the eight sources. Similar conversion processes were done for trustworthiness and final usefulness ranking performance for the set of eight sources.

In order to contrast the performance of students who did well on this task with those who did not, we established a group of higher and lower performing groups, based on the final usefulness ranking scores (step 3). Higher performers were designated as such if they performed .5 standard deviations below the mean for the entire group based on standardized scores for final ranking of usefulness. Similarly, lower performers were those who scored .5 standard deviations above the mean based on standardized scores for final ranking (recall a lower score means higher performance). This resulted in 26 higher and 23 lower performing students.

A paired-samples t-test indicated that the higher and lower performing students significantly differed on final ranking performance, $t_{(47)}$ = 2.80, p < .001. As could be expected, the higher performing (M = 14.38, SD = 2.77) scored significantly better than the lower on final ranking performance (M = 16.35, SD = 2.01).

Results indicate that higher performers were significantly better sourcing at step 1 on the task, content relevance, (M = 1.80, SD = 0.30) than lower performers (M = 1.97, SD = 0.23), $t_{(47)}$ = 2.27, p < .05. This was despite the fact that lower performers spent a longer average amount of time examining each source (M = 43.07, SD = 17.31) than higher performing evaluators (M = 29.85, SD = 22.44), $t_{(47)}$ = 1.74, p < .05.

For trustworthiness, higher and lower performing students scored similarly (M = 1.80, SD = 0.34 and M = 1.90, SD = 0.22 respectively), $t_{(47)}$ = 1.24, *ns* and spent similar amounts of time examining sources for trustworthiness (M = 47.16, SD = 28.51 and M = 45.59, SD = 13.90), $t_{(47)}$ < 1, *ns*.

Interestingly, the higher and lower sourcing groups determined by this task did not differ in their performance on a standardized reading test (Illinois State Achievement test) (M = 46.04, SD = 26.35 and M = 41.00, SD = 26.71 respectively), $t_{(44)}$ < 1, *ns*. This suggests that sourcing as assessed by this task involves literacy skills that operate beyond general reading ability as defined by standardized assessments of reading.

Our approach to ascertaining estimates for reliability of scores produced by the sourcing assessment task has been twofold. First, we have tested the same assessment task (same content) on the same users (n = 32) at two points in time. The assessments were administered one month apart.

Test-retest reliability indicated relative stability in scores over time (r_{30} =. 88). This means that students who scored high on the first administration also tended to score high on the second administration, and likewise for the lower portion of the performance continuum.

In addition, we have now created and administered this and parallel assessments across diverse samples and found similar results describing both the higher- and lower-ability students. These multiple replications speak for the veracity of the issues being measured as important skills to attend to when instructing individuals on the sourcing component of our model of multiple source comprehension.

PERSISTENT COMPLEXITIES, CHALLENGES, AND LESSONS LEARNED

Following the processes recommended under ECD, we were able to define the domain of skills that constituted competency in multiple source comprehension (e.g., student model). However, while the student model we generated depicted what an accomplished multiple source comprehender knows and can do, it did not inform us what acceptable performance for a fifth-grader would look like.

Within ECD, this issue is addressed through the provision of scaffolding and developmentally appropriate materials specified by the task models. Unfortunately, because of the lack of a strong research foundation in the area of multiple source comprehension, we had little to no guidance a priori on what materials and environments would afford fifth-grade students the opportunity to illustrate what they were capable of in a developmentally appropriate form. Decisions such as the type of instructions provided to students, how to present sources, and what information they contained required us to engage in a series of rapid prototyping studies.

Essentially, we had to use evidence generated from the multiple versions of piloted tasks not only to test out and refine potential materials and activities as a means of assessing student skill, but also as a means to refine the student model to better align with the skill set of younger learners and build the literature base.

The simultaneous process of assessment design and theoretical development was slow and extremely arduous—much more so than we had initially anticipated. However, because each element of our tasks was carefully vetted, we believe we have a much greater assurance that the performances elicited and captured by our assessments are both systematic and reproducible.

The issue of calibrating our student and task models and materials to appropriate developmental levels is also related to the second major challenge we encountered: how to operationalize the evidence statements developed to provide data that could be used to generate the interpretations model. While the evidence statements we created indicated what to look for in a student's response (e.g., the work includes information about the credibility of the author or efforts to determine credibility of the author), they did not help us determine what type of data needed to be collected, or how it should be evaluated.

Throughout this process, we had to be mindful of the fact that any performance indicators we chose had to yield data that were both manageable and interpretable in a relatively quick span of time from testing to feedback. In response, we initially adopted a "wide net" approach, collecting massive volumes of information from students in a variety of forms.

For example, in early versions of the sourcing task, we collected not only the Likert-type responses discussed above in the interpretations model, but also open-ended extended responses capturing student reasoning, as well as a host of unobtrusive navigational data (e.g., time, slick streams, rating changes).

For sourcing, decisions regarding which metrics were most useful were relatively easy as analyses revealed that many of the data streams contained redundant information.

However, in the case of the synthesis and integration component of our student model, the process has been significantly more labor intensive. Not only was it clear that open-ended extended responses were necessary, but these responses had to be coded in multiple ways to capture the various performances delineated by our student model. In order to expedite the analysis of these open-ended responses and provide timely feedback to teachers regarding student performance, it is evident that automated scoring of essays is required. We are still exploring the best method for accomplishing this.

Finally, now that we have a set of assessments for several components of our model of multiple source comprehension, we are returning to the question of determining how to relate student performance to instructional recommendations for teachers. While the assessments we developed through the ECD process afford the determination of the level of competence expressed by a student's work, additional work is needed to develop the pedagogical trajectories to provide students appropriate opportunities to learn and move from one level of performance to the next.

The specification of the knowledge and skills, and the identification of the kinds of evidence that reflect competence, has allowed us to show precisely what performances constitute complex or "deep" comprehension of the type embodied in multiple source comprehension. We think this is an excellent starting point for developing instruction and instructional trajectories.

While we are just at the beginning of this process of developing assessments of multiple source comprehension, the work is already advancing our understanding of how to theorize, measure, and instruct this construct. The work to date is also making clear how much more there is to do to identify, assess, and instruct multiple source comprehension and better prepare students for the complex literacy demands of the twenty-first century.

REFERENCES

Bransford, J. D., Brown, A. L., & Cocking, R. R. (1999). *How people learn: Brain, mind, experience, and school.* Washington, D.C.: National Academy Press.

Chi, M. T. H., Bassok, M., Lewis, M. W., Reimann, P., & Glaser, R. (1989). Self Explanations: How students study and use examples in learning to solve problems. *Cognitive Science, 13,* 145–182.

Coté, N. C., & Goldman, S. R. (1999). Building representations of informational text: Evidence from children's think-aloud protocols. In H. van Oostendorp & S. R.

Goldman (Eds.), *The construction of mental representations during reading* (pp. 169–193). Mahwah, NJ: Lawrence Erlbaum Associates.

Coté, N. C., Goldman, S. R., & Saul, E. U. (1998). Students making sense of informational text: Relations between processing and representation. *Discourse Processes, 25,* 1–53.

Goldman, S. R. (2004). Cognitive aspects of constructing meaning through and across multiple texts. In N. Shuart-Ferris & D. M. Bloome (Eds.), *Uses of intertextuality in classroom and educational research* (pp. 313–347). Greenwich, CT: Information Age Publishing.

Goldman, S. R., & Bisanz, G. (2002). Toward a functional analysis of scientific genres: Implications for understanding and learning processes. In J. Otero, J. A. León, & A. C. Graesser (Eds.), *The psychology of science text comprehension.* (pp. 19–50). Mahwah, NJ: Lawrence Erlbaum Associates.

Goldman, S. R., & Bloome, D. (2005). Learning to construct and integrate. In A. F. Healy (Ed.), *Experimental cognitive psychology and its applications* (pp. 169–182). Washington, D.C.: American Psychological Association.

Goldman, S. R., Lawless, K. A., Gomez, K. W., Braasch, J. L. G., MacLeod, S., & Manning, F. (2010). Literacy in the digital world: Comprehending and learning from multiple sources. In M. C. McKeown and L. Kucan (Eds.), *Bringing reading research to life* (pp. 257–284). New York: Guilford.

Goldman, S. R., Ozuru, Y., Braasch, J. L. G., Manning, F. H., Lawless, K. A., Gomez, K. W., & Slanovits, M. J. (in press). Literacies for learning: A multiple source comprehension illustration. To appear in N. Stein (Ed.), *Development science goes to school.* New York: Routledge.

Goldman, S. R., & Saul, E. U. (1990). Flexibility in text processing: A strategy competition model. *Learning and Individual Differences*, 2, 181–219.

Gulli, A., & Signorini, A. (May, 2005). The Indexable Web is more than 11.5 billion pages. *Proceedings of International World Wide Web Conference 2005*, Chiba, Japan.

Hartman, D. K. (1993). Intertextuality and reading: The text, the reader, the author and the context. *Linguistics in Education, 4,* 295–311.

Lawless, K. A., & Kulikowich, J. M. (1996). Understanding hypertext navigation through cluster analysis. *Journal of Educational Computing Research, 14,* 385–399.

———. (1998). Domain knowledge, interest, and hypertext navigation: A study of individual differences. *Journal of Educational Multimedia and Hypermedia, 7,* 51–70.

Lawless, K. A., & Schrader, P. G. (2008). Where do we go now? Understanding research on navigation in complex digital environments. In D. J. Leu & J. Coiro (Eds.), *Handbook of new literacies* (pp. 267-296). Hillsdale, NJ: Lawrence Erlbaum Associates.

Magliano, J. P., & Millis, K. K. (2003). Assessing reading skill with a think-aloud procedure. *Cognition & Instruction, 3,* 251–283.

Miniwatts Marketing Group (2006). *Internet world stats: Usage and population statistics.* Retrieved May 15, 2010, from www.internetworldstats.com/stats.htm

Mislevy, R. J., Steinberg, L., & Almond, R (2003). On the structure of educational assessments. *Measurement: Interdisciplinary Research and Perspective, 1*, 3–67.

O'Reilly, T. & McNamara, D. S. (2007). Reversing the reverse cohesion effect: Good texts can be better for strategic, high-knowledge readers. *Discourse Processes, 43*, 121–152.

Orr, L. (1986). Intertextuality and the cultural text in recent semiotics. *College English, 48*, 811–823.

Palincsar, A. S., & Brown, A. L. (1984). Reciprocal teaching of comprehension-fostering and comprehension-monitoring activities. *Cognition and Instruction, 1*, 117–175.

Pearson, P., & Fielding, L. (1991). Comprehension instruction. In Barr, R., M. Kamil, P. Mosenthal, and P. Pearson. (Eds.), *Handbook of reading research* (Vol. II, pp. 815–860). Mahwah, NJ: Lawrence Erlbaum Associates.

Pellegrino, J. W., Chudowsky, N., & Glaser, R. (2001). *Knowing what students know: The science and design of educational assessment.* Washington, D.C.: National Academy Press.

Pressley, M. (2000). What should comprehension instruction be the instruction of? In M. Kamil, P. B. Mosenthal, P. D. Pearson, & R. Barr (Eds.), *Handbook of reading research* (Vol. III, pp. 545-562). Mahwah, NJ: Lawrence Erlbaum Associates.

RAND Reading Study Group. (2002). *Reading for understanding: Toward an R&D program in reading comprehension.* Santa Monica, CA: Rand Education. Also available at www.rand.org/multi/achievementforall/reading/

Rouet, J-F. (2006). *The skills of document use: From text comprehension to web-based learning.* Mahwah, NJ: Lawrence Erlbaum Associates.

Tierney, R. J., & Cunningham, J. W. (1984). Research on teaching reading comprehension. In P. D. Pearson, R. Barr, M. L. Kamil, & P. Mosenthal (Eds.), *Handbook of reading research* (pp. 609-655). Mahwah, NJ: Lawrence Erlbaum Associates.

van den Broek, P., Risden, K., & Husebye-Hartman, E. (1995). The role of readers' standards for coherence in the generation of inferences during reading. In R. F. Lorch, Jr., & E. J. O'Brien (Eds.), *Sources of coherence in text comprehension* (pp. 353–373). Hillsdale, NJ: Lawrence Erlbaum Associates.

VanSledright, B. (2002a). *In search of America's past: Learning to read history in elementary school.* NY: Teachers College Press.

———. (2002b). Confronting history's interpretive paradox while teaching fifth graders to investigate the past. *American Educational Research Journal, 39*, 1089–1115.

Wiley, J., Goldman, S. R., Graesser, A. C., Sanchez, C. A., Ash, I., & Hemmerich, J. (2009). Source evaluation, comprehension, and learning in internet science inquiry tasks. *American Educational Research Journal, 46*, 1060–1160.

Chapter Two

The Case for Scenario-Based Assessments of Reading Competency

Kathleen M. Sheehan and Tenaha O'Reilly

THE CASE FOR SCENARIO-BASED
ASSESSMENTS OF READING COMPETENCY

No Child Left Behind (NCLB) has highlighted the need for new types of accountability assessments that not only provide high-quality evidence about what students know and can do but also help move learning forward. This chapter introduces a scenario-based reading assessment designed to address the tradeoffs inherent in these two goals.

The assessment is part of a research and development initiative called Cognitively Based Assessment *of, for*, and *as Learning* (CBAL, Bennett & Gitomer, 2009). CBAL assessments attempt to balance measurement and learning goals through four key innovations:

1. Assessments are based on a theory of domain competency that specifies the pivotal competencies underlying state standards;
2. Assessments include extended scenario-based tasks designed to model expert teaching practice and encourage the use of classroom activities that have been shown to support learning;
3. Assessments are administered at multiple times spaced throughout the school year so information about student achievement can be shared with teachers while there is still time to take needed instructional action; and
4. State-of-the-art automated scoring technologies are used to broaden the array of skills assessed and ensure that score reports are provided in a timely manner.

This chapter describes a CBAL summative reading assessment targeted at students in grades 7 and 8. We begin by describing innovative aspects of the assessment framework, then describe a prototype test form, and finally, summarize data collected in a series of pilot administrations.

THE ASSESSMENT FRAMEWORK

Existing accountability assessments have been characterized as representing a view of proficiency that is "a mile wide and an inch deep" (Schmidt, McKnight, & Raizen, 1997). CBAL assessments, by contrast, are designed to collect deeper evidence about a more modest number of instructionally relevant competencies. The framework developed to guide this process includes two structures: a competency model and a set of task design principles. These structures are described below.

The CBAL Reading Competency Model

The CBAL Reading Competency Model synthesizes information derived from three sources: reviews of the reading literature (O'Reilly & Sheehan, 2009), state reading standards, and reading skills specified in the Partnership for 21st Century Skills (2004, 2008).

This body of work suggests that today's educators have adopted a new definition of what constitutes proficient reading at the K-12 level. In addition to traditional reading skills such as identifying main ideas and generating needed inferences, today's students are expected to master additional higher-level thinking skills such as assessing the quality of information, recognizing and explaining the presence of fallacious reasoning, and integrating and synthesizing information from multiple texts.

Both researchers and business leaders have argued that mastery of these additional skills is essential to success in today's increasingly competitive international economy (National Center on Education and the Economy, 2006; Kirsch, Braun, Yamamoto, & Sum, 2007; Committee on Prospering in the Global Economy of the 21st Century, 2007).

Figure 2.1 provides a graphical illustration of key parts of the model. Three important sources of individual differences are highlighted: component skills, reading strategies, and knowledge of text conventions and characteristics.

The Skills Dimension

The skills dimension highlights three broad categories of skills: Prerequisite Reading Skills, Model Building Skills, and Applied Comprehension Skills. These three groups of skills are roughly similar to Chall's (1967) notion of the skill sets involved in *learning-to-read*, *reading-to-learn*, and *reading-to-do*.

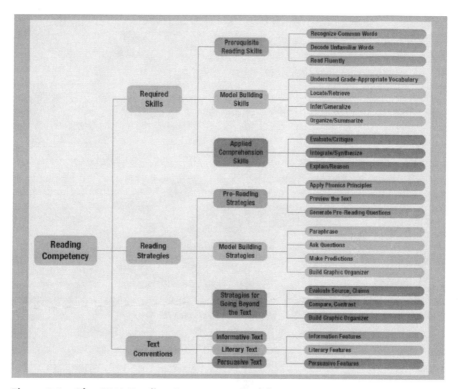

Figure 2.1. The CBAL Reading Competency Model

Prerequisite Reading Skills includes all of the skills needed to understand print, including oral reading fluency, word recognition, and decoding. Although some of these skills (e.g., decoding) are not typically addressed on high-stakes assessments, recent research has confirmed that providing feedback about students' mastery of prerequisite skills can help move learning forward because deficiencies in these skills can compromise readers' ability to efficiently apply needed higher-order skills (Perfetti, 1985; Vellutino, Tunmer, & Jaccard, 2007).

The title Model Building Skills is designed to emphasize the category's role in helping readers develop coherent mental representations of the information presented in stimulus materials. This second group includes all of the skills needed to form a coherent mental representation of a text, (i.e., its gist), including: (a) comprehending the literal meaning of individual sentences; (b) inferring the meaning of unfamiliar words; (c) using text-based inferences to infer cross-sentence links; and (d) using a text's network of hierarchical and logical relationships (i.e., its structure) to develop a more complete mental model of text content (Kintsch, 1998).

In some cases, comprehension of the gist of a text is all that is needed to completely satisfy a reader's goals. In other cases, however, readers must go beyond the literal and inferential interpretation of text in order to use the text to achieve a particular goal such as creating a presentation, writing a report, or making a decision.

Applied Comprehension Skills, as they are called in the CBAL framework, are those involved in implementing this third level of processing. They include the additional skills needed to evaluate, explain, and critique information, and to integrate and synthesize information from multiple texts.

The Strategies Dimension

While increases in skill mastery have been shown to be consistently correlated with increases in reading proficiency, researchers have also argued that skilled readers differ from less skilled readers in terms of their ability to deploy effective reading strategies when needed[1] (see McNamara, 2007).

There are two bases for this claim. First, several studies have shown that skilled readers tend to employ empirically validated reading strategies more frequently than do less skilled readers (Bereiter & Bird, 1985; Chi, Bassok, Lewis, Reimann, & Glaser, 1989; Paris & Jacobs, 1984; Pressley & Afflerbach, 1995). Second, studies have also demonstrated that direct training in reading strategy selection can lead to significant improvements in comprehension (Chi, de Leeuw, Chiu, & LaVancher, 1994; McNamara, 2004; Palinscar & Brown, 1984; Paris, Cross, & Lipson, 1984; Pressley, Wood, Woloshyn, & Martin, 1992).

As shown in figure 2.1, the competency model highlights three types of reading strategies.

The first category, called Pre-Reading Strategies, includes strategies such as setting a goal and generating hypotheses about text content from a scan of titles and headers. The second category, called Model Building Strategies, includes strategies such as asking questions, making predictions, building graphic organizers, and paraphrasing. The third category, called Strategies for Going Beyond the Text, includes additional strategies such as elaboration and using outside resources such as dictionaries and thesauruses.

The Text Dimension

The competency model also characterizes readers in terms of their knowledge of the conventions and characteristics of text that may help to facilitate comprehension. This category is called Text Conventions and reflects a large body of literature documenting significant differences in the processes engaged when reading informational versus literary texts (e.g., Graesser, McNamara, & Louwerse, 2003; Sheehan, Kostin, & Futagi, 2008a, 2008b).

When reading literary text, for example, knowledge of literary concepts such as plot and theme may help facilitate comprehension. When reading informational text, by contrast, comprehension is more likely to be facilitated by knowledge of common organizing schemas such as cause/effect, problem/ solution, and advantages/disadvantages.

Task Design Principles

In addition to providing high-quality information about where students are in their mastery of critical competencies, CBAL assessments are designed to support teaching and learning by modeling expert teaching practice and encouraging the use of classroom activities that have been shown to support learning. Task design principles intended to facilitate achievement of these goals are summarized below.

Providing a Realistic Purpose for Reading

The importance of providing a purpose for reading has been frequently noted in the literature (Alderson, 2000; Bransford, Brown, & Cocking, 1999; Pellegrino, Chudowsky, & Glaser, 2001; Pressley, 2000). CBAL incorporates these findings by providing extended, scenario-based tasks designed to simulate the types of reading activities engaged in by expert readers at the targeted grade level.

Each extended task set begins with an introductory scenario selected to give students an engaging purpose for reading a collection of related texts. Scenarios present realistic project goals designed to enhance interest and motivation and to help examinees distinguish the individual sections of a text that are likely to be more or less relevant.

Encouraging an Awareness of Text Structure

Researchers have also considered the facilitative effects of instruction focused on encouraging readers to pay closer attention to the various ways in which texts are organized (Daneman & Merikle, 1996; Pellegrino et al., 2001; Vitale & Romance, 2007; Wyman & Randel, 1998). CBAL incorporates these findings by employing graphical task formats designed to help readers become more adept at organizing and chunking information, and to encourage them to consider multiple ways of representing text (e.g., timelines, flow charts, decision trees, Venn diagrams, T-charts, hierarchical graphic organizers, etc.).

Facilitating Learning via Simulated Student Responses

Learning by observing, or vicarious learning, has been shown to be an effective instructional approach, particularly for low-proficiency students (Cox, McKendree, Tobin, Lee, & Mayes, 1999; Gholson & Craig, 2006; Muller, Sharma, Eklund, & Reimann, 2007). CBAL incorporates these findings via a new type of task called a Simulated Peer Response (SPR) task.

Each SPR task includes four parts: a complex, multipart question; a simulated student response to that question; a rubric for use in evaluating the simulated student response; and finally, one or more items designed to extract evidence of examinee proficiency relative to the task of evaluating and correcting the response. Typically, examinees will be asked to complete missing sections of the response, or to identify and correct flaws in the response.

This innovative task format offers two main benefits: (1) It enables us to pose complex, realistic problems requiring the integrated use of multiple component skills while simultaneously maintaining strict constraints on timing and scoring costs; and (2) The inclusion of a detailed scoring rubric as part of the task setup furthers the formative assessment goal of clarifying success criteria (Black & Wiliam, 1998).

A PROTOTYPE ASSESSMENT TARGETED AT SEVENTH- AND EIGHTH-GRADE READERS

Information that arrives at the end of the year cannot help teachers adjust instruction in the middle of the year. CBAL addresses the need for more timely information about students' underlying strengths and weaknesses by distributing accountability assessment over several administrations spaced throughout the school year. Resulting partial assessments are called Periodic Accountability Assessments, or PAAs. Final estimates of student competency are obtained by aggregating information from successive PAAs.

Although the total number of PAAs administered in any one school district during any one school year will be subject to a variety of economic and policy constraints, designs involving four or fewer assessments per year are most likely. For this study, we elected to investigate the two-PAA design shown in table 2.1.

This type of multiform design offers three advantages: (1) tasks can be more complex and integrative because more time is available for assessment in the aggregate; (2) intermediate results can be provided to teachers while there is still time to take appropriate instructional action; and (3) because no one assessment or occasion is determinative, a firmer evidentiary base is

Table 2.1. A summative reading assessment implemented via a two-PAA design.

Testing Occasion	Prerequisite Skills	Reading Strategies	Literary Skills & Knowledge	Informational/ Persuasive Skills & Knowledge
1	✓	✓	✓	
2	✓	✓		✓

available to support high-stakes decisions about students, teachers, and institutions at the end of the year.

Two prototype PAAs were developed for use in investigating the proposed design. Each prototype included two sections: a Spoken Response Section and a scenario-based Extended Comprehension Section. These sections are described below.

The Spoken Response Section

This section is designed to provide evidence of examinees' mastery status relative to key prerequisite reading skills such as recognizing familiar words, decoding unfamiliar words, and reading fluently. It consists of 20 real words, 20 nonsense words, and three passages that examinees are asked to read aloud.

Examinee-level data derived from this section, combined with examinee-level data derived from the Extended Comprehension Section described below, are designed to help teachers distinguish two types of struggling readers: (1) "word callers," that is, examinees who are fluent readers yet have trouble comprehending what they've read, and (2) "gap fillers," that is, examinees who must struggle to maintain a sufficient reading speed yet are still managing to grasp the literal meaning of text, possibly because they have learned to compensate for deficiencies in required prerequisite skills (see Paris, Carpenter, Paris, & Hamilton, 2005).

The Extended Comprehension Section

This section begins with an introductory scenario selected to give students a realistic purpose for reading a collection of related texts. The scenario in the Informational PAA was specified as follows: *You have to write a report about the Scientific Method for your science class. Since you enjoy reading about American History, you decide to focus your report on Ben Franklin's use of the Scientific Method. Read the following passages to learn more about the Scientific Method and about Ben Franklin's scientific experiments.*

Subsequent exercises focused on four related texts: an article about the scientific method taken from an encyclopedia, a passage about Ben Franklin's scientific experiments adapted from a social studies textbook, a newspaper article about three recent winners of the Intel Science Competition, and a diagram from a student lab report. The texts were presented with 23 associated exercises. Some of the exercises were designed to assess comprehension of individual texts in isolation; others were designed to assess the ability to integrate and synthesize information from multiple texts.

For example, one exercise required examinees to classify individual sentences from the Ben Franklin passage in terms of the particular steps of the scientific method. Because the Ben Franklin passage was *not* written to illustrate the steps of the scientific method, a correct response requires both cross-document thinking and transfer, that is, students have to apply a classification framework developed from reading one text (the encyclopedia article) to a specific "reading-to-do" problem framed in terms of a second text (the Ben Franklin passage).

METHOD

Materials

Materials consisted of two prototype scenario-based assessments developed in accordance with the hypothesized competency model. The first prototype (called PAA #1) was administered in fall 2007. It included 43 spoken response items, 13 selected response items, and 10 constructed response items. The second prototype (called PAA #2) was administered in spring 2008. It included 43 spoken response items, 23 selected response items, and 6 constructed response items.

Participants

Table 2.2 shows the numbers of students tested at each administration. All participating students were enrolled in English language arts or social studies classes taught by four different teachers from three different schools in a large northeastern U.S. school district.

Table 2.2.   Numbers of students tested at grades 7 and 8, by form.

Form	Time	Grade 7	Grade 8	Total
PAA #1	Fall '07	150	56	216
PAA #2	Spring '08	108	72	180

A total of 171 students were tested on both occasions.

Procedure

PAAs were administered via students' individual Macintosh laptops during regular classroom sessions. Students were allowed 10 minutes to complete the Spoken Response Section and 55 minutes to complete the Extended Comprehension Section.

Analysis

Psychometric analyses focused on two key properties: reliability and construct representation. Reliability was evaluated by examining internal consistency estimates calculated using Cronbach's Coefficient Alpha. As local item dependencies resulting from the scenario-based nature of the Extended Comprehension Section may have resulted in some degree of inflation, the reported Alphas for that section may be viewed as an upper bound on the true reliability of the section.

The correlation between scores earned on the Extended Comprehension sections of the first and second PAAs was also examined. This correlation provides a lower bound on the reliability of the Extended Comprehension Section because (a) several months elapsed between the two administrations, and (b) the two PAAs were designed to target somewhat different constellations of skills (see table 2.1).

Construct representation, that is, the processes, strategies, and knowledge structures involved in responding to test items (Embretson, 1983, 1998), was evaluated for the Extended Comprehension Section only.

Analyses considered the degree of consistency between examinees' observed item response patterns and a set of ideal item response patterns defined in accordance with the Model Building/Applied Comprehension distinction specified in the competency model. When a significant proportion of the observed item response patterns are consistent with the hypothesized ideal item response patterns, we have evidence that the hypothesized competencies are, in fact, involved in item solving (Tatsuoka, 1983, 1990).

RESULTS

Reliability

Internal consistency estimates calculated using Cronbach's Coefficient Alpha ranged from 0.87 to 0.92 (see table 2.3). The cross-form correlation of the Extended Comprehension Section, estimated from a total of 171 score pairs, was 0.76. These results suggest that the reliability is within the range considered acceptable for making judgments about individuals.

Table 2.3. Cronbach's Coefficient Alpha, by form and section.

Form/Section	Total Items	Coefficient Alpha
PAA # 1		
Spoken Section	43	0.91
Extended Comprehension Section	23	0.87
PAA # 2		
Spoken Section	43	0.92
Extended Comprehension Section	29	0.88

Construct Representation

Table 2.4 shows the numbers of items classified as measuring either Model Building or Applied Comprehension skill on each of the two PAAs. The table also shows the mean percent correct, by skill category, for each PAA. Note that on each PAA, and at each grade level, examinees consistently performed better on Model Building items as compared to Applied Comprehension items.

This result is consistent with the hypothesized model because Model Building skill is defined as the ability to develop an accurate mental representation of the information presented in a *single* text, and Applied Comprehension skill is defined as the ability to use such representations, when necessary, to solve complex applied problems such as evaluating assumptions and reconciling information from different texts.

Table 2.4 also shows that the increased difficulty of the Applied items, relative to the Model Building items, was more pronounced on the second PAA than on the first. This result was expected because data from the first

Table 2.4. Mean percent correct by skill category and grade level.

PAA/Skill Category	Items	Grade 7	Grade 8	Grade Level Difference
PAA #1				
Model-Building Skill	24	0.61	0.66	.05 (.26)
Applied Comprehension	6	0.45	0.53	.08 (.33)
Skill Level Difference		0.16	0.13	
		(.76)	(.55)	
PAA #2				
Model-Building Skill	16	0.64	0.74	.10 (.51)
Applied Comprehension	13	0.39	0.47	.08 (.40)
Skill Level Difference		0.27	0.28	
		(1.25)	(1.47)	

Item skill classifications were specified during item development. All constructed response items were double scored. Weighted Kappa statistics for these items ranged from 0.78 to 0.99. Numbers in parentheses are effect sizes calculated using Cohen's d.

Table 2.5.   Frequency of skill mastery patterns defined in terms of examinees' Model-Building and Applied Comprehension scores, for each of two different PAAs.

			PAA #1		PAA #2	
Pattern	*MB*	*AP*	*No.*	*Percent*	*No.*	*Percent*
1	Low	Low	55	25	39	22
2	High	Low	62	29	74	41
3	High	High	95	44	67	37
4	Low	High	4	2	0	0
Total			216	100	180	100

MB = Model Building, AP = Applied Comprehension. Low = less than 50 percent correct. High = Greater than or equal to 50 percent correct.

PAA were used to update the item writing guidelines used during development of the second PAA.

Prerequisite relationships among Model Building and Applied Comprehension items were also evaluated. In these analyses, a percent correct cutoff score of 50 percent was used to classify examinee performance in each skill area as either Low or High. Table 2.5 summarizes the resulting profiles.

Because the hypothesized cognitive model specifies that Model Building skills are prerequisite to Applied Comprehension skills, three of the specified patterns are consistent with the model and one is not. The single inconsistent pattern is Pattern 4, the only pattern that pairs a low Model Building score with a high Applied Comprehension score. The table shows that Pattern 4 was observed four times for PAA #1, and not at all for PAA #2. These results contribute to construct representation by supporting the hypothesized prerequisite relationship between Model Building skill and Applied Comprehension skill.

CONCLUSION

This chapter presented an initial look at the feasibility of employing scenario-based reading assessments for state accountability purposes. Analyses considered item response data collected for two prototype scenario-based forms administered in three different middle schools in a large northeastern U.S. school district.

Data collected in this initial, exploratory study suggest that scenario-based reading assessments can indeed provide the type of high-quality evidence needed for state accountability purposes while simultaneously supporting teaching and learning. Two types of findings support this preliminary conclusion.

First, both prototypes were delivered in accordance with strict constraints on administration times and scoring costs, and each yielded acceptable levels of reliability.

Second, analyses of the Model Building and Applied Comprehension sub-scores suggested that (a) our attempts to distinguish items requiring higher-level critical thinking and problem-solving skills have been successful, particularly on the second PAA, and (b) examinee classifications determined from the specified Model Building and Applied Comprehension subscores hold promise for assigning students to theoretically meaningful reading comprehension profiles designed to support differentiated instructional treatments.

Although these results are encouraging, certain limitations should be noted. First, available samples were relatively small, consisting of just 216 students in the fall 2007 sample, and 180 students in the spring 2008 sample. Second, samples were not randomly selected from a known population of students so they are not representative of students at the targeted grade levels. Third, while we hypothesized that subscores based on the Model Building/Applied Comprehension distinction would support differentiated instructional approaches, the study was not designed to evaluate the validity of diagnostic classifications or to measure changes in classroom practice.

Additional planned research will enable us to address these limitations while also obtaining more in-depth information about feasibility, reliability, and construct representation.

REFERENCES

Alderson, J. C. (2000). *Assessing reading*. Cambridge, UK: Cambridge University Press.

Bennett, R. E., & Gitomer, D. H. (2009). Transforming K-12 assessment. Integrating accountability testing, formative assessment, and professional support. In C. Wyatt-Smith & J. Cumming (Eds.), *Educational assessment in the 21st century* (pp. 43–61). New York: Springer.

Bereiter, C., & Bird, M. (1985). Use of thinking aloud in identification and teaching of reading comprehension strategies. *Cognition & Instruction, 2*, 131–156.

Black, P., & Wiliam, D. (1998). Assessment and classroom learning. *Assessment in Education: Principles, Policy & Practice, 5*, 7074.

Bransford, J., Brown, A., & Cocking, R. (Eds.). (1999). *How people learn: Brain, mind, experience and school*. Washington, DC: National Academies Press.

Chall, J. S. (1967). *Stages of reading development*. New York: McGraw-Hill.

Chi, M. T. H., Bassok, M., Lewis, M., Reimann, P., & Glaser, R. (1989). Self-explanations: How students study and use examples in learning to solve problems. *Cognitive Science, 13*, 145–182.

Chi, M. T. H., de Leeuw, N., Chiu, M.-H., & LaVancher, C. (1994). Eliciting self-explanations improves understanding. *Cognitive Science, 18*, 439–477.

Committee on Prospering in the Global Economy of the 21st Century (2007). *Rising above the gathering storm: Energizing and employing America for a brighter economic future.* Washington, DC: National Academies Press.

Cox, R., McKendree, J. Tobin, R., Lee, J., & Mayes, T. (1999). Vicarious learning from dialogue and discourse. *Instructional Science, 27,* 431–458.

Daneman, M., & Merikle, P. (1996). Working memory and language comprehension: A meta-analysis. *Psychonomic Bulletin & Review,* 3, 422–433.

Embretson, S. E. (1983). Construct validity: Construct representation versus nomothetic span. *Psychological Bulletin, 93,* 179–197.

———. (1998). A cognitive design system approach to generating valid tests: Application to abstract reasoning. *Psychological Methods,* 3, 300–396.

Gholson, B., & Craig, S. D. (2006). Promoting constructive activities that support vicarious learning during computer-based instruction. *Educational Psychology Review, 18,* 119–139.

Graesser, A. C., McNamara, D. S., & Louwerse, M. M. (2003). What do readers need to learn in order to process coherence relations in narrative and expository text? In A. P. Sweet & C. E. Snow (Eds.), *Rethinking reading comprehension* (pp. 82–98). New York: Guilford Press.

Kintsch, W. (1998). *Comprehension: A paradigm for cognition.* Cambridge, UK: Cambridge University Press.

Kirsch, I., Braun, H., Yamamoto, K., & Sum, A. (2007). *America's perfect storm: Three forces changing our nation's future.* Princeton, NJ: Educational Testing Service.

McNamara, D. S. (2004). SERT: Self explanation reading training. *Discourse Processes, 38,* 1–30.

———. (Ed.). (2007). *Reading comprehension strategies: Theory, interventions, and technologies.* Mahwah, NJ: Lawrence Erlbaum Associates.

Muller, D., Sharma, M., Eklund, J., & Reimann, P. (2007). Conceptual change through vicarious learning in an authentic physics setting. *Instructional Science, 35,* 519–533.

National Center on Education and the Economy. (2006). *Tough times, tough choices: The report of the New Commission on the Skills of the American Workforce.* Washington, DC.

O'Reilly, T., & Sheehan, K. M. (2009). *Cognitively based assessment of, for, and as learning: A framework for assessing reading competency.* (Number RR-09-26). Princeton, NJ: Educational Testing Service.

Palinscar, A. S., & Brown, A. L. (1984). Reciprocal teaching of comprehension-fostering and comprehension-monitoring activities. *Cognition and Instruction, 1,* 117–175.

Paris, S. G., Carpenter, R.D., Paris, A. H., & Hamilton, E.E. (2005). Spurious and genuine correlates of children's reading comprehension. In S. G. Paris & S. A. Stahl (Eds). *Children's reading comprehension and assessment* (pp. 131–160). Mahwah, NJ: Lawrence Erlbaum Associates.

Paris, S. G., Cross, D. R., & Lipson, M. Y. (1984). Informed strategies for learning: A program to improve children's reading awareness and comprehension. *Journal of Educational Psychology, 76,* 1239–1252.

Paris, S., & Jacobs, J. (1984). The benefits of informed instruction for children's reading awareness and comprehension skills. *Child Development, 55,* 2083–2093.

Partnership for 21st Century Skills (2004). *Learning for the 21st century: a report and mile guide for 21st century skills.* Washington, DC: Author. Retrieved October 15, 2008 from www.21stcenturyskills.org/images/stories/otherdocs/p21up_Report. pdf.

———. (2008). *21st century skills and English map.* Washington, DC: Author. Retrieved January 15, 2009 from: www.21stcenturyskills.org/documents/21st_century_skills_english_map.pdf.

Pellegrino, J; Chudowsky, J. N.; & Glaser, R. (Eds.) (2001). *Knowing what students know. The science and design of educational assessment.* Washington, DC: National Academy Press.

Perfetti, C. A. (1985). *Reading ability.* New York: Oxford University Press.

Pressley, M. (2000). What should comprehension instruction be the instruction of? In M. L. Kamil, P. B. Mosenthal, P. D. Pearson, & R. Barr (Eds.), *Handbook of reading research* (volume III, pp. 545–561). Mahwah, NJ: Lawrence Erlbaum Associates.

Pressley, M., & Afflerbach, P. (1995). *Verbal protocols of reading: The nature of constructively responsive reading.* Hillsdale, NJ: Lawrence Erlbaum Associates.

Pressley, M., Wood, E., Woloshyn, V. E., & Martin, V. (1992). Encouraging mindful use of prior knowledge: Attempting to construct explanatory answers facilitates learning. *Educational Psychologist, 27,* 91–109.

Schmidt, W. H., McKnight, C. C., & Raizen, S.A. (1997). *A spirited vision: An investigation of U.S. science and mathematics education.* Dordrecht, The Netherlands: Kluwer.

Sheehan, K. M., Kostin, I., & Futagi, Y. (2008a, July). *Reading level assessment for high-stakes testing applications: A second look at variation due to differences in text genre.* Paper presented at the Annual Meeting of the Society for Text and Discourse, Memphis, TN.

———. (2008b, July). *When do standard approaches for measuring vocabulary difficulty, syntactic complexity and referential cohesion yield biased estimates of text difficulty?* Poster presented at the 30th Annual Meeting of the Cognitive Science Society, Washington, D.C.

Tatsuoka, K. K. (1983). Rule space: An approach for dealing with misconceptions based on item response theory. *Journal of Educational Measurement, 20,* 345–354.

———. (1990). Toward an integration of item-response theory and cognitive error diagnosis. In N. Fredericksen, R. Glaser, A. Lesgold, and Shafto, M. G. (Eds.), *Diagnostic monitoring of skill and knowledge acquisition* (pp. 453–488). Hillsdale, NJ: Lawrence Erlbaum Associates.

Vellutino, F., Tunmer, W., & Jaccard, J.(2007). Components of reading ability: Multivariate evidence for a convergent skills model of reading development. *Scientific Studies of Reading, 11,* 3–32.

Vitale, M., & Romance, N. (2007). A knowledge-based framework for unifying content-area reading comprehension and reading comprehension strategies. In D.

S. McNamara (Ed.), *Reading comprehension strategies: Theory, interventions, and technologies* (pp. 73–104). Mahwah, NJ: Lawrence Erlbaum Associates.

Wyman, B., & Randel, J. (1998). The relation of knowledge organization to performance of a complex cognitive task. *Applied Cognitive Psychology, 12,* 251–264.

NOTE

1. Strategies are deliberate, conscious, effortful actions that successful readers implement to repair breaks in comprehension and to move understanding from a shallow to a deeper level.

Chapter Three

Assessing Comprehension Processes during Reading

Keith Millis and Joseph Magliano

Comprehension emerges from a complex set of processes that occur as one reads, leading to the construction of a coherent memory representation for a text. However, most available assessments rely on measuring comprehension *after* reading is completed using a multiple-choice format where questions are answered while the text is still available. So it is possible that students adopt test-taking strategies that compromise the assumption that students are actually relying on the memory representation for the text to answer the questions.

To be certain, there are advantages to this testing format (Freedle & Kostin, 1994; Glover, Zimmer, & Bruning, 1979; Malak & Hegeman, 1985; van den Bergh, 1990), but this approach presents serious challenges if the goal is to assess the products and processes specified by discourse theory (Magliano & Millis, 2003; Magliano, Millis, Ozuru, & McNamara, 2007).

In this chapter, we present research on a test that is designed to assess reading comprehension as it emerges during students' reading of a text and to examine some of the processes that have been identified as important for comprehension.

The approach described here bases assessment entirely on the user typing in verbal responses to questions that appear during reading of a text. It attempts to measure comprehension as it is unfolding *online*, during reading, and is based on prior research conducted in our laboratory that demonstrates that concurrent verbal protocols (e.g., think-aloud protocols) are indicative of comprehension skill (Magliano & Millis, 2003; Millis, Magliano, & Todaro, 2006).

In the test, a student reads a passage where only one sentence is shown on the screen at a time. The student progresses sentence by sentence by pressing a "next" button with the mouse. Periodically the computer interrupts with a question, and the student is required to type in an answer.

Consider figure 3.1, which provides the beginning of a text on the Spanish Civil War, questions, and a few sample answers. The first question is a very general one that prompts for the student's thoughts, whereas the second is much more specific. The answers to both questions are intuitively revealing about the level of comprehension being achieved by the student.

Consider John's response to the general prompt, "What are you thinking about now?" He essentially repeats the last sentence that he read, which was "The Nationalists' hopes were dashed." He also elaborates by stating people

The Spanish Civil War

On July 17, 1936, Spanish military forces stationed in Morocco mutinied and proclaimed a revolution against Spain's elected government. The uprising marked the beginning of the Spanish Civil War. The rebels, or Nationalists, soon found a strong leader in General Francisco Franco. Supporters of the government, known as Republicans, included most workers, liberals, socialists, communists, and Basque and Catalan separatists.

The initial goal of the Nationalists was to seize power quickly with little bloodshed. At first the Nationalist forces made great advances. Nationalist control rapidly extended across most of western and southern Spain. However, Republicans soon defeated the insurgents in eastern and northern cities. The Nationalists' hopes were dashed.

(question appears) What are you thinking about now?

John's answer: the nationalist's hopes were down. They were upset. I know that I would be.

Ella's answer: the nationalist's hopes were dashed because republicans had just defeated them, which impeded their goal of seizing power peacefully over the whole country which they were actually doing.

(passage continues)

However, the Nationalist movement had several advantages that would ensure victory. Nationalists took control of agricultural areas. There were severe shortages of food in Republican controlled areas. The Nationalist forces were more unified, and better equipped and trained, than their Republican adversaries. During this time, there was a strong anti-Communist movement growing in Europe. Consequently, the Nationalists benefited from larger amounts of foreign assistance.

(question appears) Why was more foreign assistance going toward the Nationalists?

John's answer: I think because they were winning. Winners get rewards.

Ella's answer: because republicans included communists, and Europeans hated the communists, so they were giving money to their enemies, the nationalists.

Figure 3.1. Example text, questions, and answers.

feel sad when their hopes are dashed. At least on the basis of this answer, he does not appear to be linking the last sentence he read with the earlier text.

In contrast, Ella explains why their hopes were dashed by retrieving ideas earlier stated in the text. When prompted with the more direct question, "Why was more foreign assistance going toward the Nationalists?," Ella continues to provide an explanation by bringing up ideas explicitly stated earlier in the text ("Republicans included communists," "Europeans hated communists") and reasonable inferences from world knowledge, namely that the "assistance" consisted of money, and something akin to "the enemy of your enemy is your friend." John's answer to the same question reveals, however, that he does not comprehend the text.

Below, we present research on a new reading assessment tool that exploits the approach described above. It is called the Reading Strategy Assessment Tool (RSAT; Gilliam, Magliano, Millis, Levinstein, & Boonthum, 2007; Magliano, Millis, The RSAT Development Team, Levinstein, & Boonthum, 2011). RSAT is a computer-administered program that provides an overall assessment of discourse comprehension and an assessment of some processes and strategies that are related to comprehension.

For example, on the basis of the types of answers provided by John and Ella, RSAT would be able to recognize that Ella is a better comprehender than John, and that she integrates sentences together by generating bridging inferences. John, on the other hand, makes an attempt to elaborate on the text content using world knowledge and paraphrases the explicit text, but he does little in the way of integrating the text.

RSAT is a long way from being an assessment tool with wide applications. However, it provides a step toward this goal by providing an automated assessment of constructed responses that reveals comprehension processes.

Many automated systems that classify constructed responses do so in a two-step procedure. In a first step, the system segments and classifies the contribution into categories, such as speech acts and metacognitive statements. In this step, short responses are removed as well as categories that are not addressed by the system. For example, AutoTutor (Graesser, Wiemer-Hastings, Wiemer-Hastings, Kreuz, & The Tutoring Research Group, 2000) and iSTART (McNamara, Levinstein, & Boonthum, 2004) remove short responses, metacommunicative statements, metacognitive statements, and sometimes expressive evaluations.

In the second step, the remaining content is analyzed on a conceptual level. AutoTutor, for example, computes measures of semantic similarity between the input and ideal answers to the question posed to the user.

These measures are based on techniques found in computational linguistics, artificial intelligence, and machine learning. A common technique is latent semantic analysis (LSA), which computes a metric of semantic similarity using a corpus of documents (Landauer & Dumais, 1997). If the measure of similarity between the input and an ideal answer, for example, reaches a criterion threshold, then the system deems the answer to be acceptable. If not, it is deemed unacceptable or incomplete, and the system responds accordingly.

RSAT also uses a two-step procedure. In the first step, all function words are removed from the input. This leaves content words (nouns, verbs, adjectives, and adverbs). Also, misspellings are identified and repaired by using Soundex matching (Birtwisle, 2002). In the second step, each content word is compared to the text. The program notes where in the text it had appeared—the current sentence, prior sentence(s), or not in the text at all. As will be described below, the place in the text that a word appeared is aligned with reading strategies.

For example, Ella's response to the first question contains words located a few sentences back ("seize," "power"), which indicates that she was interpreting the current sentence in the context of prior discourse. In contrast, John's response to the same question suggests that he was primarily thinking about the last sentence he read, because his contribution did not contain other words that appeared in the text besides from the last sentence.

A DESCRIPTION OF RSAT

Students read six short texts on the computer, including two narratives, two history, and two scientific expositions. The texts are grade-appropriate for tenth and eleventh graders, although the narratives are very simple (Flesch grade level around fifth grade).

Because many readability measures emphasize word frequency and sentence length in the calculations (Zakaluk & Samuels, 1988), the relatively simple nature of these texts suggests that most late adolescents will have the vocabulary necessary to understand the texts. Therefore, the test is meant to gauge comprehension when lower levels (word level, syntax) of comprehension are largely intact (Magliano & Millis, 2003). This leaves higher-order processes to be assessed, including the construction of the propositional representation of the text (i.e., textbase), the integration of propositions across large spans of text, and the generation of knowledge-based inferences.

The test-taker reads the texts one sentence at a time on the computer, because the intent is to have answers based on the student's mental representation of the text. We have verified that responses produced in this format have higher correlations with independent outcome measures than providing the student with the entire text read to this point (Gilliam et al., 2007). Students are prompted to answer questions after preselected sentences that were chosen due to causal connection to prior discourse content. After these sentences, the test-taker is asked one of two types of questions, direct and indirect.

Direct questions are phrased as *wh-* questions (why x?, when x?, what is x?, etc.) regarding an event or action explicitly mentioned up to (and including) the target sentence. Some sample direct questions are "Why do we hear thunder after the first lightning strike?"; "Why is there an increase in blood glucose with diabetes?"; "What was Louis IV trying to accomplish at the beginning of his reign?"; and "Why did the [train] cabin smell of roses?"

The purpose of direct questions is to measure the completeness and coherence of the students' discourse representation at the location when the question is posed. In particular, the questions were constructed to measure the situation model, which contains inferences regarding temporal and spatial information, characters' motivations and reasons, as well as causal connections among events and actions (Graesser, Singer, & Trabasso, 1994; Zwaan & Radvansky, 1998).

Because why-questions are known to tap causal antecedents and consequences for events and characters' actions (Graesser & Clark, 1985; Millis & Barker, 1996), the majority of the direct questions are why-questions. Nevertheless, the answers to the direct questions would come from both the textbase and the situation model.

The *indirect* question is always "What are you thinking now?," which is meant to elicit a think-aloud type of response. At these question prompts, the student is instructed "to report your thoughts regarding the current sentence in the context of the passage." The purpose of the indirect questions is to get an unbiased snapshot of the student's reading strategies (the strategies will be discussed below). This and other prompts are common in verbal protocol research where researchers are interested in the contents of working memory (Trabasso & Magliano, 1996).

We realize that any question will affect the content of individuals' working memory to some extent, so this cue was chosen to direct their answers to their understanding of the discourse. In particular, many researchers have used this approach in understanding the differences between skilled and less skilled readers (Chi, Bassok, Lewis, Reimann, & Glaser, 1989; Coté & Goldman, 1999; Magliano & Millis, 2003; Millis et al., 2006; Pressley & Afflerbach, 1995; Trabasso & Magliano, 1996; Whitney, Ritchie, & Clark, 1991).

There are tradeoffs between direct and indirect questions. The advantage of direct questions is that they can be constructed to target specific information that good readers should be able to encode. In particular, questions tapping explanatory reasoning are particularly diagnostic of comprehension and learning from discourse (Chi, deLeeuw, Chiu, & LaVancher, 1994; Coté, Goldman, & Saul, 1998; Graesser & Olde, 2003).

A disadvantage from the perspective of traditional reading assessment is that they may affect the representations that students build as they read (e.g., Callender & McDaniel, 2007; Peverly & Wood, 1999; Sagerman & Mayer, 1987). Asking questions during and after students read texts increases comprehension (van den Broek, Lorch, Linderholm, & Gustafson, 2001), and higher-level inferential questions increase comprehension to a greater extent than factual questions (Sagerman & Mayer, 1987).

An advantage of indirect questions, such as general think-aloud instructions, is that they reveal content and processes in working memory without interference, working effectively for complex tasks that can be expressed via language and are not overly constrained by the stimulus (Ericsson & Simon, 1993). A downside is that for some readers and contexts, the indirect question can elicit frustration because, due to the lack of constraints, the reader does not know what to write.

READING STRATEGIES ASSESSED BY RSAT

We use the term "reading strategies" a bit differently than others in the discourse and educational communities. Reading strategies are typically defined as actions that are somewhat effortful that are used in order to overcome barriers to understanding (Alexander & Jetton, 2003). These include taking notes, rereading, using imagery, underlining, paraphrasing, retelling, making examples, and so on. We use the word "strategy" more narrowly, namely to refer to mental processes that are implicated during reading, as the reader attempts to make sense of the printed word.

One of the strategies that RSAT attempts to measure is *bridging*. Bridging inferences refer to the process of linking current text (propositions, words) to prior text (Clark, 1975; McNamara & Magliano, 2009). Anaphor is one type of bridging inference, such as the use of pronouns to refer to previously introduced entities.

However, RSAT attempts to measure the process of integrating ideas from the prior text with the current sentence. A sentence might relate to a number of previously mentioned ideas in a number of ways. For example, it might be a causal consequence of one or more previous ideas that lie on a causal chain, a summary statement, or it might relate to the structure of the passage as a solution in a problem-solution rhetorical structure.

Ella's answer to the indirect question in figure 3.1 fits the bill because it includes explicit information from the prior text as an explanation for why the

Nationalists' hopes were dashed—the current sentence. Because some of the content that appeared in her answer appeared a few sentences back, Ella had to reinstate the content from long-term memory into working memory. She had to take this information, reason about it, and use some elements of world knowledge and common sense to form an integrated and coherent answer.

The target sentences were chosen based on a causal analysis of the texts (Trabasso, van den Broek, & Suh, 1989). We did this for several related reasons. The first is that causality is an important feature of narratives, historical accounts, and scientific discourse, and therefore should be related to the comprehension of these texts (Graesser et al., 1994; Trabasso et al., 1989).

The second is that readers are generally sensitive to ideas on a causal chain, in that they are better remembered (Trabasso & van den Broek, 1985) and are more activated in working memory (Suh & Trabasso, 1993) than ideas not on a causal chain.

The third is that skilled readers are more sensitive than less skilled readers in noticing and encoding causality (Magliano & Millis, 2003; Todaro, Millis, & Dandotkar, 2010). This last reason is especially relevant because the goal of RSAT is to measure comprehension ability.

RSAT distinguishes between local and distal bridges. Local bridges occur between the target sentence and the immediately prior sentence. Distal bridges occur between the target sentences and sentences located two or more sentences back.

Various researchers have reported evidence that skilled and less skilled readers differ on processes linked with bridging inferences. For example, less skilled readers are less likely to integrate successive ideas in a text than skilled readers (Lorch, Lorch, & Morgan, 1987). Generally, less skilled readers tend to focus more on the immediate context surrounding each sentence (Coté & Goldman, 1999; Coté, Goldman, & Saul, 1998; Rapp, van den Broek, McMaster, Kendeou, & Espin, 2007).

A second strategy assessed by RSAT is *elaboration*. Elaborative inferences are based on the reader's world knowledge of the text (e.g., Graesser, Millis, & Zwaan, 1997; McNamara & Magliano, 2009). They become activated as the text is read and may be incorporated into the mental representation of the text.

There are at least three primary distinctions between bridges and elaborations. First, unlike bridges, elaborations do not connect sentences. Rather, they are ideas from the reader's world knowledge that may temporarily become activated by a concept or proposition from the text or added to the mental representation as a dangling node.

Second, unlike bridging inferences, which contain elements directly from the text, elaborations do not express content directly from the text. Third, elaborations provide information to form the situation model and a context from which to interpret the text events.

A third strategy is *paraphrasing*. Unlike bridging and elaboration, which are based on theories of comprehension and a substantial amount of empirical evidence (e.g., McNamara & Magliano, 2009), the strategy of paraphrasing primarily arises from the method of using verbal protocols. When readers think aloud or type their thoughts as they read, they sometimes mention the sentence, in part or in its entirety, as part of their verbal protocol. Sometimes this takes the form of a summary of the sentence.

Although we do not claim that paraphrasing is something readers do implicitly under normal reading circumstances, readers often use paraphrasing as part of their self-explanations (McNamara et al., 2009). There is also evidence that the amount of paraphrasing in verbal protocols is negatively correlated with comprehension (Magliano & Millis, 2003). This negative correlation likely occurs because students who excessively paraphrase do little bridging and elaborating. This was the case for John in figure 3.1.

The strategies above, particularly bridging and elaborations, are similar to component processes measured by the comprehension test developed by Hannon and Daneman (2001). In their test, participants read sentences that contain both nonsense and real words that together specify an ordered set of relations among the concepts (e.g., "A MIRT resembles an OSTRICH but is larger and has a longer neck. A COFT resembles a ROBIN but is smaller and has a longer neck. A FILP resembles a COFT but is smaller, has a longer neck, and nests on land").

Afterward, they were tested by true/false statements that measured the reader's (1) memory for the statements (e.g., "A MIRT is larger than an OSTRICH"), (2) access of prior knowledge (e.g., A ROBIN lives in Canada, whereas a PENGUIN typically doesn't"), (3) inferences between the sentences that do not require prior knowledge (e.g., "A FLIP is smaller than a ROBIN"), and (4) integration of prior knowledge with new text information (e.g., "Like PENGUINS, MIRTS can't fly").

Scores on all of these item types predicted the Nelson Denny test of comprehension, but the items that measured the ability to integrate text information with world knowledge did the best.

Our measure of bridging and elaborations appears to be related to these components, at least to some degree. For example, in order to bridge and integrate ideas across text, one needs access to prior text (memory) and to make conceptual or logical inferences among the ideas (generation of inferences) in part by using world knowledge (integration of prior knowledge). Elaborative inferences require the access of prior knowledge, and they arise when the reader integrates the text with prior knowledge.

Hannon and Daneman's (2001) test has been criticized because of its artificial texts, and because of its reliance on problem-solving skills (Kintsch & Kintsch, 2005). Kintsch and Kintsch (2005) argue that a test that measures these components in a more natural context would be beneficial. They offer an alternative based on scoring essays using LSA, and RSAT is another.

SCORING IN RSAT

RSAT employs a "semantic benchmark" approach for indicating the presence of a strategy (Millis et al., 2004). In doing so, RSAT uses rubrics for scoring in much the same way a teacher might score an answer to a question—RSAT counts the number of content words in the answer that matches a benchmark (rubric).

For the direct questions, which are meant to measure the comprehension of the text, the benchmarks are "ideal answers" to the questions. So, the score for each direct question is the number of words in the answer that was mentioned in the ideal answer.

For the indirect questions, four scores are computed. A local bridging score is the number of content words in the answer that appear in the sentence immediately prior to the target sentence. A distal bridging score is the number of words in the answer that appear in sentences that are more than two sentences back from the target sentence. An elaboration score is the number of content words in the answer that do not appear in the text. A paraphrasing score is the number of content words in the answer that come from the target sentence.

The scores from the target sentences are averaged: An overall score for comprehension is computed from the answers to the direct questions, as well as a score for the paraphrases, local bridges, distal bridges, and elaborations from the indirect questions.

Of course, there are many methods for comparing input to stored responses. Various methods are used in intelligent tutoring systems (e.g., Graesser, Penumatsa, Ventura, Cai, & Hu, 2007) and in essay graders (e.g., Foltz, Laham, & Landauer, 1999). Methods differ on the content of the benchmarks, the method of computing similarity between the input and the benchmarks, the way that benchmarks or words are weighted, and the criterion in which an answer is deemed acceptable, to name a few.

We should note that in the brief history of RSAT, we have used LSA while exploring some of these factors (Magliano, Wiemer-Hastings, Millis, Munoz, McNamara, 2002). In Millis et al. (2004), we compared different types of semantic benchmarks that would best indicate the extent that a reader's self-explanation reflected global, integrated processing of the text. (In this context, a self-explanation is a written or oral response that is produced by a reader to comprehend a sentence in a context of the passage.)

We found that benchmarks that contained content words from the text performed just as well as intact examples of self-explanations that reflected different degrees of integrative processing. The examples were self-explanations that were previously generated by students.

However, since that time, we have dropped using LSA as the algorithm of comparing the constructed response to benchmarks in favor of the word-based procedure described above. There were two reasons for setting aside LSA. One is that LSA cosines increase with the number of words being compared, even when the words are randomly sampled from a source (e.g., Graesser et al., 2007). In many of our cases, however, a constructed response may have only a few content words.

Another reason is that LSA relies on a corpus that should be semantically aligned with the material for which it is used. For example, we constructed a LSA space to fit the semantic requirements of the texts and topics used in the study. Word-matching frees up some of these requirements, but perhaps at a cost of precision and accuracy.

RESEARCH USING RSAT

Magliano et al. (2011) have shown that RSAT predicts comprehension. In their research, university students took one of three forms of RSAT, the Gates-MacGinitie test of comprehension, and an open-ended experimenter-generated test of comprehension composed of two expository texts and short essay questions.

The open-ended test was considered the "gold standard" from which to gauge the effectiveness of RSAT and the Gates-MacGinitie. They found that the open-ended test correlated with performance on the direct questions ($r = .45$) to a degree that was comparable with the Gates-MacGinitie ($r = .52$), although the correlation was slightly lower for RSAT. (We have also found instances of near identical correlations for direct questions and the Gates-MacGinitie with open-ended tests; Millis, Perry, Gilliam, & Magliano, 2007).

Magliano et al. (2011) also showed that the strategy scores derived from the answers to the indirect questions predicted 21% of the variance on the open-ended test ($p < .001$). The predictors were the average number of content words in the answers that were also in the current sentence (paraphrase), prior sentence (local bridge), distal sentences (distal bridges), or not from the text (elaborations).

They reported positive significant slopes for bridges and elaborations and a significant negative slope for paraphrases. The positive slopes would be expected because comprehension requires integrative bridges and elaborations from world knowledge. The negative slope for paraphrases suggests that readers who primarily paraphrase the current sentence are not integrating the current sentence with the prior text.

A slightly different pattern of results occurred when they predicted the responses to the direct questions from the strategy measures collected from the indirect questions. The amount of predicted variance increased to 38%, which would be expected because the measures of strategies and comprehension are now based on the same texts. Presumably, the measures of strategy use for the texts contributed to the comprehension of those texts. (One would expect lower correlations if gathering evidence of strategy use from one set of texts to predict comprehension on another set of texts.)

However, the slope for paraphrases flipped from being a negative to a positive predictor of comprehension. The change in direction did not appear to be related to multicolinearity or suppression. Instead, we believe that paraphrasing strengthens the memory for the text (surface-level and textbase representations). This would increase the scores for the direct questions because many of the words in the ideal answers were taken from the text.

However, readers who primarily paraphrase are doing so at the expense of generating bridging and elaborative inferences, at least to some extent. Therefore, paraphrases are negative predictors of comprehension when the measurement of comprehension is not strongly tied to the memory of the explicit passage and requires other processes, such as bridging and elaboration.

When we consider total variance explained by both direct and indirect measures, RSAT accounted for a significant 34% of the variance in the open-ended test (p < .001). Clearly, the combined RSAT measures account for more variance than they do independently. We also considered the unique variance of RSAT over and above a standardized test, specifically Gates-MacGinitie, and vice versa. RSAT scores accounted for a significant and unique 14% of the variance over and above the Gates-MacGinitie test (*p* < .05), whereas Gates-MacGinitie accounted for a significant and unique 8% (*p* < .005).

Lastly, Magliano et al. (2011) reported fairly high correlations between the word count measures of the strategies and human raters for those strategies: between .46 and .70 (*p*'s < .01). These last two findings suggest that the measures of strategies reported by RSAT are valid in the sense they predict comprehension and agree with human raters of those strategies.

As mentioned above, we constructed three stimulus lists, which could be conceptualized as Forms A, B, and C. The above analyses involved an assessment of the approach, and in doing these analyses, we dummy coded for forms. When we consider the amount of variance in SA performance accounted for by each form (using direct and indirect measures), there was a significant 50%, 41%, and 40% of the variance explained by Forms A, B, and C, respectively (all p's < .005).

We have also begun to assess the reliability of RSAT with data collected from additional students. We had college students take two of the three existing forms of RSAT, each taking a different one on two consecutive days. After they completed the second administration of RSAT on the second day and a short break, they completed an open-ended test of comprehension. Because there were three forms (forms A, B, and C), there were six groups representing the different combinations (A then B, A then C, etc.).

There are a couple of findings worth mentioning. First, the strategy scores predicted the open-ended test of comprehension, thereby replicating the findings reported in Magliano et al. (2011). Second, participants generally wrote one to two fewer content words in their answers during the second administration. We believe that this reflected a type of practice effect in that they learned to express their thoughts in fewer words. Third, test-retest correlations were all statistically significant, and all but two were .50 or higher.

From the perspective of the strategy scores and the comprehension score, the highest reliability occurred for distal bridges and elaborations (both r's = .79), followed by comprehension (r = .70), paraphrase (r = .66), and local bridges (r = .51). The magnitude of these correlations was positively correlated with the magnitude of the raw scores (i.e., mean number of words in each category). Presumably, there is more error with strategies that contain fewer words.

We should note that our findings are not as robust as others reported in other chapters. We generally find correlations between the direct questions and open-ended tests of comprehension to hover around .50 (R^2 = .25). These are smaller compared to correlations produced by published comprehension tests and indicate that RSAT is undoubtedly not suitable for widespread use and high-stakes testing. However, we think this magnitude is rather encouraging given our straightforward and simple approach of using word-based matching to score constructed responses.

CONCLUSION

RSAT is in the relatively early stages of test development. We see RSAT as a valuable research tool that perhaps could eventually serve alongside multiple-choice tests. Many tests of comprehension have a general comprehension scale as well as a vocabulary scale, but no other measure of the processes implicated during comprehension.

RSAT contains both. It has a measure of comprehension as well as snapshots of the reader trying to integrate the text using bridging and elaborative inferences. This makes RSAT unique in the world of assessment. However, unique does not necessarily mean better. RSAT has the potential to be useful to the extent that it affords something that traditional multiple-choice formats do not.

Indeed, we believe that providing measures of comprehension processes and strategies can be useful for researchers and educators (see also Hannon & Daneman, 2001). We should note that because most models of comprehension assume that readers bridge and elaborate (McNamara & Magliano, 2009), RSAT is relatively model-neutral, which adds to its appeal as a research tool.

In addition, researchers who are developing reading interventions can use these metrics to examine treatment effects. For example, we are exploring ways that RSAT comprehension and processing measures can assess readers' change self-explanations as a function of iSTART, a computer program that teaches self-explanation and reading strategies (McNamara et al., 2004).

For reading educators, the strategy scores might lead to focused interventions. For example, a high paraphrase score together with low bridging and elaboration scores would inform the instructor that the student needs remedial work on integrating sentences together and with activating world knowledge. A comprehension score by itself would not provide this level of diagnosticity (Magliano et al., 2007). Therefore, researchers and educators would both benefit with assessments of the processes (strategies) of comprehension rather than merely an assessment of the end product.

A second potential advantage of RSAT is that it measures comprehension as it occurs. Most tests measure comprehension with multiple-choice items after the test passage is read. But in most cases, readers can go back to the passage to answer the questions. If the test permits, a savvy student might even read the questions before reading the test passage.

In addition, the multiple-choice format allows readers to recognize the correct answer even when they did not encode that information during comprehension. Therefore, it is uncertain as far as the extent that the test is measuring test-taking strategies rather than the end product of comprehending a passage (Farr, Pritchard, & Smitten, 1990).

In RSAT, however, students cannot go back and reread text to answer a question, and they cannot know the questions ahead of reading. This is one advantage of computer-based administration.

We should point out that the goal to measure comprehension during comprehension may not be shared by all researchers. In fact, measuring end products might be considered the bottom line because they represent what is ultimately achieved from the acts of comprehension. However, as with most cognitive processes, comprehension is achieved with processes that take time and resources to complete.

It is plausible that most comprehension processes occur during the course of reading, but there might be others that occur afterward, such as reflection and insight. Reflecting and achieving various amounts of insight may occur minutes or days after reading, and the processes that make up reflecting might be the same as those implicated during reading. Clearly, as researchers, we need to decide *when* it is best to test in addition to *what* should be measured based on assessment goals (Magliano et al., 2007).

One of our bigger challenges has been to arrive at a valid measure of elaboration. Our current measure is limited for a couple of reasons. First, any content word that does not appear in the text is counted as an elaboration. Therefore, synonyms would be counted as an elaboration even though most researchers would not count synonyms as evidence of elaborative processing. For example, John's use of the word "down" for "dashed" in figure 3.1 would be counted as an instance of elaboration. Adding synonyms to the benchmarks and bringing LSA back to the mix might alleviate this problem (e.g., see McNamara, Boonthum, Levinstein, & Millis, 2007).

Second, all elaborations are counted as being equally relevant to the text, although it is clearly not the case. Just as relevant associations and elaborations are related to comprehension, unrelated or "off the wall" associations should also be diagnostic of comprehension (Trabasso & Magliano, 1996). However, the relationship between the presence and relevance of elaborations and overall comprehension might be subtle.

For example, Rapp et al. (2007) discuss identifying two types of struggling readers based on eye movements and think-aloud protocols. One group focused processing on the current sentence, doing little by way of integrating it with prior text. The other group showed evidence of going beyond the current sentence (like better readers), but these "activities were frequently unsuccessful or invoked inappropriate background knowledge" (Rapp et al., 2007, p. 304). The second group presumably generated fewer relevant elaborations than the better readers.

An implication for RSAT is that assessment accuracy would be increased if we could assess the relevancy of the elaborations. We have tried to empirically identify relevant from irrelevant elaborations by first having human raters classify them into one or the other category; however, raters could not reliably agree on the extent that an elaboration was relevant.

There are also issues related to ecological validity when readers answer questions during comprehension. Readers are not accustomed to stopping in the middle of reading to answer questions. This could affect measurement in several ways.

First, if the reader is in "flow" while reading, then answering questions could be highly disruptive. The disruptions might interfere with comprehension or at least be annoying. In this case, the instrument would probably underestimate the skills of the reader.

Second, the questions might affect the motivation or the metacognitive monitoring of the student. The questions might increase motivation if the student is doing well or if they are within the skill level of the student. They might decrease motivation if the reader perceives the questions to be too easy or too difficult, or irrelevant to the task.

Lastly, as mentioned earlier, the questions could change the reading strategy of the reader (Callender & McDaniel, 2007; Sagerman & Mayer, 1987).

We acknowledge that RSAT presents a simple way to classify thoughts that people have during comprehension. It is simple because it relies only on word matching; that is, matching content words that are typed in with a "bag of words" representing sentences and ideas.

As mentioned above, we have previously used latent semantic analysis to provide a metric of semantic similarity between the constructed responses and the "bags of words," but in our experiences, both approaches tended to predict comprehension to about the same extent (e.g., Magliano & Millis, 2003). It is also simple in that other components of language representation are not taken into consideration, such as syntax, as well as other types of reading strategies (rereading, underlining, asking questions, etc.). Of course, it is an open question as to the extent that including these other components would add to the predictive validity of the instrument.

In conclusion, we believe that RSAT provides a "proof of concept" that constructed responses to different types of questions during comprehension can be used to assess overall comprehension and certain strategies.

Although the goals of reading assessments and surrounding political climates have changed across time (Pearson & Hamm, 2005), various forms of constructed responses have been used for years. One limiting factor in their use has been costs surrounding scoring. The computerized scoring procedure used by RSAT is a simple first step for classifying constructed responses for the presence of online strategies.

We are not arguing against selected response formats. Indeed, we agree with Campbell (2005), who argues that both should be considered because both types of responses have strengths and weaknesses.

However, we think that one important consideration of assessments is that they are constructed from an evidence-based approach (Mislevy, 1993;

Pellegrino & Chudowsky, 2003) that emphasizes an understanding of the *student*, the *task*, and principles for *interpreting data*. The evidence-based approach together with a simple classification algorithm has led RSAT to be sufficient for many assessment needs. Of course, more sophisticated natural language processing and artificial intelligence will be needed to ascertain more fine-tuned discriminations, if they are needed.

We understand that the approach here will break under conditions where more precision is needed. However, we are interested in seeing how far this relatively simple approach will go.

REFERENCES

Alexander, P., & Jetton, T. L. (2003). Learning from traditional and alternative texts: New conceptualizations for the information age. In A. C. Graesser, M. A. Gernsbacher, & S. R. Goldman (Eds.), *Handbook of discourse processes* (pp. 199–241). Mahwah, NJ: Lawrence Erlbaum Associates.

Birtwisle, M. (2002). The Soundex Algorithm. Retrieved from: www.comp.leeds .ac.uk/matthewb/ar32/basic_soundex.htm.

Callender, A. A., & McDaniel, M. A. (2007). The benefits of embedded question adjuncts for low and high structure builders. *Journal of Educational Psychology, 99,* 339–348.

Campbell, J. R. (2005). Single instrument, multiple measures: Considering the use of multiple item formats to assess reading comprehension. In S. G. Paris & S. A. Stahl (Eds.), *Children's reading comprehension and assessment* (pp. 347–368). Mahwah, NJ: Lawrence Erlbaum Associates.

Chi, M., Bassok, M., Lewis, M. W., Reimann, R., & Glaser, R. (1989). Self-explanation: How students study and use examples in learning to solve problems. *Cognitive Science, 13,* 145–182.

Chi, M. T. H., de Leeuw, N., Chiu, M., & LaVancher, C. (1994). Eliciting self-explanations improves understanding. *Cognitive Science, 18,* 439–477.

Clark, H. H. (1975). Bridging. In R. C. Schank & B. L. Nash-Webber (Eds.), *Theoretical issues in natural language processing* (pp. 169–174). New York: Association for Computing Machinery.

Coté, N., & Goldman, S. R. (1999). Building representations of informational text: Evidence from children's think-aloud protocols. In H. van Oostendorp & S. R. Goldman, *The construction of mental representations during reading*, (pp. 169–193). Mahwah, NJ: Lawrence Erlbaum Associates.

Coté, N., Goldman, S. R., & Saul, E. U. (1998). Students making sense of informational text: Relations between processing and representation. *Discourse Processes, 25,* 1–53.

Ericsson, K. A., & Simon, H. A. (1993). *Protocol analysis: Verbal reports as data.* Cambridge, MA: MIT Press.

Farr, R., Pritchard, R., & Smitten, B. (1990) A description of what happens when an examinee takes a multiple-choice reading comprehension test. *Journal of Educational Measurement, 27*, 209–226.

Foltz, P. W., Laham, D., & Landauer, T. K. (1999). Automated essay scoring: Applications to educational technology. In *Proceedings of EdMedia World Conference on Educational Multimedia, Hypermedia, & Telecommunications,* Seattle, WA.

Freedle, R., & Kostin, I. (1994). Can multiple-choice reading tests be construct valid? *Psychological Sciences, 5*, 107–110.

Gilliam, S., Magliano, J. P., Millis, K. K., Levinstein, I., & Boonthum, C. (2007). Assessing the format of the presentation of text in developing a Reading Strategy Assessment Tool (RSAT). *Behavior Research Methods, Instruments, & Computers, 39*, 199–204.

Glover, J. A., Zimmer, J. W., & Bruning, R. H. (1979). Utility of the Nelson-Denny as a predictor of structure and themanticity in memory for prose. *Psychological Reports, 45*, 44–46.

Graesser, A. C., & Clark, L. C. (1985). *Structures and procedures of implicit knowledge.* Norwood, NJ: Ablex.

Graesser, A. C., Millis, K. K., Zwaan, R. A. (1997). Discourse comprehension. *Annual Review of Psychology, 48*, 163–189.

Graesser, A. C., & Olde, B. A. (2003). How does one know whether a person understands a device? The quality of the questions the person asks when the device breaks down. *Journal of Educational Psychology, 95*, 524–536.

Graesser, A. C., Penumatsa, P., Ventura, M., Cai, Z., & Hu, X. (2007). Using LSA in AutoTutor: Learning through mixed-initiative dialogue in natural language. In T. K. Landauer, D. S. McNamara, S. Dennis, & W. Kintsch (Eds.), *Handbook of latent semantic analysis* (pp. 243–262). Mahwah, NJ: Lawrence Erlbaum Associates.

Graesser, A. C., Singer, M., & Trabasso, T. (1994). Constructing inferences during narrative text comprehension. *Psychological Review, 101*, 371–395.

Graesser, A. C., Wiemer-Hastings, K., Wiemer-Hastings, P., Kreuz, R., & The Tutoring Research Group (2000). AutoTutor: A simulation of a human tutor. *Journal of Cognitive Systems Research, 1*, 35–51.

Hannon, B., & Daneman, M. (2001). A new tool for measuring and understanding individual differences in the component processes of reading comprehension. *Journal of Educational Psychology, 1*, 103–128.

Kintsch, W., & Kintsch, E. (2005). Comprehension. In S. G. Paris & S. A. Stahl (Eds.), *Children's reading comprehension and assessment* (pp. 71–92). Mahwah, NJ: Lawrence Erlbaum Associates.

Landauer, T. K., & Dumais, S. T. (1997). A solution to Plato's problem: The latent semantic analysis theory of acquisition, induction and representation of knowledge. *Psychological Review, 104*, 211–240.

Lorch, R. F., Lorch, E. P., & Morgan, A. M. (1987). Task effects and individual differences in on-line processing of the topic structure of a text. *Discourse Processes, 10*, 63–80.

Magliano, J. P., & Millis, K. K. (2003). Assessing reading skill with a think-aloud procedure. *Cognition and Instruction. 21*, 251–283.

Magliano, J. P., Millis, K. K., Ozuru, Y., & McNamara, D. S. (2007). A multidimensional framework to evaluate assessment tools. In D. S. McNamara (Ed.), *Reading comprehension strategies: Theories, interventions, and technologies*, (pp. 107–136). Mahwah, NJ: Lawrence Erlbaum Associates.

Magliano, J. P., Millis, K. K., The RSAT Development Team, Levinstein, I., & Boonthum, C. (2011). Assessing comprehension during reading with the reading strategy assessment tool (RSAT). *Metacognition and Learning*.

Magliano, J. P., Wiemer-Hastings, K., Millis, K. K., Munoz, B. D., & McNamara, D. (2002). Using latent semantic analysis to assess reader strategies. *Behavior Research Methods, Instruments, and Computers, 34*, 181–188.

Malak, J., & Hegeman, J. N. (1985). Using verbal SAT scores to predict Nelson-Denny scores for reading placement. *Journal of Reading, 28*, 301–304.

McNamara, D. S., Boonthum, C., Levinstein, I., & Millis, K. (2007). Evaluating self-explanations in iSTART: Comparing word-based and LSA algorithms. In T. K. Landauer, D. S. McNamara, S. Dennis, and W. Kintsch (Eds.), *Handbook of latent semantic analysis*, (pp. 247–242). Mahwah, NJ: Lawrence Erlbaum Associates.

McNamara, D. S., Boonthum, C., Kurby, C. A., Magliano, J., Pillarisetti, S., & Bellissens, C. (2009). Interactive paraphrase training: The development and testing of an iSTART module. In V. Dimitrova, R. Mizoguchi, B. du Boulay, & A. C. Graesser (Eds.), *Artificial intelligence in education: Building learning systems that care, from knowledge representation to affective modeling* (pp. 181–188). Amsterdam, The Netherlands: IOS Press.

McNamara, D. S., Levinstein, I. B., & Boonthum, C. (2004). iSTART: Interactive strategy trainer for active reading and thinking. *Behavioral Research Methods, Instruments, & Computers, 36,* 222–233.

McNamara, D. S., & Magliano, J. P. (2009). Towards a comprehensive model of comprehension. In B. Ross (Ed.), *The psychology of learning and motivation* (Vol. 51, pp. 297–384). New York: Elsevier Science.

Millis, K. K., & Barker, G. (1996). Question answering for expository texts. *Discourse Processes, 21,* 57–84.

Millis, K. K., Kim, H. J., Todaro, S. Magliano, J., Wiemer-Hastings, K., & McNamara, D. (2004). Identifying reading strategies using latent semantic analysis: Comparing semantic benchmarks. *Behavior Research Methods, Instruments, & Computers, 36,* 213–221.

Millis, K. K., Magliano, J., & Todaro, S. (2006). Measuring discourse-level processes with verbal protocols and latent semantic analysis. *Scientific Studies of Reading, 10,* 225–240.

Millis, K., Perry, P., Gilliam, S., & Magliano, J. (2007, July). *Taking on multiple-choice tests: The reading strategy assessment tool (RSAT).* Paper presented at the Annual Meeting of the Society for Text and Discourse, Glasgow, Scotland.

Mislevy, R. J. (1993). Foundations of a new test theory. In N. Frederikson, R. J. Mislevy, I. I. Bejar (Eds.), *Tests theory for a new generation of tests.* Hillsdale, NJ: Lawrence Erlbaum Associates.

Pearson, P. D., & Hamm, D. P. (2005). The assessment of reading comprehension: A review of practices–past, present, and future. In S. G. Paris & S. A. Stahl (Eds.),

Children's reading comprehension and assessment (pp. 13–70). Mahwah, NJ: Lawrence Erlbaum Associates.

Peverly, S. T., & Wood, R. (1999). The effects of adjunct questions and feedback on improving the reading comprehension skills of learning-disabled adolescents. *Contemporary Educational Psychology, 26*, 25–43.

Pellegrino, J. W., & Chudowsky, N. (2003). The foundations of assessment. *Interdisciplinary Research and Perspectives, 1*, 103–148.

Pressley, M., & Afflerbach, P. (1995). *Verbal protocols of reading: The nature of constructively responsive reading*. Hillsdale, NJ: Lawrence Erlbaum Associates.

Rapp, D. N., van den Broek, P., McMaster, P., Kendeou, P., & Espin, C. A. (2007). Higher-order comprehension processes in struggling readers: A perspective for research and intervention. *Scientific Studies of Reading, 11*, 289–312.

Sagerman, N., & Mayer, R. E. (1987). Forward transfer of different reading strategies evoked by adjunct questions in science text. *Journal of Educational Psychology, 79*, 189–191.

Suh, S., & Trabasso, T. (1993). Inferences during reading: Converging evidence from discourse analysis, talk-aloud protocols, and recognition priming. *Journal of Memory and Language, 32*, 279–301.

Todaro, S., Millis, K., & Dandotkar, S. (2010). The impact of semantic relatedness and causal relatedness and reading skill on standards of coherence. *Discourse Processes, 47*, 421–446.

Trabasso, T., & Magliano, J. P. (1996). Conscious understanding during text comprehension. *Discourse Processes, 21*, 255–288.

Trabasso, T., & van den Broek, P. (1985). Causal thinking and the representation of narrative events. *Journal of Memory and Language, 24*, 612–630.

Trabasso, T., van den Broek, P., & Suh, S., (1989). Logical necessity and transitivity of causal relations in stories. *Discourse Processes, 12*, 1–25.

van den Bergh, H. (1990). On the construct validity of multiple-choice items for reading comprehension. *Applied Psychological Measurement, 14*, 1–12.

van den Broek, P., Lorch, R. F., Jr., Linderholm, T., & Gustafson, M. (2001). The effects of readers' goals on inference generation and memory for texts. *Memory & Cognition, 29*, 1081–1087.

Whitney, P., Ritchie, B. G., & Clark, M. B. (1991). Working memory capacity and the use of elaborative inferences. *Discourse Processes, 14*, 133–145.

Zakaluk, B. L., & Samuels, J. (1988). *Readability: Its past, present and future*. Newark, DE: International Reading Association.

Zwaan, R. A., & Radvansky, G. A. (1998). Situation models in language comprehension and memory. *Psychological Bulletin, 123*, 162–185.

Chapter Four

Searching for Supplementary Screening Measures to Identify Children at High Risk for Developing Later Reading Problems[1]

Donald L. Compton, Amy M. Elleman,
and Hugh W. Catts

The use of IQ-achievement discrepancy procedures for the identification of children with learning disabilities (LD), and more specifically reading disabilities (RD), has come under widespread and persistent criticism (e.g., Fletcher, Coulter, Reschly, & Vaughn, 2004; Francis et al., 2005; Stanovich & Siegel, 1994; Stuebing et al., 2002; Vellutino, Scanlon, & Lyon, 2000).[2] With the recent reauthorization of the Individuals with Disabilities Education Act (IDEA, 2004), states now have the option of discontinuing use of IQ-achievement discrepancy procedures as part of the RD identification process in favor of a response to intervention (RTI) approach.

RTI is based on the premise that students are identified as RD when their response to an effective educational intervention is dramatically inferior to that of peers (e.g., Berninger & Abbott, 1994; D. Fuchs, Mock, Morgan, & Young, 2003; L. Fuchs, 2003; L. Fuchs & Fuchs, 1998; Vaughn & Fuchs, 2003; Vellutino & Scanlon, 1987). An important feature of RTI is a multi-tier structure: primary intervention (Tier 1) refers to classroom instruction; secondary intervention (Tier 2) usually involves more intensive small-group instruction; and tertiary intervention (Tier 3) denotes most intensive instruction, often special education.

Proponents of the use of RTI for prevention and disability identification claim it has many advantages over the IQ-achievement discrepancy approach. These include a stronger focus on prevention, earlier identification of children with disabilities, and an assessment process with clearer implications for academic programming.

The success of prevention models such as RTI hinges on an accurate determination of which children are at risk for future difficulty (e.g., Compton, Fuchs, Fuchs, & Bryant, 2006; Fuchs & Fuchs, 2007; McCardle, Scarborough, & Catts, 2001). Correct identification of children at risk for reading difficulty (RD) in kindergarten to second grade can trigger early intervention prior to the onset of significant problems, which, in turn, can place children on the path of normal reading development.

Universal screening is a principal means of identifying at-risk children (see Glover & Albers, 2007). It usually involves precursor measures of literacy (e.g., phonemic awareness, letter-naming fluency, concepts about print, word reading) and the use of a cut-point to demarcate risk and nonrisk (for a review, see Jenkins, Hudson, & Johnson, 2007). There is growing evidence that multivariate screening batteries can accurately identify children at high risk of developing early word reading difficulties (Catts, Fey, Tomblin, & Zhang, 2002; Compton et al., 2010; Compton et al., 2006; O'Connor and Jenkins, 1999).

However, there is a group of students who do not display reading difficulties until later in elementary school, with a majority of these students exhibiting comprehension difficulties (see Catts & Hogan, 2002; Catts, Hogan, & Adlof, 2005; Leach, Scarborough, & Rescorla, 2003). These so-called "late-emerging" RD (LERD) children present a particular challenge to the early identification and prevention aims of RTI.

For RTI to work effectively, procedures for determining RD risk in the early elementary grades (typically kindergarten through second grade) must yield a high percentage of true positives [e.g., sensitivity rates above 90% (Jenkins, 2003)] while identifying a manageable risk pool by limiting false positives (see Compton et al., 2006; Compton et al., 2010).

However, children with LERD, by definition, are not identified as at risk during early screening procedures and therefore represent false negatives. These false negatives undermine the intent of the RTI process by depriving at-risk children of the early intervention they require (Jenkins, 2003; Torgesen, 2002).

In this chapter, we provide a brief rationale supporting the existence of LERD subgroups, give estimates of prevalence rates of these subgroups, and speculate on some measures that could be added to early screening batteries to increase the identification accuracy of children at risk of developing later difficulties in reading.

Within an RTI model, early identification of children at high risk for developing later comprehension difficulties is considered the first step in a general prevention model in which at-risk children receive systematic treatment aimed at improving reading and reading-related skills (e.g., language skills) resulting in normal developmental trajectories over time.

THE RATIONALE FOR THREE SUBGROUPS OF LERD

Comprehending written material requires the coordination of a complex set of skills. Thus, there are potentially multiple sources of comprehension failure (Cain, Oakhill, & Bryant, 2000; Gersten & Baker, 1999; Oakhill, Cain, & Yuill, 1998; Perfetti, Marron, & Foltz, 1996; Pressley, 2000; Stanovich, West, Cunningham, Cipielewski, & Siddiqui, 1996).

Word reading skills are strongly associated with comprehending text, particularly in the early stages of reading development (Perfetti, 1985; Shankweiler et al., 1999; Shankweiler & Fowler, 2004; Vellutino, Scanlon, & Tanzman, 1994). Yet, developmental studies provide evidence of significant independence between reading comprehension and word recognition (Cain et al., 2000; Catts et al., 2005; Nation, 2005), particularly as children become older.

Specifically, the correlation between word identification and reading comprehension skills shifts around fourth grade, when word reading accuracy and reading comprehension are influenced by different skill sets (Betjemann, Keenan, Fazendeiro, & Olson, 2002), leading to stronger correlations between reading comprehension and language skill (e.g., listening comprehension) and weaker correlations between reading comprehension and word identification (Aaron, Joshi, & Williams, 1999; Catts et al., 2005; Stanovich, Cunningham, & Freeman, 1984; Stitch & James, 1984).

This partial independence between reading comprehension and word recognition skills that changes across development allows for the possibility of three major LERD subgroups: (1) LERD with only comprehension problems (LERD-C); (2) LERD with only word reading problems (LERD-W); and (3) LERD with both reading comprehension and word reading problems (LERD-CW). The question then is whether these major subgroups are found in the population of school-age children.

Prevalence Rates of LERD Subgroups

Little is currently known about the nature of children who change classification from typically developing in primary grades to RD in the intermediate grades (e.g., Leach et al., 2003; Lipka, Lesaux, & Siegel, 2006; Wright, Fields, & Newman, 1996). Estimates suggest that the prevalence of LERD ranges from 20% to 50% of those identified with RD in elementary school.

Previously, the high prevalence of such children had been attributed to flaws in the identification process (e.g., overlooked due to their high intelligence, good behavior, or compensatory strategies). However, after conducting a retrospective analysis of school records, Leach et al. (2003) found that LERD children had no identifiable deficits until fourth or fifth grade. Leach et al. concluded that these students were indeed late emerging, not late identified.

Lipka et al. (2006) extended the work of Leach et al. by using a longitudinal, population-representative sample. They, too, found that students not identified until fourth grade showed no indicators of an RD in second grade.

More recently, we (Compton, Fuchs, Fuchs, Elleman, & Gilbert, 2008) explored the stability of latent classes associated with RD and typically developing children across time (grades 1–4). Results indicated that late emergers fit the profile described by Leach et al. and Lipka et al.; namely, performance was in the normal range across various reading measures in first and second grades, but it was significantly below the normal range in fourth grade. As with Leach et al. and Lipka et al., our findings indicate the existence of a developmental class of children who are late emerging—not simply late-identified RD.

Having identified a population of children that fit the LERD profile, we next explore whether there is evidence to suggest three major subgroups within the population of children exhibiting LERD. Of 31 late-emerging students identified in grades 4 and 5 in the Leach et al. (2003) study, 11 (36%) were poor decoders, 10 (32%) had a specific comprehension deficit, and 10 (32%) had difficulty with both decoding and comprehension. Although findings indicated many children who exhibit late-emerging RD have difficulty understanding text, more than two-thirds of this group also had difficulty with word identification and decoding.

Lipka et al. (2006) also reported subgroups of LERDs who were poor decoders, had a specific comprehension deficit, or both poor decoding and comprehension. Results from these studies indicate that subgroups based on word reading and comprehension skill exist within the LERD population.

More recently, Catts, Compton, Tomblin, and Bridges (2011) employed mixture latent Markov modeling to examine the stability of latent classes associated with RD and typical development across time (grades 2–10) and to identify the prevalence of the three LERD subgroups.

In these analyses, 493 children were initially recruited as part of an epidemiologic study of language impairment in kindergarten, involving a stratified cluster sample of 7,218 children (Tomblin et al., 1997). Children were assessed in grades 2, 4, 8, and 10. A weighting procedure, correcting for oversampling of children at risk for developing language impairment, was used to estimate the prevalence of LERD in the overall population based on the epidemiologic study (see Catts et al., 2005; Catts, Fey, Zhang, & Tomblin, 1999).

Overall, 85% of the population remained in the same class (i.e., stable) across grades 2–10 (69% typically developing; 16% RD). The remaining 15% of the sample made a class transition across time. Table 4.1 provides a description of the six major latent classes, population estimates for each class, and the point at which transition occurred.

The stable early-identified RD class comprised a mix of RD-word reading only and RD-reading comprehension and word reading, and there was movement between the RD classes as a function of time.

Approximately 13% of the population transitioned from the typically developing class to one of the LERD classes, with comprehension deficits (LERD-C & LERD-CW) making up the largest transitioning group (8.5% of the population). Further, the LERD population represented nearly 50% of the total sample identified with RD [LERD/(LERD + early-identified RD)]. It is noteworthy that 4% of the population showed LERD in word reading skill only, indicating a class of children who develop word reading problems later in school. Finally, almost 2% of the population transitioned from RD to typically developing across time.

The vast majority of transitions took place between grades 2–4, with far fewer occurring between grades 4–8, and a negligible number occurring between grades 8–10. In addition, transitions were generally followed by stable class membership, meaning that once a child transitioned from, say, typically developing to LERD-C, he or she tended to stay in that class.

Results indicate that LERD occurs frequently (13% of the population using a -1 *SD* cut-off on latent indicators of reading); represents approximately 50% of children who will ultimately develop RD; and comprises at least three important subgroups (i.e., LERD-C, LERD-W, & LERD-CW).

However, we currently know little about the mechanisms that cause children to transition from typically developing to RD, whether these mechanisms vary across LERD subgroups, and the best means to identify and teach each of the subgroups. In the remainder of this chapter, we explore child-level variables that may be associated with each LERD subtype. Unique characteristics, or sets of characteristics, may in turn help researchers identify potential measures to be added to screening batteries with the intent of identifying early children at high risk for developing LERD.

Table 4.1. Population prevalence and grade of transition for the six major subgroups of readers.

Latent Classes (Subgroups)	Population Prevalence (%)	Transition Grade
Stable Subgroups		
TD → TD	68.6	NA
RD → RD	16.3	NA
Late Emerging RD		
TD → LERD-C	6.9	4 & 8
TD → LERD-W	4.7	4
TD → LERD-CW	1.6	4
Late Emerging TD		
RD → TD	1.9	4 & 8

Note. TD = Typically Developing, RD = Reading Disabled; LE = Late Emerging, C = Comprehension, W = Word, CW = Comprehension and Word.

Child Variables for Identifying LERD Subgroups

Scarborough (2003) has distinguished between two broad categories of skills (with associated subprocesses) influencing reading development: language comprehension (including background knowledge, vocabulary, grammar language structure, verbal reasoning, and literacy knowledge) and word reading (including phonological awareness, decoding, and sight recognition).

In the development of skilled readers, the various subprocesses that constitute these two domains become increasingly interwoven to form a highly interdependent set of processes. Yet, in children with RD, these various subprocesses may be less interdependent, allowing for wide variation among skills, thereby potentially leading to LERD subgroups. From an early identification standpoint, we assume that deficits in certain subprocesses uniquely predict LERD subgroup membership and distinguish these children from those who will develop typically.

We understand that the subprocesses that accurately distinguish children who will develop LERD from those who are typically developing are by necessity different from those used to identify children at risk for developing early-identified RD. Therefore, we need to expand upon our corpus of measures used to identify children at risk for early word reading difficulties.

Our early identification model assumes that in a majority of children who will develop LERD, deficits are intrinsic to the child and can be detected prior to development of reading failure. However, we must consider alternative models in which LERD develops through the experience of learning to read.

A clear set of early predictors may not exist that accurately identify children at high risk of LERD. For instance, Stanovich et al. (1996) argued that individual differences in reading experience affect both the development of cognitive processes and knowledge bases that support further gains in comprehension growth. Thus, reading practice can spur increases in vocabulary and declarative knowledge that underlie future increases in comprehension efficiency. Therefore deficits in these knowledge domains would not likely exist until children have had ample literacy opportunities.

Given our assumption that early markers of LERD do indeed exist, we use the Scarborough framework to identify potential subprocesses that influence the development of reading and may form the basis for the identification of children at risk for developing LERD.

We expand upon Scarborough's list of subprocesses affecting word reading and comprehension skills in two important ways. In terms of word reading skills, we focus on the development of subword orthographic-phonological connections that allow advanced word reading skills to develop.

From the perspective of comprehension skills, we include executive function, which has been hypothesized by Cutting and colleagues (Cutting,

Materek, Cole, Levine, & Mahone, 2009; Sesma, Mahone, Levine, Eason, & Cutting, 2009) to distinguish children with comprehension deficits from children with word reading deficits. Following Cutting, we include the following as executive function skills related to reading measures: working memory, inferential reasoning, planning (i.e., developing and using reading strategies), sequencing/organizing, attention, and monitoring information.

We believe this conceptualization is supported by studies demonstrating that children with poor comprehension have difficulty engaging in active strategies to enhance understanding, retain information, and circumvent comprehension failures (see Baker & Anderson, 1982; Palincsar & Brown, 1984; Pazzaglia, Cornoldi, & DeBeni, 1995; Yuill & Oakhill, 1991). We provide further details regarding the relationship between these variables and reading skill development below.

Word Recognition Processes

Acquiring a lexical system of representations that permits efficient word recognition is an essential part of learning to read. As children learn to read, this lexical representation system changes in two important ways (Ehri, 1992; Perfetti, 1991, 1992).

First, there is a continuous increase in the absolute number of orthographically addressable entries, often referred to as "word-specific" representations. Word-specific representations are considered to be less dependent on phonological processes because those representations have been supplanted by specific connections linking spelling directly to pronunciations (Ehri, 1992; Perfetti, 1992; Reitsma, 1983; Share, 1995).

A second change in the lexicon that occurs as children learn to read is an increase in the overall quantity and quality of subword orthographic-phonological connections. Subword connections between orthographic and phonological codes likely exist at the level of individual letter-phonemes, letter cluster-phonemes, letter cluster-rimes, and letter cluster-syllables (Berninger, 1994; Ehri, 1992).

These subword connections between orthographic and phonological units form what Gough and colleagues (Gough & Hillinger, 1980; Gough, Juel, & Griffith, 1992; Gough & Walsh, 1991; Gough & Wren, 1998) have referred to as the *cipher*. The cipher is best conceptualized as a set of abstract context-dependent relationships between orthography and phonology that are "implicit, very numerous, and very fast" (Gough et al., 1992, p. 38).

Early connections are initially based on simple one-to-one correspondences that are relatively insensitive to orthographic context (see Share, 1995). With increased print experiences, these initially incomplete and oversimplified representations become sophisticated context-dependent connections.

Thus, two lexical acquisition systems are at work as a child learns to read—the addition of word-specific entries and the expansion of subword orthographic-phonological connections. These acquisition systems are mutually facilitative: "The more powerful the context-sensitive decoding rules (or analogic capabilities), the more entries the learner can acquire. And the more entries, the more powerful the decoding rules" (Perfetti, 1992, pp. 161–162).

Disruptions in either of the two acquisition systems should compromise the other system and affect reading development. For instance, early deficits in phonological processing have been causally linked to poor word identification through a mechanism that disrupts the development of decoding skills (Brady & Shankweiler, 1991; Shankweiler et al., 1999; Siegel, 1989, Stanovich & Siegel, 1994; Torgesen, 2000; Vellutino et al., 1996).

Specifically, deficits in the ability to recognize and manipulate the phonemes of words are believed to disrupt the acquisition of spelling-to-sound (i.e., orthographic-phonological connections) translation routines that form the basis of early decoding (Bus & van Ijzendoorn, 1999; Metsala, Stanovich, & Brown, 1998).

Deficits in basic decoding limit the growth of orthographic knowledge in children with RD and result in a tendency to process only partial information about words (Ehri & Saltmarsh, 1995). Thus, early-identified RD is often associated with deficits in phonological processing skills, namely phonemic awareness, that disrupt the acquisition of subword orthographic-phonological connections and, in turn, limit the number of word-specific entries.

However, there is evidence to indicate the possibility of disassociation between phonological and orthographic processes, giving rise to RD groups that show differential performance across these skills (e.g., phonological RD versus surface RD). We suspect that relative differences in phonological and orthographic processing skills exist between LERD subgroups with word-reading deficits (LERD-W & LERD-CW) versus LERD subgroups without word-reading deficits (typically developing & LERD-C), as well as between LERD subgroups and typically developing children.

In the case of LERD-W, it may be that this subgroup of children has adequate early phonological awareness skills that support early development of simple orthographic-phonological subword connections that facilitate basic decoding skill acquisition and word reading development, but has deficits in processes that support the long-term development of advanced orthographic-phonological connections (see Ehri, 1992; Perfetti, 1992).

Less is known about the processes, in addition to phonemic awareness, that support the long-term development of advanced subword orthographic-phonological connections necessary for the formation of fully specified word-specific representations in the lexicon. Certainly more advanced metalinguistic skills such as morphological awareness skills (e.g., Carlisle, 2000) are possible candidates, as are processes such as rapid automatized naming (Bowers & Wolf, 1993) and orthographic awareness (Roman, Kirby, Parrila, Wade-Woolley, & Deacon, 2009).

Unfortunately, basic work examining factors that contribute to the reading of complex multisyllabic words (e.g., studies exploring the reality of the basic orthographic syllabic structure of words) unexpectedly stopped in the late 1980s to early 1990s. It may be that this type of work is necessary in the study of children with LERD-W and LERD-CW.

Language Comprehension Skill

In Scarborough's (2003) framework, various language subprocesses support children's ability to comprehend text. The language subprocesses in Scarborough's model include vocabulary, morphological processing, syntactic processing, listening comprehension, domain-specific knowledge, and verbal reasoning.

We predict that early differences in language skill explains differences between LERD subgroups with (LERD-C & LERD-CW) and without (LERD-W) comprehension skill deficits and also help separate children who will develop later comprehension problems from typically developing children. However, we do not know whether single or multiple measures of language processing are required to accurately distinguish LERD-C and LERD-CW subgroups from typically developing children. We briefly review evidence supporting each of the potential subprocesses as an early predictor of LERD with comprehension skill deficits.

Vocabulary is recognized as an important skill related to early reading development (Beck, McKeown, & Kucan, 2008; Molfese & Molfese, 2004). Knowledge of word meanings and their semantic associations is strongly linked to individual differences in reading and listening comprehension (Carroll, 1993; Farr, 1968; Nation & Snowling, 1998, 1999), even when items on the vocabulary test do not overlap with words on the comprehension test.

Given that poor comprehenders tend to have poor vocabulary, it is widely accepted that poor early vocabulary skill should act as a strong indicator of risk for future reading comprehension problems (see Perfetti et al., 1996). In addition, vocabulary differences can be reliably measured in young children, and vocabulary skills tend to be relatively stable over time. Thus, there is reason to believe that adding tests of receptive and/or expressive vocabulary to early screening batteries may help identify the two LERD subgroups with comprehension deficits.

An evolving literature suggests that individual differences in morphological skills are associated with reading comprehension. While morphological awareness makes its largest contribution to reading comprehension through its impact on vocabulary, it makes a unique contribution to reading comprehension as well (Nagy, Berninger, & Abbott, 2006).

Also, time intervals may exist of especially marked growth for specific aspects of morphology. Anglin (1993), for example, found that knowledge of prefixed and suffixed words increased sharply from grades 3–5, when the relation between morphological skill and comprehension surpassed the unique contribution of phonological awareness in typically developing students (Carlisle & Fleming, 2003; Green et al., 2003). For students at risk for RD, morphological awareness was strongly and increasingly correlated with reading comprehension at grades 2 and 4, but it only accounted for unique variance in reading comprehension at grade 2 (Nagy, Berninger, Abbott, Vaughan, & Vermeulen, 2003).

The difference in the relation between morphological awareness and comprehension across typically developing students and those at risk for RD at grade 4 suggests that morphological awareness may be important in reading development. Clearly, there appear to be important relations between morphological process and reading comprehension in the middle elementary grades, but scant evidence exists to support the use of morphological awareness as an early screener (e.g., kindergarten through first grade) for designating LERD (LERD-C and LERD-CW) risk. More work in this area would appear warranted.

Syntactic processing refers to the ability to use grammatical rules that set constraints on how words are organized in sentences. The ability to interpret syntactically complex sentences has been found deficient in RD children (Byrne, 1981; Vogel, 1975), although such weakness may be driven primarily by constraints in phonological and working memory (Crain & Shankweiler, 1988; Perfetti, Landi, & Oakhill, 2005). There is also speculation that the poor syntactic processes found in poor comprehenders may be due to limited reading experience (Nation, Snowling, & Clarke, 2005).

However, Scarborough (1998) reported that early sentence imitation, which relies on syntactic processing and phonological memory, was one of the best predictors of later reading. In addition, Adlof and Catts (2009) have shown evidence of grammatical problems in tense marking in third- to fourth-grade poor comprehenders. So while the literature is equivocal regarding the predictive nature of syntactic processing on later comprehension problems, it seems reasonable to include measures of syntactic processing skill in early screening batteries.

Listening comprehension is highly correlated with reading comprehension, with the correlation increasing as children become more skilled at reading (Curtis, 1980; Stitch & James, 1984; Joshi, Williams, & Wood, 1998). The strong tendency for reading comprehension deficits to be accompanied by listening comprehension deficits holds across the range of IQ. Further, as children become older, oral language skills such as listening comprehension may be a primary factor limiting their reading comprehension.

Compton et al. (2008) found that fourth-grade children identified as LERD scored significantly below typically developing children on listening comprehension in the fall of first grade. However, using first-grade listening comprehension to predict membership in LERD and typically developing groups resulted in unacceptable rates of false positives.

Thus, we argue that listening comprehension should certainly be placed at the top of any list of measures used to identify children at risk for developing LERD (LERD-C & LERD-CW). However, we wonder whether other measures, in conjunction with listening comprehension, can be identified to help improve the predictive accuracy of LERD classification.

Perfetti et al. (1996) have argued, " . . . the component that may be the most important (to reading comprehension) and least interesting is domain knowledge" (p. 142). Numerous studies (Anderson, Reynolds, Schallert, & Goetz, 1977; Anderson, Spiro, & Anderson, 1978; Spilich, Vesonder, Chiesi, & Voss, 1979) show that declarative knowledge influences reading comprehension.

Readers with high levels of declarative knowledge consistently demonstrate stronger comprehension and retention than readers with low levels of knowledge (Langer, 1981; Pearson, Hanson, & Gordon, 1979). Good and poor readers differ not only in amount of knowledge but also in how they make use of it to facilitate comprehension (Bransford, Stein, Shelton, & Owings, 1981; Oakhill, 1984).

In the same vein, research has shown that when poor readers are prompted to use their prior knowledge or are helped to build knowledge, their comprehension improves (e.g., Dole, Valencia, Greer, & Wardop, 1991; Neuman, 1988; Recht & Leslie, 1988). High levels of domain-specific knowledge for vocabulary and concepts yield benefits for comprehending related texts.

For example, young children who already know a lot about dinosaurs can learn new information about dinosaurs more readily than adults who know little about dinosaurs (Chi, 1978). The question then is whether early measures of declarative knowledge can effectively distinguish children at risk for developing LERD from a typically developing child, or whether declarative-knowledge deficits develop over time due to lack of reading experience.

The relation between reasoning/IQ and reading comprehension skill in typically developing and RD children is strong (e.g., Oakhill & Cain, 2000; Swanson & Alexander, 1997). This relation is understood to reflect similar demands on "high-order" cognitive processes (van den Bos, Brand-Gruwel,

& Lind, 1998). We include IQ because of its strong link with reading comprehension and because poor comprehenders tend to perform lower on IQ compared to chronological age– and comprehension age–matched controls (Stothard & Hulme, 1996).

We suspect that there is considerable overlap between vocabulary, listening comprehension, and IQ in terms of early prediction of LERD risk. However, we are unfamiliar with any study that has attempted to use these three measures to predict group membership in LERD and typically developing groups.

Executive Function

We follow Cutting and colleagues (Cutting, Eason, Young, & Alberstadt, 2008; Sesma et al., 2009) in hypothesizing additional processes affecting reading comprehension, including those in the "executive function" category, although they are not always labeled as such. These include working memory, inferential reasoning, attention, planning (developing and using reading strategies), organizing, and monitoring information. Many of these processes seem to require different aspects of neurocognitive functioning (Willcutt et al., 2001).

Whereas the multifactorial nature of executive function has been demonstrated (e.g., Pennington, 1997; Willcutt et al., 2001), it has been criticized as weakly defined and overly broad. Nevertheless, we include it in the proposal because it has been recently linked to comprehension problems in children, especially through verbal working memory, the ability to make inferences, and the ability to plan, organize, and monitor.

Cutting et al. and Sesma et al. reported that executive function is uniquely associated with reading comprehension deficits in children. Based on the research of Cutting and colleagues, we expect LERD-C and LERD-CW children to perform lower than typically developing, LERD-W, and early-identified RD students on executive functioning tasks.

The ability to make and understand inferences has long been hypothesized as critical in cognitive models of reading comprehension. Numerous studies have demonstrated this in adult skilled readers (e.g., Kintsch, 1998; Schmalhofer & Perfetti, 2007). In the literature on children with reading comprehension problems, inference making has been implicated, via executive function (e.g., Oakhill, 1993; Oakhill & Garnham, 1988; Oakhill & Yuill, 1996; Perfetti et al., 1996; Swanson & Alexander, 1997), although this link has not been well studied.

For example, Oakhill and Yuill (1996) found that children with a specific comprehension deficit had difficulty answering inferential questions but could answer literal questions. Dennis and Barnes (1993) found that children with hydrocephalus who showed specific comprehension deficits had difficulty understanding and making inferences, adversely affecting their comprehension.

Oakhill & Yuill (1996) and Perfetti et al. (1996) hypothesized that difficulties in inference making are linked to difficulties in verbal working memory, another aspect of executive function (holding information long enough to make inferences). However, Swanson and Alexander (1997) found that a comprehension deficit group was impaired in inference making, which was separate from working memory.

Although the literature suggests the importance of inference generation to comprehension, this issue has not been assessed in sufficient depth or applied to LERD. So while it may be difficult to accurately assess inferencing skills in young children, there is some reason to think that these skills may help distinguish children at risk for LERD from typically developing children (see Elleman, Compton, Fuchs, Fuchs, & Bouton, in press).

Working memory refers to one or more systems of limited capacity that store and manipulate information. Studies have reported strong correlations between reading comprehension and working memory (e.g., Brady, 1986; Chiappe, Hasher, & Siegel, 2000; Fletcher, 1985; Gottardo, Stanovich, & Siegel, 1996; Just & Carpenter, 1992; Savage, Lavers, & Pillay, 2006; Swanson, 1993, 1996, 1999, 2003; Waters & Caplan, 1996). Further, working memory accounts for variance in comprehension well beyond the modest correlation observed with simple rote-memory measures such as digit span (Daneman & Carpenter, 1980).

The correlation between working memory and reading comprehension reflects the involvement of working memory in most component processes of comprehension—retrieving word meanings and keeping them activated; forming a coherent representation of the discourse and keeping it activated; integrating currently activated information with subsequent information, etc. (Nation, Adams, Bowyer-Crain, & Snowling, 1999; Baddeley 1986, 1996, 2003a, 2003b; Gathercole & Baddeley, 1993).

We are most interested in aspects of verbal working memory because it has been shown to be more closely related to language processing, and more specifically, reading ability (Nation et al., 1999; Perfetti, 1985; Siegel & Ryan, 1989). We predict the two LERD subgroups with comprehension deficits would show greater working memory deficits than typically developing children. In addition, we have been able to reliably measure working memory capacity in younger children that would allow its use as an early predictor of LERD.

Planning, organizing/sequencing, and monitoring, as well as strategy generation, have also been found to be important for reading comprehension (Ferstl et al., 2007; Cutting et al., 2009).

Ability to monitor while reading (comprehension monitoring; e.g., Oakhill & Yuill, 1996; Perfetti et al., 1996; Cain, Oakhill, & Bryant, 2004; Oakhill, Hartt, & Samols, 2005; Ruffman, 1996), knowledge and use of reading strategies to clarify text and to compensate for weaknesses (e.g., Cain et al., 2004; Oakhill et al., 2005; Swanson & Trahan, 1996; Walczyk, Marsiglia, Johns, & Bryan, 2004), and ability to organize what has been read (see Cornoldi, De Beni, & Pazzaglia, 1996) predict comprehension and have been conceptualized as dependent on executive function (Ferstl, 2007; Swanson, 1999).

Knowledge of reading strategies as assessed by questionnaires designed to reflect the "ability to monitor, adjust, and regulate . . . cognitive actions in regard to" reading (Swanson & Trahan, 1996; p. 336), such as knowing when to reread and finding the main idea/topic, differentiate impaired and skilled comprehenders (Swanson & Trahan, 1996; Swanson, 1999). Knowledge of reading strategies also has a strong impact on comprehension abilities in older readers (Willson & Rupley, 1997), and it has separate predictive power from working memory (Swanson & Trahan, 1996).

Comprehension monitoring has also been shown to differentiate good and poor comprehenders (Cain et al., 2004; Oakhill et al., 2005). While these skills are paramount to skilled reading, we doubt whether there are adequate proxies for this type of behavior that can be administered to children in kindergarten through second grade. Therefore we question whether these skills could realistically be assessed in an early screening battery.

Comprehending text requires the simultaneous coordination of multiple processes that may be dependent on attention. We propose that individual differences in attentive behavior are associated with variance in reading comprehension and may discriminate between the LERD subgroups with comprehension deficits and typically developing readers.

Few studies have examined the relation between attention and reading comprehension (as does Cutting & Scarborough, 2006) with most relevant work done with attention deficit hyperactivity disorder (ADHD) populations (see Lorch et al., 2004). However, an argument can be made linking comprehension development and sustained attention. In addition, teacher and parent questionnaires of attention have been used successfully with children in kindergarten through second grades.

CONCLUSION

In this chapter we have made a case for attempting to expand universal screening batteries to include measures to distinguish children at high risk for LERD from typically developing children and children at risk for early

RD. Within an RTI framework, correct identification of children at risk for developing LERD in kindergarten through second grade allows early intervention before the onset of significant reading comprehension and word reading problems, which, in turn, can place children on the path of normal reading development.

To support this view, we presented evidence to support the existence of LERD, and more specifically, subgroups of LERD. Catts et al. (2011) estimate the overall prevalence of LERD to be equal to the prevalence rate of early-identified RD, and that using a criteria of −1 SD below the mean on standardized tests, approximately 7% of the school-age population would develop LERD-C, 5% LERD-W, and 2% LERD-CW. In looking for early predictors of LERD, we assumed that deficits in certain subprocesses uniquely predict LERD subgroup membership and distinguish these children from those who will develop typically.

In addition, we understand that the subprocesses that accurately distinguish children who will develop LERD from those who are typically developing are by necessity different from those used to identify children at risk for developing early-identified RD. Therefore we attempted to expand upon our corpus of measures used to identify children at risk for early word reading difficulties.

We also assume, perhaps incorrectly, that in a majority of children who will develop LERD, deficits are intrinsic to the child and can be detected prior to development of reading failure. However, we recognize the influence of instruction on both the academic and cognitive profiles of children.

At this point, there is little direct evidence in the literature to guide our choice of potential new measures to add to screening batteries to identify early children at risk for developing LERD.

Our initial thoughts are that measures tapping skills associated with the development of advanced orthographic-phonological connections, vocabulary, syntactic processing, listening comprehension, working memory, and attention should help distinguish LERD groups from typically developing and early-identified RD. Multivariate prediction studies are needed to evaluate whether any of the measures, or a combination of measures, can correctly distinguish children at risk of LERD from typically developing and children at risk of early-identified RD.

REFERENCES

Aaron, P. G., Joshi, M., & Williams, K. A. (1999). Not all reading disabilities are alike. *Journal of Learning Disabilities, 32*, 120–137.

Adlof, S., & Catts, H. (2009, November). Morphosyntax in children with specific reading comprehension deficits. Paper presented at the Annual Conference of the American Speech-Language-Hearing Association, New Orleans, LA.

Anderson, R. C., Reynolds, R. E., Schallert, D. L., & Goetz, E. T. (1977). Frameworks for comprehending discourse. *American Educational Research Journal, 14,* 367–381.

Anderson, R. C., Spiro, R. J., & Anderson, M. C. (1978). Schemata as scaffolding for the representation of information in connected discourse. *American Educational Research Journal, 15,* 433–440.

Anglin, J. M. (1993). Vocabulary development: A morphological analysis. *Monographs of the Society of Research in Child Development, 58* (Serial No. 238).

Baddeley, A. D. (1986). *Working memory.* Oxford: Clarendon Press.

———. (1996). Exploring the central executive. *Quarterly Journal of Experimental Psychology A: Human Experimental Psychology, 49,* 5–28.

———. (2003a). Working memory: Looking back and looking forward. *Nature Reviews Neuroscience, 4,* 829–839.

———. (2003b). Working memory and language: An overview. *Journal of Communication Disorders, 36,* 189–208.

Baker, L., & Anderson, R. I. (1982). Effects of inconsistent information on text processing: Evidence for comprehension monitoring. *Reading Research Quarterly, 22,* 281–294.

Beck, I. L., McKeown, M. G., & Kucan, L. (2008). *Creating robust vocabulary: Frequently asked questions and extended examples.* New York: Guilford Press.

Berninger, V. W. (1994). *The varieties of orthographic knowledge I: Theoretical and developmental issues.* Dordrecht, The Netherlands: Kluwer Academic Publishers.

Berninger, V. W., & Abbott, R. D. (1994). Redefining learning disabilities: Moving beyond aptitude-achievement discrepancies to failure to respond to validated practice. In G. R. Lyon (Ed.), *Frames of reference for the assessment of learning disabilities: New views on measurement issues* (pp. 163–184). Baltimore, MD: Paul H. Brookes Publishing Co.

Betjemann, R. S., Keenan, J. M., Fazendeiro, T., & Olson, R. K. (2002, May). *Reading and listening comprehension in normal readers and children with reading disability.* Paper presented at the Seventy-Fourth Meeting of the Midwestern Psychological Association, Chicago, IL.

Bowers, P., & Wolf, M. (1993). Theoretical links among naming speed, precise timing mechanisms, and orthographic skill in dyslexia. *Reading and Writing: An International Journal, 5,* 69–85.

Brady, S. A. (1986). Short-term memory, phonological processing, and reading ability. *Annals of Dyslexia, 36,* 138-153.

Brady, S. A., & Shankweiler, D. P. (Eds.) (1991). *Phonological processes in literacy: A tribute to Isabelle Y. Liberman.* Hillsdale, NJ: Lawrence Erlbaum Associates.

Bransford, J. D., Stein, B. S., Shelton, T. S., & Owings, R. A. (1981). Cognition and adaptation: The importance of learning to learn. In J. Harvey (Ed.), *Cognition, social behavior, and the environment* (pp. 92–110). Hillsdale, NJ: Lawrence Erlbaum Associates.

Bus, A. G., & Ijzendoorn M. H. (1999). Phonological awareness and early reading: A meta-analysis of experimental training studies. *Journal of Educational Psychology, 91,* 403–414.

Byrne, B. (1981) Deficient syntactic control in poor readers: is a weak phonetic memory code responsible? *Applied Psycholinguistics, 2,* 201–212.

Cain, K., Oakhill, J., & Bryant, P. (2000). Investigating the causes of reading comprehension failure: The comprehension-age match design. *Reading and Writing: An Interdisciplinary Journal, 12,* 31–40.

———. (2004). Children's reading comprehension ability: Concurrent prediction by working memory, verbal ability, and component skills. *Journal of Educational Psychology, 96,* 31–42.

Carlisle, J. F. (2000). Awareness of the structure and meaning of morphologically complex words: Impact on reading. *Reading and Writing, 12,* 169–190.

Carlisle, J. F., & Fleming, J. (2003). Lexical processing of morphologically complex words in the elementary years. *Scientific Studies of Reading, 7,* 239–253.

Carroll, J. B. (1993). *Human cognitive abilities: A survey of factor analytic studies.* New York: Cambridge University Press.

Catts, H. W., Compton, D. L., Tomblin, J. B., & Bridges, M. (2011, submitted). *Prevalence and nature of late-emerging poor readers.*

Catts, H. W., Fey, M. E., Tomblin, J. B., & Zhang, X. (2002). A longitudinal investigation of reading outcomes in children with language impairments. *Journal of Speech, Language, and Hearing Research, 45,* 1142–1157.

Catts, H. W., Fey, M. E., Zhang, X., & Tomblin, J. B. (1999). Language basis of reading and reading disabilities. *Scientific Studies of Reading, 3,* 331–361.

Catts, H. W., & Hogan, T. P. (2002, June). *The fourth grade slump: Late emerging poor readers.* Poster presented at the Annual Conference of the Society for the Scientific Study of Reading, Chicago, IL.

Catts, H. W., Hogan, T. P., & Adlof, S. M. (2005). Developmental changes in reading and reading disabilities. In H. Catts & A. Kamhi (Eds.), *Connections between language and reading disabilities* (pp. 50–71). Mahwah, NJ: Lawrence Erlbaum Associates.

Chi, M. T. H. (1978). Knowledge structures and memory development. In R. S. Siegler (Ed.), *Children's thinking: What develops?* (pp. 73–96). Hillsdale, NJ: Lawrence Erlbaum Associates.

Chiappe, P., Hasher, L., & Siegel, L.S. (2000). Working memory, inhibitory control, and reading disability. *Memory and Cognition, 28,* 8–17.

Compton, D. L., Fuchs, D., Fuchs, L. S., Bouton, B., Gilbert, J. K., Barquero, L., & Crouch, R. C. (2010). Selecting at-risk readers in first grade for early intervention: Eliminating false positives and exploring the promise of a two-stage screening process. *Journal of Educational Psychology, 102,* 327–340.

Compton, D. L., Fuchs, D., Fuchs, L. S., & Bryant, J. D. (2006). Selecting at-risk readers in first grade for early intervention: A two-year longitudinal study of decision rules and procedures. *Journal of Educational Psychology, 98,* 394–409.

Compton, D. L., Fuchs, D., Fuchs, L. S., Elleman, A. M., & Gilbert, J. K. (2008). Tracking children who fly below the radar: Latent transition modeling of students with late-emerging reading disability. *Learning and Individual Differences, 18,* 329–337.

Cornoldi, C., De Beni, R., & Pazzaglia, F. (1996). Profiles of reading comprehension difficulties: An analysis of single cases. In C. Cornoldi, & J. Oakhill (Eds.), *Reading comprehension difficulties: Processes and intervention.* (pp. 113–136). Mahwah, NJ: Lawrence Erlbaum Associates.

Crain, S., & Shankweiler, D. (1988). Syntactic complexity and reading acquisition. In G. M. Green & A. Davison (Eds.), *Linguistic complexity and text comprehension: Readability issues reconsidered* (pp. 167–192). Hillsdale, NJ: Lawrence Erlbaum Associates.

Curtis, M. E. (1980). Development of components of reading skill. *Journal of Educational Psychology, 72,* 656–669.

Cutting, L. E., Eason, S. H., Young, K., & Alberstadt, A. L. (2008). Reading comprehension: Cognition and neuroimaging. In K. Pugh K. & P. McCardle (Eds.). *How children learn to read: Current issues and new directions in the integration of cognition, neurobiology and genetics of reading and dyslexia research and practice* (pp. 195–213). Mahwah, NJ: Lawrence Erlbaum Associates.

Cutting, L. E., Materek, A., Cole, C. A. S., Levine, T., & Mahone, E. M. (2009). Effects of language, fluency, and executive function on reading comprehension performance. *Annals of Dyslexia. 59,* 34–54.

Cutting, L. E., & Scarborough, H. S. (2006). Prediction of reading comprehension: Relative contributions of word recognition, language proficiency, and other cognitive skills can depend on how comprehension is measured. *Scientific Studies of Reading, 10,* 277–299.

Daneman, M., & Carpenter, P. (1980). Individual differences in working memory and reading. *Journal of Verbal Learning and Verbal Behavior, 19,* 450–466.

Dole, J. A., Valencia, S. W., Greer, E. A., & Wardop, J. L. (1991). Effects of two types of prereading instruction on the comprehension of narrative and expository text. *Reading Research Quarterly, 26,* 142–159

Ehri, L. C. (1992). Reconceptualizing the development of sight word reading and its relationship to recoding. In P. B. Gough, L. C. Ehri, & R. Treiman (Eds.), *Reading acquisition* (pp. 107–144). Hillsdale, NJ: Lawrence Erlbaum Associates.

Ehri, L. C., & Saltmarsh, J. (1995). Beginning readers outperform older disabled readers in learning to read words by sight. *Reading and Writing: An Interdisciplinary Journal, 7,* 295–326.

Elleman, A. M., Compton, D. L., Fuchs, D., Fuchs, L. S., Bouton, B. (in press). Exploring dynamic assessment as a means of identifying children at-risk of developing comprehension difficulties. *Special Issue on Dynamic Assessment in the Journal of Learning Disabilities.*

Farr, R. C. (1968). The convergent and discriminant validity of several upper level reading tests. *Yearbook of the National Reading Conference, 17,* 181–191.

Ferstl, E. C. (2007). The functional neuroanatomy of text comprehension: What's the story so far? In F. Schmalhofer, & C. A. Perfetti (Eds.), *Higher level language processes in the brain: Inference and comprehension processes* (pp. 53–102). Mahwah, NJ: Lawrence Erlbaum Associates.

Fletcher, J. M. (1985). Memory for verbal and nonverbal stimuli in learning disability subgroups: Analysis of selective reminding. *Journal of Experimental Child Psychology, 40,* 244–259.

Fletcher, J. M., Coulter, W. A., Reschly, D. J., & Vaughn, S. (2004). Alternative approaches to the definition and identification of learning disabilities: Some questions and answers. *Annals of Dyslexia, 54,* 304–331.

Francis, D. J., Fletcher, J. M., Stuebing, K. K., Lyon, G. R., Shaywitz, B. A., & Shaywitz, S. E. (2005). Psychometric approaches to the identification of LD: IQ and achievement scores are not sufficient. *Journal of Learning Disabilities, 38,* 98–108.

Fuchs, D., Mock, D., Morgan, P. L., & Young, C. L. (2003). Responsiveness-to-intervention: Definitions, evidence, and implications for the learning disabilities construct. *Learning Disabilities Research and Practice, 18,* 151–171.

Fuchs, L. S. (2003). Assessing intervention responsiveness: Conceptual and technical issues. *Learning Disabilities Research and Practice, 18,* 172–186.

Fuchs, L. S., & Fuchs, D. (1998). Treatment validity: A unifying concept for the identification of learning disabilities. *Learning Disability Research and Practice, 14,* 204–219.

———. (2007). Progress monitoring within a multi-tiered prevention system. *Perspectives, 33,* 43–47.

Gathercole, S. E., & Baddeley, A. D. (1993). *Working memory and language.* Hillsdale, NJ: Lawrence Erlbaum Associates.

Gersten, R., & Baker, S. (1999). *Two decades of research in learning disabilities: Reading comprehension, expressive writing, problem solving, self-concept. Keys to successful learning: A national summit on research in learning disabilities.* New York: National Center for Learning Disabilities.

Glover, T., & Albers, C. (2007). Considerations for evaluating universal screening assessments. *Journal of School Psychology, 45,* 117–135.

Gottardo, A., Stanovich, K. E., & Siegel, L. S. (1996). The relationships between phonological sensitivity, syntactic processing, and verbal working memory in the reading performance of third-grade children. *Journal of Experimental Child Psychology, 63,* 563–582.

Gough, P. B., & Hillinger, M. L. (1980). Learning to read: An unnatural act. *Bulletin of the Orton Society, 30,* 179–236.

Gough, P. B., Juel, C., & Griffith, P. L. (1992). Reading, spelling, and the orthographic cipher. In P. B. Gough, L. C. Ehri, & R. Treiman (Eds.), *Reading acquisition* (pp. 35–48). Hillsdale, NJ: Lawrence Erlbaum Associates.

Gough, P. B., & Walsh, M. A. (1991). Chinese, Phoenicians, and the orthographic cipher of English. In S. A. Brady & D. P. Shankweiler (Eds.), *Phonological processes in literacy: A tribute to Isabelle Y. Liberman* (pp. 199–209). Hillsdale, NJ: Lawrence Erlbaum Associates.

Gough, P. B., & Wren, S. (1998). The decomposition of decoding. In C. Hulme & M. Joshi (Eds.), *Reading and spelling: Development and disorders* (pp. 19–32). Mahwah, NJ: Lawrence Erlbaum Associates.

Green, L., McCutchen, D., Schwiebert, C., Quinlan, T., Eva-Wood, A., & Juelis, J. (2003). Morphological development in children's writing. *Journal of Educational Psychology, 95,* 752–761.

Jenkins, J. R. (2003, December). *Candidate measures for screening at-risk students.* Paper presented at the Conference on Response to Intervention as Learning Disabilities Identification, Sponsored by the National Research Center on Learning Disabilities, Kansas City, MO.

Jenkins, J. R., Hudson, R. F., & Johnson, E. S. (2007). Screening for service delivery in a response-to-intervention (RTI) framework. *School Psychology Review, 36,* 582–600.

Joshi, R. M., Williams, K. A., & Wood, J. R. (1998). Predicting reading comprehension from listening comprehension: Is this the answer to the IQ debate? In C. Hulme and R. M. Joshi (Eds.), *Reading and spelling: Development and disorders* (pp. 319–327). Mahwah, NJ: Lawrence Erlbaum Associates.

Just, M., & Carpenter, P. A. (1992). A capacity theory of comprehension: Individual differences in working memory. *Psychological Review, 99,* 122–149.

Kintsch, W. (1998). *Comprehension: A paradigm for cognition.* Cambridge, UK: Cambridge University Press.

Langer, J. (1981). From theory to practice: A prereading plan. *Journal of Reading, 24,* 152–156

Leach, J. M., Scarborough, H. S., & Rescorla, L. (2003). Late-emerging reading disabilities. *Journal of Educational Psychology, 95,* 211–224.

Lipka, O., Lesaux, N. K., & Siegel, L. S. (2006). Retrospective analyses of the reading development of grade 4 students with reading disabilities: Risk status and profiles over 5 years. *Journal of Learning Disabilities, 39,* 364–378.

Lorch, E. P., Eastham, D., Milich, R., Lemberger, C. C., Sanchez, R. P., Welsh, R., & van den Broek, P. (2004). Difficulties in comprehending causal relations among children with ADHD: The role of cognitive engagement. *Journal of Abnormal Psychology, 113,* 56–63.

McCardle, P., Scarborough, H. S., & Catts, H. W. (2001). Predicting, explaining, and preventing children's reading difficulties. *Learning Disability Research and Practice, 16,* 230–239.

Metsala, J. L., Stanovich, K. E., & Brown, G. D. A. (1998). Regularity effects and the phonological deficit model of reading disabilities: A meta-analytic review. *Journal of Educational Psychology, 90,* 279–293.

Molfese, V. J., & Molfese, D. L. (2004). Screening early reading skills in preschool children: Get Ready to Read. *Journal of Psychoeducational Assessment, 22,* 136–150.

Nagy, W., Berninger, V., & Abbott, R. D. (2006). Contributions of morphology beyond phonology to literacy outcomes of upper elementary and middle-school students. *Journal of Educational Psychology, 98,* 134–147.

Nagy, W., Berninger, V., Abbott, R., Vaughan, K., & Vermeulen, K. (2003). Relationship of morphology and other language skills to literacy skills in at-risk second-grade readers and at-risk fourth-grade writers. *Journal of Educational Psychology, 95,* 730–742.

Nation, K. (2005). Children's reading comprehension difficulties. In M. Snowling & C. Hulme, (Eds.), *The science of reading: A handbook* (pp. 248–266). Oxford: Blackwell.

Nation, K., Adams, J. W., Bowyer-Crane, C. A., & Snowling, M. J. (1999). Working memory deficits in poor comprehenders reflect underlying language impairments. *Journal of Experimental Child Psychology, 73,* 139–158.

Nation, K., & Snowling, M. J. (1998). Semantic processing and the development of word-recognition skills: Evidence from children with reading comprehension difficulties. *Journal of Memory and Language, 39,* 85–101.

———. (1999). Developmental differences in sensitivity to semantic relations among good and poor comprehenders: Evidence from semantic priming. *Cognition, 70,* B1-13.

Nation, K., Snowling, M. J., & Clarke, P. (2005). Production of the English past tense by children with language comprehension impairments. *Journal of Child Language, 32,* 117–137.

Neuman, S. B. (1988). Enhancing children's comprehension through previewing. *National Reading Conference Yearbook, 37,* 219–224.

Oakhill, J. (1984). Inferential and memory skills in children's comprehension of stories. *British Journal of Educational Psychology, 54,* 31–39.

———. (1993). Children's difficulties in reading comprehension. *Educational Psychology Review. Special Issue: European Educational Psychology, 5,* 223–237.

Oakhill, J., & Cain, K. E. (2000). Investigating the causes of reading comprehension failure: The comprehension-age match design. *Reading and Writing, 12,* 31–40.

Oakhill, J., Cain, K., & Yuill, N. (1998). Individual differences in children's comprehension skill: Toward an integrative model. In C. Hulme & R. M. Joshi (Eds.), *Reading and spelling: Development and disorders* (pp. 343–368). Mahwah, NJ: Lawrence Erlbaum Associates.

Oakhill, J., & Garnham, A. (1988). *Becoming a skilled reader.* Cambridge, MA: Basil Blackwell.

Oakhill, J., Hartt, J., & Samols, D. (2005). Levels of comprehension monitoring and working memory in good and poor comprehenders. *Reading and Writing, 18,* 657–686.

Oakhill, J., & Yuill, N. (1996). Higher order factors in comprehension disability: Processes and remediation. In C. Cornoldi, & J. Oakhill (Eds.), *Reading comprehension difficulties: Processes and intervention.* (pp. 69–92). Mahwah, NJ: Lawrence Erlbaum Associates.

O'Connor, R. E., & Jenkins, J. R. (1999). The prediction of reading disabilities in kindergarten and first grade. *Scientific Studies of Reading, 3,* 159–197.

Palincsar, A. S., & Brown, A. L. (1984). Reciprocal teaching of comprehension-foster and comprehension-monitoring activities. *Cognition and Instruction, 1,* 117–175.

Pazzaglia, F., Cornoldi, C., & DeBeni, R. (1995). Knowledge about reading and self-evaluation in reading disabled children. In T. E. Scruggs & M. A. Mastropierir (Eds.), *Advances in learning and behavioral disabilities* (Vol. 9, pp. 91–118). Greenwich, CT: JAI Press.

Pearson, P. D., Hanson, J., & Gordon, C. (1979). The effect of background knowledge on young children's comprehension of explicit and implicit information. *Journal of Reading Behavior, 9,* 201–209.

Pennington, B. F. (1997). Dimensions of executive functions in normal and abnormal development. In N. A. Krasnegor & G. R. Lyon (Eds.), *Development of the prefrontal cortex: Evolution, neurobiology, and behavior* (pp. 265–281). Baltimore: Brookes.

Perfetti, C. A. (1985). *Reading ability.* New York, NY: Oxford University Press.

———. (1991). Representations and awareness in the acquisition of reading competence. In L. Rieben & C. A. Perfetti (Eds.), *Learning to read: Basic research and its implications* (pp. 33–46). Hillsdale, NJ: Lawrence Erlbaum Associates.

———. (1992). The representation problem in reading acquisition. In P. B. Gough, L. C. Ehri, & R. Treiman (Eds.), *Reading acquisition* (pp. 145–174). Hillsdale, NJ: Lawrence Erlbaum Associates.

Perfetti, C. A., Landi, N., & Oakhill, J. (2005). The acquisition of reading comprehension skill. In M. Snowling & C. Hulme (Eds.), *The science of reading: A handbook* (pp. 227–247). Oxford: Blackwell.

Perfetti, C. A., Marron, M. A., & Foltz, P. W. (1996). Sources of comprehension failure: Theoretical perspectives and case studies. In C. Cornoldi & J. Oakhill (Eds.), *Reading comprehension difficulties: Processes and interventions* (pp. 137–165). Mahwah, NJ: Lawrence Erlbaum Associates.

Pressley, M. (2000). What should comprehension instruction be the instruction of? In M. L. Kamil, P. B. Mosenthal, P. D. Pearson, & R. Barr, (Eds.), *Handbook of reading research* (Vol. III, pp. 545–562). Mahwah, NJ: Lawrence Erlbaum Associates.

Recht, D. R., & Leslie, L. (1988). Effect of prior knowledge on good and poor readers' memory of text. *Journal of Educational Psychology, 80,* 16–20.

Reitsma, P. (1983). Printed word learning in beginning readers. *Journal of Experimental Child Psychology, 36,* 321–339.

Roman, A. A., Kirby, J. R., Parrila, R. K., Wade-Woolley, L., & Deacon, S. H. (2009). Toward a comprehensive view of the skills involved in word reading in grades 4, 6, and 8. *Journal of Experimental Child Psychology, 102,* 96–113.

Ruffman, T. (1996). Reassessing children's comprehension-monitoring skills. In C. Cornoldi & J. Oakhill (Eds.), *Reading comprehension difficulties: Processes and intervention.* (pp. 33–67). Mahwah, NJ: Lawrence Erlbaum Associates.

Savage, R., Lavers, N., & Pillay, V. (2006). Working memory and reading difficulties: What we know and what we don't know about the relationship. *Educational Psychology Review, 19,* 185–221.

Scarborough, H. S. (1998). Predicting the future achievement of second graders with reading disabilities: Contributions of phonemic awareness, verbal memory, rapid naming, and IQ. *Annals of Dyslexia, 48,* 115–136.

———. (2003). Connecting early language and literacy to later reading (dis)abilities: Evidence, theory, and practice. In S. B. Neuman & D. K. Dickinson (Eds.), *Handbook of early literacy research* (pp. 97–110). New York, NY: Guilford.

Schmalhofer, F., & Perfetti, C. A. (2007). Neural and behavioral indicators of integration processes across sentence boundaries. In F. Schmalhofer & C. A. Perfetti

(Eds.), *Higher level language processes in the brain: Inference and comprehension processes.* (pp. 161–188). Mahwah, NJ: Lawrence Erlbaum Associates.

Sesma, H. W., Mahone, E. M., Levine, T., Eason, S. H., & Cutting, L. E. (2009). The contribution of executive skills to reading comprehension. Child Neuropsychology. 15, 232–246.

Shankweiler, D., & Fowler, A. E. (2004). Questions people ask about the role of phonological processes in learning to read. *Reading & Writing, 17*, 483–515.

Shankweiler, D., Lundquist, E., Katz, L., Stuebing, K. K., Fletcher, J., Brady, S., & Shaywitz, B. A. (1999). Comprehension and decoding: Patterns of association in children with reading difficulties. *Scientific Studies of Reading, 3,* 69–64.

Share, D. L. (1995). Phonological recoding and self-teaching: Sine qua non of reading acquisition. *Cognition, 55*, 151–218.

Siegel, L. S. (1989). IQ is irrelevant to the definition of learning disabilities. *Journal of Learning Disabilities, 22,* 469–479.

Siegel, L. S., & Ryan, W. B. (1989). The development of working memory in normally achieving and subtypes of learning disabilities. *Child Development, 60,* 973–980.

Spilich, G. J., Vesonder, G. T., Chiesi, H. L., & Voss, J. F. (1979). Text processing of domain related information for individuals with high and low domain knowledge. *Journal of Verbal Learning and Verbal Behavior, 18,* 275–290.

Stanovich, K. E., Cunningham, A. E., & Freeman, D. J. (1984). Intelligence, cognitive skills and early reading progress. *Reading Research Quarterly, 19*, 278–303.

Stanovich, K. E., & Siegel, L. S. (1994). Phenotypic performance profile of children with reading disabilities: A regression-based test of phonological-core variable-difference model. *Journal of Educational Psychology, 86,* 24–53.

Stanovich, K. E., West, R. F., Cunningham, A. E., Cipielewski, J., & Siddiqui, S. (1996). The role of inadequate print exposure as a determinant of reading comprehension problems. In C. Cornoldi & J. Oakhill (Eds.), *Reading comprehension difficulties: Processes and interventions* (pp. 15-68). Mahwah, NJ: Lawrence Erlbaum Associates.

Stitch, T. G., & James, J. H. (1984). Listening and reading. In P.D. Pearson (Ed.), *Handbook of reading research* (pp. 293–317). New York: Longman Press.

Stothard, S. E., & Hulme, C. (1996). A comparison of reading comprehension and decoding difficulties in children. In C. Cornoldi & J. Oakhill (Eds.), *Reading comprehension difficulties: Processes and interventions* (pp. 93–112). Mahwah, NJ: Lawrence Erlbaum Associates.

Stuebing, K. K., Fletcher, J. M., LeDoux, J. M., Lyon, G. R., Shaywitz, S. E., & Shaywitz, B. A. (2002). Validity of IQ-discrepancy classifications of reading disabilities: A meta-analysis. *American Educational Research Journal, 39,* 469–518.

Swanson, H. L. (1993). Working memory in learning disability subgroups. *Journal of Experimental Child Psychology, 56,* 87–114.

———. (1996). Individual and age-related differences in children's working memory. *Memory and Cognition, 24,* 70–82.

———. (1999). Reading comprehension and working memory in learning-disabled readers: Is the phonological loop more important than the executive system? *Journal of Experimental Child Psychology, 72,* 1–31.

———. (2003). Age-related differences in learning disabled and skilled readers' working memory. *Journal of Experimental Child Psychology, 85,* 1–31.

Swanson, H. L., & Alexander, J. E. (1997). Cognitive processes as predictors of word recognition and reading comprehension in learning-disabled and skilled readers: Revisiting the specificity hypothesis. *Journal of Educational Psychology, 89,* 128–158.

Swanson, H. L., & Trahan, M. (1996). Learning disabled and average readers' working memory and comprehension: Does metacognition play a role? *British Journal of Educational Psychology, 66,* 333–355.

Tomblin, J. B., Records, N., Buckwalter, P., Zhang, X., Smith, E., & O'Brien, M. (1997). Prevalence of specific language impairment in kindergarten children. *Journal of Speech, Language, and Hearing Research, 40,* 1245–1260.

Torgesen, J. K. (2000). Individual differences in response to early interventions in reading: The lingering problem of treatment resisters. *Learning Disabilities Research & Practice, 15,* 55–64.

———. (2002). Empirical and theoretical support for direct diagnosis of learning disabilities by assessment of intrinsic processing weaknesses. In R. Bradley, L. Danielson, & D. P. Hallahan (Eds.), *Identification of learning disabilities: Research to practice* (pp. 565–613). Mahwah, NJ: Lawrence Erlbaum Associates.

van den Bos, K. P., Brand-Gruwel, A., & Lind, E. A. (1998). Text comprehension strategy instruction with poor readers. *Reading and Writing, 10,* 471–498.

Vaughn, S., & Fuchs, L. S. (2003). Redefining learning disabilities as inadequate response to intervention: The promise and potential problems. *Learning Disabilities Research and Practice, 18,* 137–146.

Vellutino, F. R., & Scanlon, D. M. (1987). Phonological coding, phonological awareness, and reading ability: Evidence from a longitudinal and experimental study. *Merrill Palmer Quarterly, 33,* 321–363.

Vellutino, F. R., Scanlon, D. M., & Lyon, G. R. (2000). Differentiating between difficult-to-remediate and readily remediated poor readers: More evidence against the IQ-discrepancy definition of reading disability. *Journal of Learning Disabilities, 33,* 223–238.

Vellutino, F. R., Scanlon, D. M., Sipay, E. R., Small, S. G, Pratt, A., Chen, R., & Denckla, M. B. (1996). Cognitive profiles of difficult-to-remediate and readily remediated poor readers: Early intervention as a vehicle for distinguishing between cognitive and experiential deficits as basic causes of specific reading disability. *Journal of Educational Psychology, 88,* 601–638.

Vellutino, F. R., Scanlon, D. M., & Tanzman, M. S. (1994). Components of reading ability: Issues and problems in operationalizing word identification, phonological coding, and orthographic coding. In G. R. Lyon (Ed.), *Frames of reference for the assessment of learning disabilities* (pp 279–232). Baltimore, MD: Paul H. Brookes Publishing Co.

Vogel, S. A. (1975). *Syntactic abilities in normal and dyslexic children.* Baltimore, MD: University Park Press.

Walczyk, J. J., Marsiglia, C. S., Johns, A. K., & Bryan, K. S. (2004). Children's compensations for poorly automated reading skills. *Discourse Processes, 37,* 47–66.

Waters, G., & Caplan, D. (1996). The measurement of verbal working memory capacity and its relation to reading comprehension. *The Quarterly Journal of Experimental Psychology, 49*, 51–79.

Willcutt, E. G., Pennington, B. F., Boada, R., Tunick, R. A., Ogline, J., Chhabildas, N. A., & Olson, R. K. (2001). A comparison of the cognitive deficits in reading disability and attention-deficit/hyperactivity disorder. *Journal of Abnormal Psychology, 110*, 157–172.

Willson, V. L., & Rupley, W. H. (1997). A structural equation model for reading comprehension based on background, phonemic, and strategy knowledge. *Scientific Studies of Reading, 1*, 45–63.

Wright, S. F., Fields, H., & Newman, S. P. (1996). Dyslexia: Stability of definition over a five year period. *Journal of Research in Reading, 19*, 46–60.

Yuill, N., & Oakhill, J. (1991). *Children's problems in text comprehension*. Cambridge, England: Cambridge University Press.

NOTES

1. This research was supported in part by Grant R305G050101 from the U.S. Department of Education, Institute of Education Sciences; and Core Grant HD15052 from the National Institute of Child Health and Human Development to Vanderbilt University. Statements do not reflect the position or policy of these agencies, and no official endorsement by them should be inferred.

2. Although this chapter addresses issues relevant to LD identification, our discussion is specific to reading disability (RD); therefore, we use RD for the remainder of the chapter.

Chapter Five

Assessment and Instruction Connections: The Impact of Teachers' Access and Use of Assessment-to-Instruction Software

Carol McDonald Connor, Frederick J. Morrison, Barry Fishman, and Christopher Schatschneider[1]

One of the most difficult tasks teachers face is using assessment information to inform instruction (Roehrig, Bohn, Turner, & Pressley, 2008). And yet accumulating evidence shows that planning and implementing instructional strategies and content using knowledge about students' skills and weaknesses can promote stronger student achievement (Deno et al., 2002; Fuchs, Fuchs, & Phillips, 1994). The purpose of this study is to examine teachers' use of Assessment-to-Instruction (A2i) software, which is designed to help them use assessment results to guide their literacy instruction.

Many children fail to reach proficient levels in reading because they do not receive the amount and type of instruction they need (Foorman, Francis, Fletcher, Schatschneider, & Mehta, 1998; Morrison, Bachman, & Connor, 2005; Vellutino et al., 1996). Research indicates that, unlike with spoken language, for most children, reading must be taught directly and explicitly (National Reading Panel, 2000; Rayner, Foorman, Perfetti, Pesetsky, & Seidenberg, 2001).

Research over the past decades has revealed important insights into this process and the fundamental role skilled reading plays in school success (Connor, Morrison, & Katch, 2004; Connor, Morrison, & Petrella, 2004; Neuman & Dickinson, 2001; Rayner et al., 2001). Whereas much of the research has focused on school reform (Ross, Smith, Slavin, & Madden, 1997) and curriculum-based instruction (Foorman et al., 1998), attending to individual children by assessing the progress they make on key literacy skills may yield even stronger results (Connor, Morrison, & Katch, 2004; Juel & Minden-Cupp, 2000; Torgesen, 2000).

Accumulating evidence shows that the effect of a particular instructional practice may depend on the skill level of the student. We and others have given this phenomenon various labels: child characteristic-by-instruction type (child-by-instruction) interactions (Connor, Morrison, & Katch, 2004; Connor, Morrison, & Petrella, 2004; Connor, Morrison, & Slominski, 2006; Juel & Minden-Cupp, 2000), individual response to intervention (Torgesen, 2000), and aptitude-by-treatment interactions (Cronbach & Snow, 1969).

Recent randomized control field trials have provided evidence that such child-by-instruction interactions may be causally related to the widely varying levels of student achievement observed within and between classrooms and schools (Connor, Morrison, Fishman, Schatschneider, & Underwood, 2007; Connor et al., 2009). The implication is that the effect of particular instructional strategies depends on students' language and literacy skills. Thus, patterns of instruction that are effective for one child may be ineffective for another that shares the classroom but has different language and literacy skills.

However, individualizing instruction in line with these child-by-instruction interactions is highly complex, and it demands skills and knowledge that many classroom teachers lack. Most particularly and germane to this study, many teachers have difficulty translating assessment results into effective instruction for their students (Roehrig, Bohn, et al., 2008). To individualize or differentiate instruction based on children's language and literacy skills demands highly sophisticated knowledge of assessment and how to interpret the results.

A number of progress-monitoring assessments are in general use that can inform teachers' instructional decision making. Among these are DIBELS (Good & Kaminski, 2002), AIMSWEB (http://aimsweb.com/), and Think-Link Learning (http://www.thinklinklearning.com/about.php). All three can be administered via the web.

DIBELS, as an example, is a battery of curriculum-based assessments (Deno et al., 2002) that is appropriate from kindergarten through at least third grade. The assessments are administered quickly and provide benchmark information that categorizes students' skills as "green," which indicates students are not at risk for reading difficulties, "yellow," which indicates some risk, and "red," which indicates high risk.

The results also provide recommended homogeneous skill-based groupings and information about the specific skills that deserve attention, in particular letter-sound knowledge, decoding nonsense words, and oral reading fluency.

The assessment package, however, provides no specific links between the assessment results and the amounts and types of instruction that, based on research evidence, might be required to bring individual students' reading skills to the green level. For teachers, making these connections appropriately appears to be among the most difficult aspects of using assessment to inform instructional decisions (Roehrig, Duggar, Moats, Glover, & Mincey, 2008).

A2i uses inputted student assessment scores to compute recommended amounts and types of instruction for each student, based on research models (Connor, Morrison, & Katch, 2004). A2i software was designed to help teachers translate assessment results into specific recommendations for reading instruction. Indexed to their core reading curriculum, teachers also used the software to plan daily instruction and monitor students' progress.

Although we used formal standardized measures in the study, potentially any valid and reliable reading progress monitoring assessment, such as DIBELS, may be used with A2i. A2i includes an online semantic matching task, the *Word Match Game*, which assesses students' vocabulary skills. Both reading and vocabulary scores are required for the A2i recommendation algorithms.

In six cluster randomized control field trials (one in kindergarten, three in first grade, one in second, and one in third), teachers who individualized instruction using A2i were more effective increasing their students' reading skills than were teachers in the business-as-usual control groups (Al Otaiba et al., in 2011; Connor et al., 2007; Connor, Morrison, et al., 2011) or alternative treatment control groups (Connor, Morrison, et al., in review).

Moreover, across studies, within the treatment group, the more that teachers used A2i and the more precisely they provided the recommended amounts and types of instruction, the greater were students' reading skill gains.

A2i enhancements were recommended by teachers and incorporated into the software. These included progress-monitoring graphing capabilities in addition to easy access to students' scores and the assessment-guided recommendations page. Using these features, teachers were able to examine and monitor both reading and vocabulary skill growth.

In this study, we investigated the extent that first-grade teachers used the Child Information Screen page, which displayed the child's test scores and the progress-monitoring graphing features. We also examined how and when teachers used the Classroom View, which provided the assessment-guided recommendations and student grouping features. We then examined whether using these features to a greater extent was associated with stronger student outcomes.

We hypothesized that these two features of A2i make using assessment results more salient. Thus, the more that teachers used these assessment features, the more effective their instruction might be and, hence, the stronger their students' reading skill outcomes.

The following research questions guided this investigation:

1. What is the nature and variability of teachers' use of the A2i software and, specifically, the assessment components of the software (as found on the

Classroom View and child add-edit page, which include the children's assessment information, progress-monitoring graphs, recommendations for
instruction, and grouping features)?
2. Is greater use of the A2i assessment components associated with stronger
student reading outcomes?

METHODS

The research reported in this chapter was conducted in a large ethnically and
economically diverse school district in Florida in two separate studies. Study
1 (Connor et al., 2009) was conducted in 2005–2006 in 17 schools, with 47
teachers, and 616 first-grade students. Study 2 (Connor, Morrison, et al.,
2011) was conducted in 2006–2007 in seven schools with 25 teachers (n =
14 in the treatment group) and 396 first-grade students.

For each study, schools were matched and paired on key indicators, including percentage of children qualifying for the free and reduced-price lunch
program, participation in the federal Reading First instructional program, and
school performance on the state-mandated achievement test in third-grade
reading. One school from each pair was randomly assigned to the treatment
group. All of our participating schools had students living in poverty, with
poverty rates that ranged from 4% to 96%.

In Study 2, two schools were Reading First/Title I schools and 60% and
87% of the students qualified for the federal free or reduced-price lunch
program, respectively, a widely used marker of school socioeconomic status.
For two more schools, more than one-third of the students received free or
reduced lunch, and in the remaining three schools, 12%, 9%, and 4% of students, respectively, received free or reduced lunch.

PARTICIPANTS

All of the students assigned to participating teachers were invited to join the
study, including children for whom English was a second language or who
qualified for special services. In Study 2, parental consent was obtained for
83% of the students.

Over the course of the school year, 22 children in treatment classrooms
and 24 children in the control classrooms left the district, which is about 11%
attrition. We judged this to be an acceptable rate given the sociodemographic
characteristics of the schools. None of the teachers left the study. The split
between boys and girls was even. Approximately 34% of children qualified

for free or reduced lunch. Fifty-four percent were African American, 37% were European American, and the remaining children belonged to other ethnic groups.

INTERVENTION

A2i software is web-based and uses students' fall vocabulary and letter-word reading scores in algorithms. These algorithms are based on growth models developed in our previous research (Connor, Morrison, & Katch, 2004). Using the algorithms, A2i computes recommended amounts and types of instruction for each child in the classroom. An additional algorithm then assigns children to smaller homogeneous skill groups based on reading scores (the teacher decides on the number of groups and can change group membership).

The Classroom View shows the recommended amounts of instruction for each child. Students' scores, including progress-monitoring graphs, are accessed by clicking the child's name, which takes the teacher to the "Child Information Screen" page. From this page, teachers access students' scores and progress-monitoring graphs, which are the two aspects of A2i examined in this study. Screen shots, using pseudonyms for the children, are provided for the Classroom View (top), the Child Information Screen page (bottom left,) and the graph (bottom right) (see figure 5.1).

The software presents a catalog of activities indexed to the schools' core reading curriculum. This functionality is embedded in lesson-planning software so teachers can schedule, plan, and print daily lesson plans.

All literacy activities are indexed to the dimensions of instruction (Connor, Morrison, & Katch, 2004), including teacher- versus child-managed instruction, code- versus meaning-focused instruction, and change in instruction over time.

Teacher- versus child-managed instruction identifies who is responsible for focusing the students' attention on the learning activities at hand—the teacher or the student (Connor, Morrison, & Katch, 2004; Morrison et al., 2005). Teacher-managed instruction may be highly interactive, such as when the teacher is leading a discussion. Child-managed instruction includes activities where students are expected to work independently or with peers.

Code-focused instruction includes those activities that are designed to help students achieve proficient phonological decoding and word reading skills, including letter-sound connections, phonological awareness, print awareness, repeated reading of words, and other word-level activities specifically designed to teach children how to read words fluently (National Reading Panel,

Figure 5.1.   Screenshots of Classroom View, Child Information Screen page, and graph from A2i software

2000). Meaning-focused instruction is designed to teach children how to extract and construct meaning from text (Snow, 2001). This includes explicit instruction in comprehension strategies, discussion, reading aloud, peer reading, building vocabulary, independent reading, and so on (Connor, Morrison, & Petrella, 2004).

Change over time captures the impact of changing the focus or amount of instruction over the school year (Connor, Morrison, & Katch, 2004). For example, decreasing the amount of teacher-managed instruction and increasing child-managed instruction may promote student learning (i.e., release of responsibility) (Pearson & Gallagher, 1983).

These dimensions operate simultaneously so that any language arts activity falls in one of four sectors. For example, children reading together in the library corner during center time would be participating in a child-managed/ meaning-focused activity. The teacher instructing the children in how to segment or blend phonemes in words would be a teacher-managed/code-focused activity.

About the Algorithms

In an earlier study (Connor, Morrison, & Katch, 2004), hierarchical linear models (HLM) predicted students' letter-word reading outcomes with a high degree of precision (Morrison et al., 2005). These models form the foundation of the A2i algorithms in the present study and are designed to make predictions based on a mixture of known and computed variables. In this way, the models are analogous to the dynamic system forecasting models that meteorologists use to predict the trajectory of hurricanes (Rhome, 2007).

However, rather than predict students' achievement, we want to predict the amounts and types of instruction. Assuming that all children have a range of potential achievement trajectories (Raudenbush, 2008), the algorithms or dynamic forecasting intervention models predict the amounts and types of instruction required to push achievement to children's highest potential level.

In the 2004 study, we found that children who began first grade with lower letter-word reading skills demonstrated stronger letter-word reading growth in classrooms where they spent greater amounts of time in teacher-managed/ code-focused instruction than did students in classrooms with less time receiving such instruction.

The opposite held for students with high initial letter-word reading skills. For them, *less* time in teacher-managed/code-focused activities was related to greater letter-word growth. For children with higher fall vocabulary scores, spending more time all year long in child-managed/meaning-focused instruction was associated with stronger letter-word reading skill growth.

In contrast, for children with low initial vocabulary scores, having less time in child-managed/meaning-focused activity in the fall, then spending steadily more time until reaching high amounts in the spring, was associated with stronger letter-word reading skill growth. Using more recent data (Connor et al., 2009), we found a main effect for teacher-managed/meaning-focused small group instruction and an interaction for child-managed/code-focused activities.

For the latter, more time in child-managed/code-focused activities was positively associated with reading gains, but only for students with reading skills below grade-level expectations. For children reading at or above grade level, child-managed/code-focused activities had a negative association with reading skill growth.

The A2i dynamic forecasting intervention models use these associations to compute recommended specific daily amounts (in minutes) of all four categories of instruction as a function of students' fall letter-word reading, passage comprehension, and vocabulary scores and target child outcome. For all children, the target outcome is to achieve at least grade level and a minimum of one school year's growth in reading achievement by the end of first grade. In this way, the instructional goals for all children—both high and lower performing students—are addressed.

Taking into account child-by-instruction interactions makes planning for each student in the classroom highly complex for teachers because each student has a unique pattern of instruction that will be most optimal for him or her, based on assessed reading and vocabulary scores, particularly in more heterogeneous classrooms. Moreover, these amounts will change from month to month.

A2i also includes planning software so teachers can schedule and organize an uninterrupted block of time devoted to literacy instruction and can accomplish daily or weekly lesson planning using the indexed core reading curriculum materials as well as other materials. There are online resources, including videos of teachers implementing individualized instruction and a discussion board.

RESEARCH DESIGN

We used a cluster randomized design with schools assigned to treatment and wait-list control conditions. The study was conducted over two years.

During year 1, teachers in the treatment condition received training and classroom-based support designed to help them implement the A2i recommended amounts of instruction to the children in their classroom. The teachers in the control group followed district guidelines and did not receive A2i support. Both groups of teachers provided a 120-minute block of time dedicated to literacy instruction, used an evidence-based core reading curriculum, and did approximately 45 minutes of small group instruction. Both groups of teachers had access to child progress-monitoring information through the district-administered DIBELS (Good & Kaminski, 2002).

During the second year of Study 2, teachers in the wait-list control group received the training and A2i software. For this study, amounts and types of teacher-managed/code-focused and child-managed/meaning-focused activities were recommended. The new algorithms were tested in a subsequent study.

DATA COLLECTION AND ANALYSIS

Student Outcomes

Students' language and literacy skills were assessed in the fall, and again in the winter and spring, using a battery of language and literacy assessments, including tests from the *Woodcock Johnson Tests of Achievement-III* (WJ, Mather & Woodcock, 2001). The WJ was selected because it is widely used in schools and for research. It is psychometrically strong (reliabilities on the tests used ranged from .81 to .94), and subtests are brief. All assessments were administered to children individually by a trained researcher in a quiet location near the students' classrooms.

We assessed students' word reading skills using the *Letter-Word Identification test*, which asks children to recognize and name increasingly unfamiliar letters and words out of context. To assess expressive vocabulary, we used the *Picture Vocabulary test*, which asks children to name pictures of increasingly unfamiliar objects (see table 5.1). The letter-word identification grade equivalent (GE) and the picture vocabulary age equivalent (AE) scores were entered into the A2i software and could be viewed on the Child Information Screen.

These scores were used to compute recommended amounts of each instruction type for children in the treatment and control classrooms (comparison teachers did not have access to the scores). These recommendations were

Table 5.1. Descriptive statistics for child and teacher variables.

	Total Mean (SD)		Treatment Mean (SD)		Control Mean (SD)	
Child Outcome Measures	*Fall*	*Spring*	*Fall*	*Spring*	*Fall*	*Spring*
WJ Letter Word W	417.50	463.25	417.41	464.86	417.61	461.20
	(30.66)	(26.12	(29.64)	(24.98)	(32.01)	(27.44)
WJ Picture	481.47	487.00	481.39	486.48	481.59	487.66
Vocabulary W	(9.50)	(9.87)	(9.23)	(9.38)	(9.86)	(10.83)

Teacher Variables (minutes from September to May)	*Mean*	*Std. Deviation*	*Minimum*	*Maximum*
Classroom View Minutes	147.80	203.51	11.50	721.75
Child Information Screen Minutes	49.80	37.42	1.00	141.25
Total Time Using A2i Minutes	526.50	567.76	.00	1,927.00

Note. Control teachers were coded 0 on the A2i teacher variables used in the model so that these variables also represent the groups. The means and standard deviations provided above are only for the 14 teachers in the treatment group.

viewed on the Classroom View page. Midyear, children were readministered the alternate form of the Letter-Word Identification and Picture Vocabulary tests. New scores were entered in A2i, and recommended amounts for every child were recomputed using the new scores.

The treatment group teachers first gained access to algorithm recommendations and assessment information provided by A2i software in September 2006 and used the software continuously through May 2007. The control group teachers were provided written reports of the assessment results for their students in the fall, winter, and spring of each study year.

Teachers' Use of A2i

A2i automatically tracks teachers' use of the software, including the date and time they logged on, the pages they visited, and the amount of time spent on each page. A sample of the output is provided in table 5.2. Total amounts of time spent using A2i include all of the time from log on to log out, or if the teacher does not log out, one minute after the last click of the mouse for each session. Total time includes time spent viewing the online resources, using the discussion board, and accessing the assessment and planning features of A2i.

Classroom View time includes the total amount of time teachers spent viewing the Classroom View screen, including changing student group membership. Teachers access the Child Information Screen from the Classroom View page by clicking the students' name. Time spent on this page includes viewing students' scores and accessing reading and vocabulary progress-monitoring graphs.

RESULTS

Hierarchical linear modeling (HLM, Raudenbush, Bryk, Cheong, Congdon, & du Toit, 2004) results for two level models (children nested in classrooms) revealed that A2i-guided individualized instruction promoted stronger student reading growth compared to the control group. Controlling for student initial reading and vocabulary skills, we confirmed a significant effect of treatment (treatment group = 1, control group = 0) with a treatment coefficient of 3.77 (df = 23, $p = .054$, effect size d = .23) (Connor, Morrison, et al., 2011).

Nature and Variability in Teachers' A2i Use

Even with the support of A2i software and professional development, individualizing instruction proved challenging for a few of the teachers in the study. Treatment teachers used A2i software, on average, for a total of 560 minutes from September 1 to May 31 (range 12.5 to 1,927 minutes, See table 5.1 and figure 5.2). This is considerably higher than A2i use in Study 1, when teachers used the software for an average of 180 minutes for the entire year.

Teachers used the Classroom View for 147 minutes and the Child Information Screen for 141 minutes, on average (see figure 5.3). Again, there was substantial between-teacher variability. Means, ranges, and standard deviations are provided in table 5.1.

Only three of the 14 treatment teachers used the software for less than 100 minutes, while the remaining teachers used the software for at least 200 minutes (see figure 5.2). Five teachers used the software for 500 minutes or more from September to May. Of note, teachers who used all the features of A2i were also more likely to spend greater time using the Classroom View ($r = .858$, $p < .001$).

There was no significant relation between time spent using the Classroom View and time spent using the Child Information Screen features (see figure 5.3). Overall, Study 2 teachers were likely more consistent in their implementation of individualized instruction than were Study 1 teachers, as evidenced by more consistent and greater time spent using A2i.

Relation of A2i Use and Student Outcomes

Two-level HLM, controlling for students' fall vocabulary and reading scores, revealed the more that teachers accessed the Child Information Screen pages, the greater their students' reading skill growth (i.e., residualized change). The results are provided in table 5.3 and figure 5.4. The effect size comparing students in the control group and students whose teachers spent very little time on the Child Information Screen compared with teachers who spent about 140 minutes using the page was moderate ($d = .44$). Time spent on the Classroom View page was not significantly associated with students' reading growth.

DISCUSSION

Overall, we confirmed that individualizing instruction based on students' reading and vocabulary scores was associated with stronger student reading skill growth (Connor, Morrison, et al., 2011). A closer look at teachers' use of the design aspects of A2i, which were developed to make accessing and using assessment data to inform instruction more salient, revealed that teachers accessed these features frequently. Indeed, teachers spent almost 40% of their

Table 5.2. Example transcript from the Assessment-to-Instruction teacher use log

Teacher ID	Session	Action Date and Time	URL to	URL to Area	URL to SubArea	Query String	Comments	URL to Page
	25048	10/24/2006 6:50	/A2I/ClassroomView.aspx	A2I	Classroom View		Arrived at Classroom View	ClassroomView.aspx
	25048	10/24/2006 6:50	/A2I/admin/UserAccess/Child_AddEdit.aspx	A2I	Child Information	?cid=1057	Arrived at Child Information	Child_AddEdit.aspx
	25048	10/24/2006 6:51	/A2I/ClassroomView.aspx	A2I	Classroom View		Arrived at Classroom View	ClassroomView.aspx
	25048	10/24/2006 6:52	/A2I/admin/UserAccess/Child_AddEdit.aspx	A2I	Child Information	?cid=1060	Arrived at Child Information	Child_AddEdit.aspx
	25048	10/24/2006 6:52	/A2I/ClassroomView.aspx	A2I	Classroom View		Arrived at Classroom View	ClassroomView.aspx
	25048	10/24/2006 6:53	/A2I/admin/UserAccess/Child_AddEdit.aspx	A2I	Child Information	?cid=10645	Arrived at Child Information	Child_AddEdit.aspx
	25048	10/24/2006 6:53	/A2I/ClassroomView.aspx	A2I	Classroom View		Arrived at Classroom View	ClassroomView.aspx
	25048	10/24/2006 6:53	/A2I/admin/UserAccess/Child_AddEdit.aspx	A2I	Child Information	?cid=17056	Arrived at Child Information	Child_AddEdit.aspx
	25048	10/24/2006 6:54	/A2I/ClassroomView.aspx	A2I	Classroom View		Arrived at Classroom View	ClassroomView.aspx
	25048	10/24/2006 6:54	/A2I/admin/UserAccess/Child_AddEdit.aspx	A2I	Child Information	?cid=18055	Arrived at Child Information	Child_AddEdit.aspx
	25048	10/24/2006 6:54	/A2I/ClassroomView.aspx	A2I	Classroom View		Arrived at Classroom View	ClassroomView.aspx
	25048	10/24/2006 6:55	/A2I/admin/UserAccess/Child_AddEdit.aspx	A2I	Child Information	?cid=91059	Arrived at Child Information	Child_AddEdit.aspx
	25048	10/24/2006 6:55	/A2I/ClassroomView.aspx	A2I	Classroom View		Arrived at Classroom View	ClassroomView.aspx

Teacher ID	Date/Time	URL		Content	?cid	Action	Page
25048	10/24/2006 6:55	/A2I/admin/UserAccess/Child_AddEdit.aspx	A2I	Child Information	?cid=21074	Arrived at Child Information	Child_AddEdit.aspx
25048	10/24/2006 6:56	/A2I/ClassroomView.aspx	A2I	Classroom View		Arrived at Classroom View	ClassroomView.aspx
25048	10/24/2006 6:56	/A2I/admin/UserAccess/Child_AddEdit.aspx	A2I	Child Information	?cid=61061	Arrived at Child Information	Child_AddEdit.aspx
25048	10/24/2006 6:56	/A2I/ClassroomView.aspx	A2I	Classroom View		Arrived at Classroom View	ClassroomView.aspx
25048	10/24/2006 6:56	/A2I/admin/UserAccess/Child_AddEdit.aspx	A2I	Child Information	?cid=21069	Arrived at Child Information	Child_AddEdit.aspx
25048	10/24/2006 6:56	/A2I/ClassroomView.aspx	A2I	Classroom View		Arrived at Classroom View	ClassroomView.aspx
25048	10/24/2006 6:57	/A2I/admin/UserAccess/Child_AddEdit.aspx	A2I	Child Information	?cid=1752	Arrived at Child Information	Child_AddEdit.aspx
25048	10/24/2006 6:57	/A2I/ClassroomView.aspx	A2I	Classroom View		Arrived at Classroom View	ClassroomView.aspx
26994	1/10/2007 7:13	/A2I/Home.aspx	A2I	iSi Content		Arrived at Home.aspx	Home.aspx
26994	1/10/2007 7:13	/A2I/resourcesHome.aspx	A2I	iSi Content		Arrived at resourcesHome.aspx	resourcesHome.aspx
26994	1/10/2007 7:14	/A2I/assess.aspx	A2I	iSi Content		Arrived at Using Assessment to Guide Instruction: Introduction	assess.aspx
26994	1/10/2007 7:14	/A2I/assess_cba.aspx	A2I	iSi Content		Arrived at Using Assessment to Guide Instruction: Initial Sound Fluency	assess_cba.aspx

Note. Teacher identification numbers have been removed and child identification number (?cid) have been changed to preserve confidentiality.

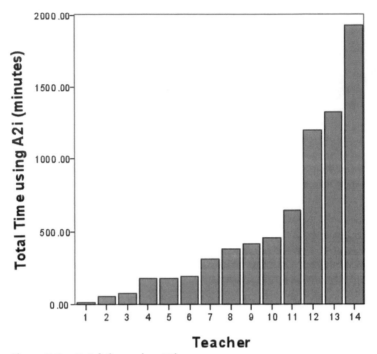

Figure 5.2.   Total time using A2i

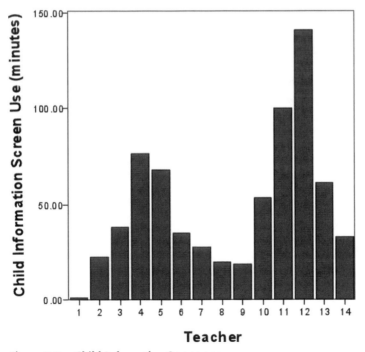

Figure 5.3.   Child Information Screen use

Table 5.3.   HLM results relating teacher A2i use, in minutes, with students' WJ Word Identification W score.

Fixed Effect	Coefficient	Standard Error	d.f.	p-value
Intercept	461.18	1.19	22	< .001
Child Level Variables				
Fall Letter-word W Score	.63	.03	391	< .001
Fall Vocabulary W Score	.16	.09	391	.08
Classroom Level Variables				
Classroom View (minutes)	−.01	.005	22	.10
Child Information Screen	.05	.02	22	.05
Random Effect	Variance	d.f.	Chi-square	p-value
Child Level	275.74			
Classroom level	3.87	22	33.65	.05

Deviance = 3354.10

time, on average, using pages that provided information about the reading and vocabulary skills of their students.

When teachers used the Child Information Screens of the A2i software more frequently, their students were more likely to make greater gains in word reading skills. Thus, the specific access to student scores and progress-monitoring graphs appeared to be related to the efficacy of teachers' instruction. By implication, tailoring instruction to meet students' instructional needs may have been facilitated by the software, thus contributing to the significant effect of treatment.

Consider that when teachers accessed the Child Information Screen, they were able to view the students' scores, including grade equivalents, and compare growth in skill to the target line of growth set by the algorithms of the software. These salient cues of good versus inadequate progress, coupled

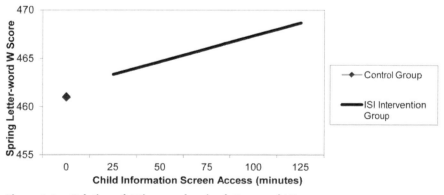

Figure 5.4.   Relation of A2i use and spring letter-word W score

with students' reading skill level (in grade and age equivalents), appear to be important.

Both treatment and control teachers had access to DIBELS data. However, DIBELS benchmarks grouped children by red (at high risk for reading failure), yellow (at moderate risk for reading failure) and green (not at risk for reading failure) levels. In contrast, the A2i scores in age and grade equivalents differentiated between children who were reading at more typical levels compared to children who were reading above or well below grade expectations on a continuous scale.

Arguably, teachers might provide more challenging reading material for a first grader who they see is reading at a third-grade level than one who is only identified as in the green zone. It may be that A2i's use of grade and age equivalents allowed teachers to better calibrate their reading instruction to the individual skill levels of their students. This is in contrast to the DIBELS results that focused principally on whether the child was struggling with reading or not.

As a personal performance system (Ericsson, 2006), A2i was designed to scaffold use of assessment to guide instruction including creating flexible homogeneous skill-based groups, which according to the effective schools research is associated with stronger student outcomes (Taylor, Pearson, Clark, & Walpole, 2000; Wharton-McDonald, Pressley, & Hampston, 1998). It was also designed to improve teachers' focus on organization and to encourage their planning through other design features, which research also reveals is associated with more effective instruction (Borko & Niles, 1987; Brophy, 1985; Cameron, 2004; Cameron, Connor, & Morrison, 2005; Fuchs et al., 1994).

For these reasons, the software may have promoted more effective teaching overall as well as supporting individualized instruction and the use of assessment to inform instruction. Further research on these questions is currently under way.

In general, the results of this study show that we can make the practice of using assessment data to guide instruction more accessible to teachers. When assessment information becomes more accessible, we can potentially help teachers increase the efficacy of their classroom practices and enhance students' outcomes.

These findings are particularly encouraging because they come within the context of a randomized control field trial conducted in generally higher-poverty schools. Replicating and extending previous findings, the results provide additional evidence regarding the causal implications of child-by-instruction interactions and show assessment-guided individualized instruction may promote stronger literacy outcomes.

REFERENCES

Al Otaiba, S., Connor, C. M., Folsom, J. S., Greulich, L., Meadows, J., & Li, Z. (2011). Assessment data-informed guidance to individualize kindergarten reading instruction: Findings from a cluster-randomized control field trial. *Elementary School Journal, 111,* 535–560.

Borko, H., & Niles, J. (1987). Descriptions of teacher planning: Ideas for teachers and research. In V. Richardson-Koehler (Ed.), *Educators' handbook: A research perspective* (pp. 167–187). New York: Longman.

Brophy, J. E. (1985). Classroom management as instruction: Socializing self-guidance in students. *Theory into Practice, 24,* 233–240.

Cameron, C. E. (2004, April). *Variation in teacher organization.* Paper presented at the Conference on Human Development, Washington, D.C..

Cameron, C. E., Connor, C. M., & Morrison, F. J. (2005). Effects of variation in teacher organization on classroom functioning. *Journal of School Psychology, 43,* 61–85.

Connor, C. M., Morrison, F. J., Fishman, B. Crowe, E. C., Al Otaiba, S., & Schatschneider, C. (in review). A longitudinal randomized control study on the impact of effective instruction on students' reading from 1st through 3rd grade: Inoculation, accumulation, or both?

Connor, C. M., Morrison, F. J., Fishman, B. J., Schatschneider, C., & Underwood, P. (2007). The early years: Algorithm-guided individualized reading instruction. *Science, 315,* 464–465.

Connor, C. M., Morrison, F. J., & Katch, E. L. (2004). Beyond the reading wars: The effect of classroom instruction by child interactions on early reading. *Scientific Studies of Reading, 8,* 305–336.

Connor, C. M., Morrison, F. J., & Petrella, J. N. (2004). Effective reading comprehension instruction: Examining child by instruction interactions. *Journal of Educational Psychology, 96,* 682–698.

Connor, C. M., Morrison, F. J., Schatschneider, C., Toste, J., Lundblom, E. G., Crowe, E. & Fishman, B. (2011). Effective classroom instruction: Implications of child characteristic by instruction interactions on first graders' word reading achievement. *Journal for Research on Educational Effectiveness, 4,* 173–207.

Connor, C. M., Morrison, F. J., & Slominski, L. (2006). Preschool instruction and children's literacy skill growth. *Journal of Educational Psychology, 98,* 665–689.

Connor, C. M., Piasta, S. B., Fishman, B., Glasney, S., Schatschneider, C., Crowe, E., & Morrison, F. J. (2009). Individualizing student instruction precisely: Effects of child by instruction interactions on first graders' literacy development. *Child Development, 80,* 77–100.

Cronbach, L. J., & Snow, R. E. (1969). *Individual differences in learning ability as a function of instructional variables* (ERIC Document reproduction service no. ED 029 001). Stanford, CA: Stanford University, School of Education.

Deno, S. L., Espin, C. A., Fuchs, L. S., Shinn, M. R., Walker, H. M., & Stoner, G. (2002). Evaluation strategies for preventing and remediating basic skill deficits. In M. R. Shinn, H. M. Walker, & G. Stoner (Eds.), *Interventions for academic and behavior problems II: Preventive and remedial approaches* (pp. 213–241). Washington, D.C.: National Association of School Psychologists.

Ericsson, K. A. (Ed.). (2006). *The Cambridge handbook of expertise and expert performance*. New York: Cambridge University Press.

Foorman, B. R., Francis, D. J., Fletcher, J. M., Schatschneider, C., & Mehta, P. (1998). The role of instruction in learning to read: Preventing reading failure in at risk children. *Journal of Educational Psychology, 90*, 37–55.

Fuchs, L. S., Fuchs, D., & Phillips, N. (1994). The relation between teachers' beliefs about the importance of good student work habits, teacher planning, and student achievement. *Elementary School Journal, 94*, 331–345.

Good, R. H., & Kaminski, R. A. (2002). *Dynamic Indicators of Basic Early Literacy Skills (DIBELS) 6th Edition*. Eugene, OR: Institute for Development of Educational Achievement.

Juel, C., & Minden-Cupp, C. (2000). Learning to read words: Linguistic units and instructional strategies. *Reading Research Quarterly, 35*, 458–492.

Mather, N., & Woodcock, R. W. (2001). *Woodcock Johnson III Tests of Achievement: Examiner's manual*. Itasca, IL: Riverside.

Morrison, F. J., Bachman, H. J., & Connor, C. M. (2005). *Improving literacy in America: Guidelines from research*. New Haven, CT: Yale University Press.

National Reading Panel (2000). *National Reading Panel report: Teaching children to read: An evidence-based assessment of the scientific research literature on reading and its implications for reading instruction* (NIH Pub. No. 00-4769). Washington D.C.: U.S. Department of Health and Human Services, National Institutes of Health, National Institute of Child Health and Human Development.

Neuman, S. B., & Dickinson, D. K. (2001). *Handbook of early literacy research*. New York: Guilford Press.

Pearson, B. D., & Gallagher, M. C. (1983). The instruction of reading comprehension. *Contemporary Educational Psychology, 8*, 317–344.

Raudenbush, S. W. (2008, August). *Causal inference in multilevel settings*. Paper presented at the American Psychological Association Conference, Boston, MA.

Raudenbush, S. W., Bryk, A. S., Cheong, Y. F., Congdon, R., & du Toit, M. (2004). *HLM6: Hierarchical linear and nonlinear modeling*. Lincolnwood, IL: Scientific Software International.

Rayner, K., Foorman, B. R., Perfetti, C. A., Pesetsky, D., & Seidenberg, M. S. (2001). How psychological science informs the teaching of reading. *Psychological Science in the Public Interest, 2*, 31-74.

Rhome, J. R. (2007). Technical summary of the National Hurricane Center track and intensity models. Retrieved October 12, 2008, from www.nhc.noaa.gov/model-summary.shtml

Roehrig, A. D., Bohn, C. M., Turner, J., & Pressley, M. (2008). Mentoring beginning primary teachers for exemplary teaching practices. *Teaching and Teacher Education, 24,* 684–702.

Roehrig, A. D., Duggar, S. W., Moats, L. C., Glover, M., & Mincey, B. (2008). When teachers work to use progress monitoring data to inform literacy instruction: Identifying potential supports and challenges. *Remedial and Special Education, 29*, 364–382.

Ross, S. M., Smith, L. J., Slavin, R. E., & Madden, N. A. (1997). Improving the academic success of disadvantaged children: An examination of success for all. *Psychology in the Schools, 34*, 171–180.

Snow, C. E. (2001). *Reading for understanding*. Santa Monica, CA: RAND Education and the Science and Technology Policy Institute.

Taylor, B. M., Pearson, D. P., Clark, K., & Walpole, S. (2000). Effective schools and accomplished teachers: Lessons about primary-grade reading instruction in low-income schools. *Elementary School Journal, 101*, 121–165.

Torgesen, J. K. (2000). Individual differences in response to early intervention in reading: The lingering problem of treatment resisters. *Learning Disabilities Research and Practice, 15*, 55–64.

Vellutino, F. R., Scanlon, D. M., Sipay, E. R., Small, S. G., Pratt, A., Chen, R., & Denckla, M. B. (1996). Cognitive profiles of difficult to remediate and readily remediated poor readers: Early intervention as a vehicle for distinguishing between cognitive and experiential deficits as basic causes of specific reading disability. *Journal of Educational Psychology, 88*, 601–638.

Wharton-McDonald, R., Pressley, M., & Hampston, J. M. (1998). Literacy instruction in nine first-grade classrooms: Teacher characteristics and student achievement. *Elementary School Journal, 99*, 101–128.

NOTE

1. We would like to thank the ISI Project team, as well as Andy Godsberg and Colleen Peterson for their work on A2i and ISIOnline. Additionally, we thank the children, parents, teachers, and school administrators without whom this research would not have been possible. This study was funded by grants R305H04013 and R305B070074, "Child by Instruction Interactions: Effects of Individualizing Instruction" from the U.S. Department of Education, Institute for Education Sciences, and by grant R01HD48539 from the Eunice Kennedy Shriver National Institute for Child Health and Human Development, and, in part, by a predoctoral training grant R305B04074, from the Institute of Education Sciences. The opinions expressed are ours and do not represent views of the funding agencies.

Chapter Six

Multiple Bases for Comprehension Difficulties: The Potential of Cognitive and Neurobiological Profiling for Validation of Subtypes and Development of Assessments

Laurie E. Cutting and Hollis S. Scarborough

WHAT SKILLS AND KNOWLEDGE CONTRIBUTE TO SUCCESSFUL COMPREHENSION?

The Simple View of Reading (Hoover & Gough, 1990) is widely accepted and has received solid empirical support from many investigations of samples of child and adult readers (e.g., Carver, 1997, 2003; Catts, Adlof, & Weismer, 2006; Curtis, 1980; Cutting & Scarborough, 2006; Francis, Fletcher, Catts, & Tomblin, 2005; Goff, Pratt, & Ong, 2005; Joshi, Williams, & Wood, 1998; Sabatini, Sawaki, Shore, & Scarborough, 2010; Shankweiler, Lundquist, Katz, Stuebing, & Fletcher, 1999; Vellutino, Tunmer, Jaccard, & Chen, 2007).

According to this model, reading comprehension is viewed as the product of two factors: word recognition/decoding skill and listening comprehension. Hence, reading comprehension disabilities (RCDs) can stem from weaknesses in either or both of these two components. Indeed, consistent with the model, there is now a great deal of evidence that some students have "general" reading disabilities (GRD) marked by impairment both in recognizing printed words and in understanding text.

Others exhibit "specific" word-level deficits (S-WLD), such that poor decoding and identification of printed words are demonstrated in conjunction with satisfactory comprehension; and others display specific reading comprehension disabilities (S-RCD) that are characterized by intact word reading skills but deficient understanding of text (e.g., Cain & Oakhill, this volume; Leach, Scarborough, & Rescorla, 2003; Nation & Snowling, 1998; 1999; Torppa et al., 2007).

Nevertheless, when considering the nature of the comprehension problems of GRD and S-RCD students, too little attention has been paid, we think, to the longstanding view that the listening comprehension component does not represent a monolithic capability. Rather, as stated by Gates (1949), it encompasses many "types of thinking, evaluating, judging, imaging, reasoning, and problem-solving."

The Simple View model achieved its eloquent simplicity by intentionally collapsing all this acknowledged complexity into a single listening comprehension factor. This step made an invaluable contribution to the field by directing attention so clearly to the contrast between reading-specific bottom-up factors versus nonspecific top-down factors.

Nevertheless, given recent advances in research on RCDs, the time has perhaps arrived when it may be fruitful to take a closer look at the roles of subcomponents of listening comprehension in order to more fully understand failures of reading comprehension and design better diagnostic assessments of them.

As a starting point, as illustrated in figure 6.1, we can hypothesize that the understanding of spoken language requires (in addition to the perception of the speech input itself, of course) the availability of stored knowledge of many kinds of information (especially background facts and concepts, word meanings, and so forth), plus the accurate and efficient processing of information in various ways (including syntactic and morphological analyses, verbal reasoning, retention in memory, and so forth).

Figure 6.1 thus retains the Simple View model at its core but breaks out the listening comprehension component into a set of subcomponents that most researchers would probably accept as potential contributors to comprehension.[1] If these sources of comprehension difficulty are not entirely interdependent but instead can be dissociated from one another, then it is probable that the bases for reading comprehension difficulties may be quite different across individual students. For instance, the major obstacle to understanding might be inadequate vocabulary and background knowledge in some cases, but insufficient verbal reasoning and memory skills for other students.

Few would quarrel with the inclusion of background knowledge and oral language proficiency (vocabulary and sentence processing) as important components of listening comprehension. Lexical, morphological, and syntactic skills have been shown to predict reading comprehension well in numerous studies (e.g., Carlisle, 1993; Catts, Fey, Zhang, & Tomblin, 1999; Juel, 1988; Nation, Adams, Bowyer-Crane, & Snowling, 1999; Nation & Snowling, 1998, 1999; Ricketts, Nation, & Bishop, 2007; Scarborough, 1990).

Background knowledge also has a strong relation to comprehension (e.g., Best, Floyd, & McNamara, 2008; Samuelstuen & Braten, 2005; Snow, 2002; Taboada, Tonks, Wigfield, & Guthrie, 2009; van den Broek, 2010) and is closely linked to vocabulary breadth (e.g., see National Reading Panel, 2000;

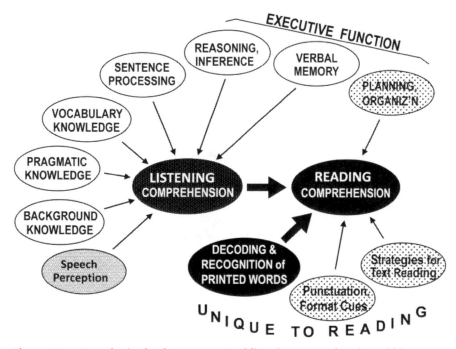

Figure 6.1. Hypothesized subcomponents of listening comprehension within an expanded simple model of reading comprehension

Snow, 2002; Stahl & Nagy, 2006), presumably because exposure to life experiences and formal instruction typically introduce learners simultaneously to new knowledge domains and the terminology associated with each.

The remaining two subcomponents of listening comprehension in figure 6.1—verbal memory and inferential reasoning—are particularly interesting from the perspective of clinical neurobiology and neuropsychology. That is because these kinds of cognitive abilities, along with planning and organizational skills, are often cited as defining characteristics associated with the umbrella domain of "executive function."

EF "refers to a set of cognitive processes utilized in the management of goal-directed behaviors and in the development and implementation of an approach to completing tasks . . . it is a multidimensional construct, separable from (but dependent on) core 'ingredient' skills such as vocabulary, visuo-spatial skills, and intelligence" (Locascio, Mahone, Eason, & Cutting, 2010).

Although many reading researchers would agree that these factors contribute to comprehension, and thus have investigated them in relation to reading skills, they are not always labeled or discussed in reference to EF (see Ferstl, 2007 for a discussion of this issue). There are sound reasons for doing so, however, even though EF is sometimes legitimately criticized as lacking a well-specified consensus definition (see Burgess, 1997; McCloskey, Perkins, & Van Divner, 2009).

Most importantly, EF has a strong biological basis for tying together the set of cognitive skills it encompasses, which may superficially seem to have little in common. The concept of EF grew out of studies of individuals with lesions of the prefrontal cortex. These patients exhibited marked difficulties in higher-order cognitive skills such as inhibition, working memory, planning, organizing, inferential reasoning, and self-monitoring.

The hypothesis that these EF functions are subserved by the prefrontal cortex has been corroborated by neuroimaging studies in healthy adults and children. For example, that research has demonstrated that the dorsal prefrontal cortex is associated with performance on the nonlinguistic Tower of London test of planning, organization, and strategy usage (e.g., Lazerson et al., 2000) and with measures of both linguistic and nonlinguistic inferential reasoning (e.g., Ferstl, 2007; Kroger et al., 2002; Mason & Just, 2004). The common biological underpinnings of these cognitive skills suggest that it would be helpful to study EF as a cohesive, neurobiologically based construct.

It bears noting that in figure 6.1, we chose not to link the planning/organization/sequencing skill set with listening comprehension, but rather have drawn the arrow directly to reading comprehension and stippled that oval (and the others that pertain to reading-specific skills). This reflects our hypothesis presumption that this facet of EF affects literacy skills much more than oral comprehension.

In particular, it is probably associated with the application of comprehension strategies during text reading, which have been shown to be related to successful understanding of written passages (National Reading Panel, 2000). For example, inefficiency in planning and organization may result in difficulties with organizing and summarizing material during reading, and difficulties with monitoring may result in inability to detect and repair inconsistencies in comprehension.

Indeed, at the behavioral level, it has been empirically demonstrated that reading comprehension differences are related to EF skills. In particular, research has shown that inferential reasoning, verbal working memory, and planning, organization, and sequencing are often deficient in students with RCDs (e.g., Locascio et al., 2010; Nation et al., 1999; Oakhill, 1993; Oakhill & Garnham, 1988; Oakhill & Yuill, 1996; Perfetti, Marron, & Foltz, 1996; Sesma, Mahone, Levin, Eason, & Cutting, 2008; Swanson, 1999; Swanson & Alexander, 1997; Swanson & Trahan, 1996).

In our research samples, both EF and language-skill deficits have been associated with poor reading comprehension. We have identified and compared

Table 6.1.   Research samples.

	N	Age/Grade	Source(s)
Sample A	97	7-16 years	Cutting & Scarborough (2006); Rimrodt, Lightman, Roberts, Denckla, & Cutting (2005)
Sample B	63	9-14 years	Cutting, Materek, Cole, Levine, & Mahone (2009)
Sample C	169	10-14 years	Locascio, Mahone, Eason, & Cutting (2010)
Sample D	191	4th-5th grade	Leach, Scarborough & Rescorla (2003)

GRD and S-RCD groups within the four samples listed in table 6.1, and we will use data from those samples to illustrate the ideas in this chapter.

For instance, figure 6.2 compares subgroups from Samples B, C, and D to illustrate that GRD and S-RCD students are similarly impaired, relative to typically developing classmates, in their performance on reading comprehension measures, but differ markedly on tests that require them to read aloud lists of words or pseudowords.

In each sample, the typically developing (TD) unimpaired reader group included students who scored at or above the 37th or 40th percentile (depending on the sample) on standardized tests of both reading comprehension and word/pseudoword reading.

For assignment to the GRD group, a preponderance of scores had to be at or below the 25th percentile on both kinds of measures. Assignment to the S-RCD subgroup required scores at or above the 37th to 40th percentile on word recognition/decoding tests and at or below the 25th percentile for reading comprehension (for at least two such measures out of the several that were administered to Samples A and C).

Although the test batteries (and exact percentile cutoffs) were not identical from study to study, they had much in common, and this is reflected in the similarity of results across samples.

As can be seen in figure 6.3, the GRD and S-RCD groups both showed weaker performance than the TD groups in two aspects of oral language (vocabulary and sentence processing) and on two EF tasks that are often used clinically (Tower of London and Perceptual Mazes). Moreover, these are indications that the S-RCD group, on average, may be more impaired in EF skills than the GRD group.

Group comparisons of this sort cannot reveal, however, *whether oral language and EF deficits actually coexist in individuals with RCDs*. If EF is a distinct (but perhaps somewhat overlapping with oral language) construct related to reading comprehension, we should expect to see dissociations between oral language and EF skills when data are examined at an individual level. New research suggests that such dissociations can indeed occur.

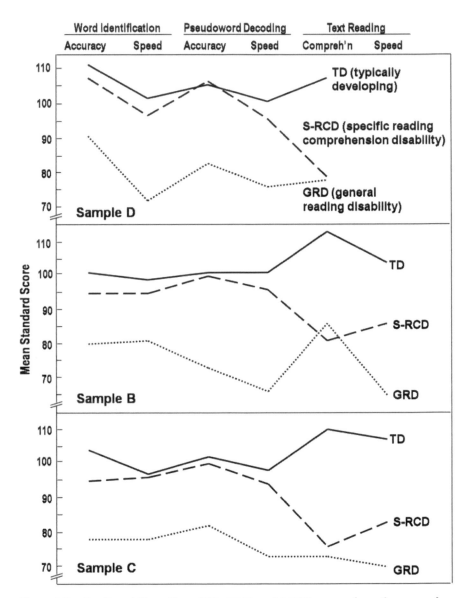

Figure 6.2. Reading skill profiles of TD, GRD, and S-RCD groups from three samples

For example, figure 6.4 shows the bivariate distribution for one language score (a vocabulary measure on the *Peabody Picture Vocabulary Test,* or *PPVT*) and one EF measure (a measure of planning and organization, the *D-KEFS Tower Test*) that were administered to Sample C. The correlation

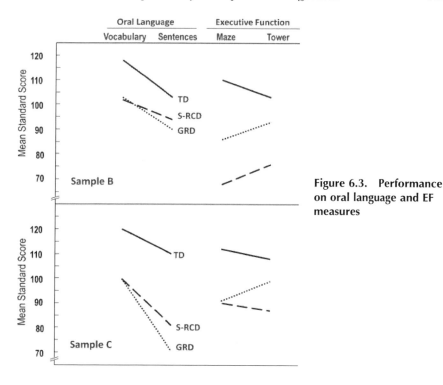

Figure 6.3. Performance on oral language and EF measures

between these two variables is .32 ($p < .001$), and their correlations with the five reading comprehension scores ranged from .57 to .69 ($p < .001$) for the PPVT and .21 to .26 ($p < .02$) for the Tower test.

In the figure, we have highlighted two areas of the distribution. The upper left quadrant includes several GRD and S-RCD individuals with above-average EF scaled scores (11 or higher) and weak vocabulary standard scores (below 90), suggesting that their comprehension difficulties stemmed mainly from weak linguistic proficiency rather than a lack of the kinds of strategic planning and problem-solving capabilities that are required to do well on the Tower test.

In contrast, the lower right quadrant includes some individuals with the opposite pattern of scores: average or above-average vocabulary knowledge (PPVT standard scores greater than 100) but poor performance on the Tower test (scaled score of 8 or lower). Comparatively speaking, a large proportion of individuals with GRDs show weaknesses in both (or neither) of these skills, while those with S-RCD had a greater tendency to have specific weaknesses in either EF or vocabulary, and to fall in the highlighted areas of the figure.

More specifically, each pattern of dissociation was shown by only 4.4% of the 45 students with GRD, most of whom were instead either weak in both

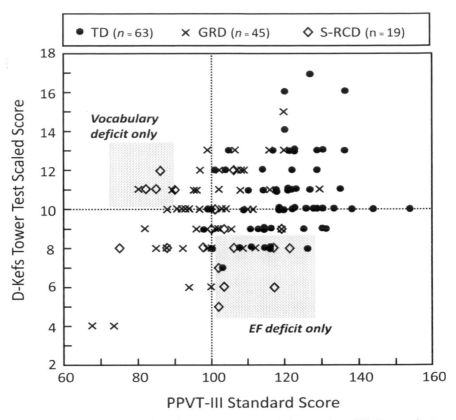

Figure 6.4. Scatterplot of the relation between vocabulary and EF skills in sample C

skills or unimpaired in both (because word recognition/decoding deficits were responsible for their low scores in reading comprehension). Of the 19 S-RCD students, however, seven (36.8%) exhibited the EF-only deficit profile and three (15.8%) the vocabulary-only pattern.

These preliminary findings suggest, first of all, that it is not uncommon for a child with a reading comprehension problem, especially one with S-RCD, to be unimpaired in vocabulary knowledge. Second, these findings suggest that the comprehension problems of S-RCD and GRD might not be entirely the same with regard to their bases, with narrower ("specific") areas of weakness seen more often for the former, and broader deficit profiles more typically occurring among the latter.

In short, the group and individual data that we have summarized suggest that reading comprehension is influenced not just by language proficiency but also by a reader's EF skills. This suggests that impaired reading comprehension can stem from different impairments that are currently lumped together within the Simple View.

While this streamlined model is a useful framework for predicting reading comprehension, it is not as helpful a guide to a full understanding of the bases for failures of reading comprehension in ways that inform the design of appropriate interventions. The Simple View is limited, therefore, as a guide to assessment—and in particular to diagnostic assessment—of reading comprehension differences. We thus turn next to issues pertaining to assessment.

LIMITED AGREEMENT AMONG CONVENTIONAL ASSESSMENTS OF READING COMPREHENSION

Several recent papers by us (Cutting & Scarborough, 2006) and others (Francis et al., 2006; Keenan, Betjemann, Wadsworth, DeFries, & Olson, 2006) have focused attention on the troubling fact that when several tests of reading comprehension are administered to a sample, there is much less agreement among the test results than we had presumed. Hence, existing tests have been found to differ considerably about whether a given student's reading comprehension would be considered impaired or not (Rimrodt, Lightman, Roberts, Denckla, & Cutting, 2005).

This is illustrated in figure 6.5 by Venn diagrams for two samples. The one on the left shows data from Sample A, in which students were given tests of reading comprehension from the *Gates-MacGinitie* (G-M), the *Wechsler Individual Achievement Test* (WIAT), and the *Gray Oral Reading Test* (GORT). The other shows results from Sample C, in which the reading comprehension subtest of the *Woodcock Reading Mastery Test* (WRMT) was administered in lieu of the WIAT.

In both samples, we identified all students whose scores were at or below the 25th percentile on any of the three tests, and then tallied the agreements and disagreements across tests for these students. In Sample A, there were 52 such students; of them, just 25% were identified by all three tests, and another 27% by two of the three, leaving fully 48% whose comprehension difficulties were identified by only one of the three tests. Similarly, in Sample C, of the 57 children with any low score(s), only 21% were low on all three tests, 33% on two tests, and fully 46% on just one of the three tests.

It is tempting to imagine that these variations in diagnostic classification occurred merely because borderline cases met criteria on one test but not another. We have not found this to be the case, however. Instead, when there is disagreement, students who show impaired reading comprehension on one test appear adequately competent on the other, and vice versa. This finding is illustrated for Samples A and B by the bar graphs in figure 6.5.

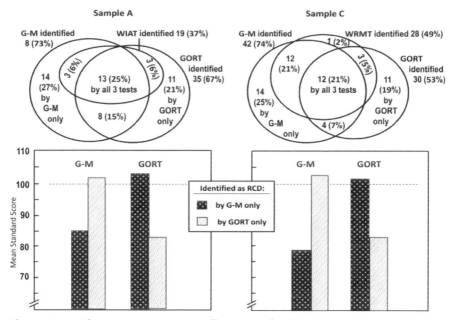

Figure 6.5.   **(Dis)agreement among reading comprehension tests**

An alternative explanation for the disagreements among test results is that different tests have been constructed to align with different conceptualizations of what reading comprehension entails and which component skills contribute to comprehension difficulty. When an assessment of reading comprehension is designed, the product will reflect how much weight the designer gives to these multiple components in the construction of items.

To date, there is evidence that existing assessments differ in their relative demands for decoding skills, vocabulary knowledge, and sentence processing proficiency (Cutting & Scarborough, 2006; Francis et al., 2006; Keenan et al., 2006). More research is needed along these lines to compare tests with respect to their relative demands for EF skills (relative to word recognition and language abilities).

In light of what we now know, the hypothesis can be entertained that the low scorers on different tests of reading comprehension may represent subtypes of RCD. At present, it is customary to use a 2 x 2 classification of reading ability differences based on the relative strengths and weaknesses in word recognition/decoding (WRD) versus reading comprehension (e.g., Catts et al., 1999; Shankweiler et al., 1999), yielding subgroups that we have called TD, GRD, S-WRD, and S-RCD in our samples.

As reviewed by Cain and Oakhill (this volume) and also illustrated in figure 6.1, there is now abundant evidence for S-RCD as a distinct type with its own cognitive profile (figure 6.3). However, the fact that EF and language skills are both lower, on average, for students with S-RCD than for TD groups does not necessarily mean that deficiencies in both language and EF are implicated when reading comprehension disabilities cannot be attributed to word recognition deficits, as in S-RCD.

It is also possible, as suggested by figure 6.4, that three subtypes (language-only, EF-only, and combined) can be distinguished *within* the S-RCD classification. To explore this interesting idea further in future research, the defining subcomponents of each type must first be established, the reliability of subtyping classifications demonstrated, differences among reading comprehension tests in detecting language- and EF-related comprehension deficits explored, and the diagnostic utility investigated.

In seeking to understand disagreements among assessments of comprehension, consideration should also be given, we feel, to the relative demands for various cognitive skills that are imposed by different kinds of reading material. For example, expository texts may make substantially greater demands for EF skills than do narrative texts (Eason, Geist, Goldberg, & Cutting, 2009), and this could produce discrepant results for reading comprehension tests that require reading of only narrative passages versus those that use informational texts.

Such differences could be especially marked for older students, because children are increasingly required to read expository material as they transition from "learning to read" in the primary grades to "reading to learn" (Chall, 1983). In addition, longer passages may place greater EF demands on a reader. Hence, disagreements between tests that use texts of different lengths would be expected, and indeed have been observed (Keenan, Betjemann, & Olson, 2008).

Let us suppose that when tests of reading comprehension produce discrepant results, the disagreements can be traced to differences in the extent to which test item difficulty reflects unequal demands for various component skills such as word recognition/decoding versus language proficiency versus EF. From a research or clinical standpoint, this poses a clear dilemma. It is not possible at this juncture to say that some of the tests are "better" than others with regard to construct or criterion validity. To do so would require the field to reach consensus on a better-defined construct of reading comprehension than we now have.

At present, therefore, when different researchers use different reading comprehension tests and arrive at different conclusions (e.g., about instruction outcomes, gender differences, etc.), it is not clear whether the choice of assessment may account for study-to-study differences in results. Similarly, when clinicians administer only a single test of reading comprehension, it is clear that this means that some students will be deemed unimpaired, even though another test would have identified a substantial comprehension problem.

The ideal solution would be the development of a single assessment tool that demonstrably aligns well with a consensus construct; fortunately an initiative of that sort was recently launched by the U. S. Institute of Education Sciences. Meanwhile, the problem can be addressed by basing clinical and research decisions on results from more than one test. Although this involves undesirable costs (especially in test administration time), it is currently the best option.

Even if an excellent summative assessment of reading comprehension were available, it would probably not be sufficient for differentiating subtypes of disabled readers and RCDs. For that purpose, a diagnostic instrument would also be needed to differentiate profiles of poor readers.

In this regard, one approach to validation that has not been employed is to examine how well test results align with biological markers of the underlying cognitive abilities that influence test performance. For instance, the three skill domains that we have focused on—word recognition/decoding, oral language, and EF—have been linked to various different brain systems, both anatomically and functionally. Thus, anomalous brain functioning in these areas may provide biological explanatory power for why an individual has difficulty in decoding print, language proficiency, making inferences, or planning and organizing behavior.

Combining different reading comprehension assessments with not only cognitive function but underlying biology may be able to tell us how, for example, the different aspects of listening/reading comprehension are best represented in terms of *brain system requirements* to perform them. Having a cohesive biological model may allow us to determine that higher-order components of reading comprehension, such as employing reading strategies and making inferences, both rely on the same general brain systems and regions that are associated with EF.

This knowledge could help refine the way we categorize various components of reading comprehension—and thus the way we design assessments. One could envision some aspects of reading comprehension measures that are particularly difficult for individuals who struggle with EF (and, consequently, those reading-related skills that allow students to employ reading strategies); in this case, anomalies on neurobiological measures in the brain areas associated with EF (prefrontal cortex) should be present.

This same approach could be taken for the elements of oral language that are important for reading comprehension. Thus, we propose that by having the ability to map onto brain systems the basic cognitive elements important for higher-level reading processes (such as comprehension monitoring and reading strategies), more parsimonious reading comprehension assessments could be developed.

Using these types of assessments to identify these children provides a target for intervention, as such knowledge would aid in our ability to zero in on students' specific cognitive deficits in order to provide intervention for weaknesses on particular aspects of reading comprehension.

REFERENCES

Best, R. M., Floyd, R. G., & McNamara, D. S. (2008). Differential competencies contributing to children's comprehension of narrative and expository texts. *Reading Psychology, 29,* 137–164.

Burgess, P. W. (1997) Theory and methodology in executive function research. In P. Rabbitt (Ed.), *Methodology of frontal and executive function* (pp. 81–16). Hove, UK: Psychology Press.

Carlisle, J. F. (1993). Selecting approaches to vocabulary instruction for the reading disabled. *Learning Disabilities Research and Practice, 8,* 97–105.

Carver, R. P. (1997). Predicting reading levels in grades 1 to 6 from listening level and decoding level: Testing theory relevant to the simple view of reading. *Reading and Writing: An Interdisciplinary Journal, 10,* 121–154.

———. (2003). The highly lawful relationships among pseudoword decoding, word identification, spelling, listening, and reading. *Scientific Studies of Reading, 7,* 127–154.

Catts, H. W., Adolf, S. A., & Weismer, S. E. (2006). Language deficits in poor comprehenders: A case for the simple view of reading. *Journal of Speech, Language, and Hearing Research, 49,* 278–293.

Catts, H. W., Fey, M. E., Zhang, X., & Tomblin, J. B. (1999). Language basis of reading and reading disabilities: Evidence from a longitudinal investigation. *Scientific Studies of Reading, 3,* 331–361.

Chall, J. S. (1983) *Stages of reading development.* New York: McGraw-Hill.

Curtis, M. (1980). Development of components of reading skill. *Journal of Educational Psychology, 72,* 656–669.

Cutting, L. E., & Scarborough, H. S. (2006). Prediction of reading comprehension: Relative contributions of word reading, language proficiency, and other cognitive skills can depend on how comprehension is measured. *Scientific Studies of Reading, 10,* 277–299.

Dunn, L. M., & Dunn, L. M. (1997). *Peabody Picture Vocabulary Test—Third Edition.* Circle Pines, MN: American Guidance Service.

Eason, S. H., Geist, M., Goldberg, L. F., & Cutting, L. E. (2009, February). *Reader-text interactions in reading comprehension.* Poster presented at the 37th Annual Meeting of International Neuropsychological Society, Atlanta, GA.

Ferstl, E. C. (2007). The functional neuroanatomy of text comprehension: What's the story so far? In F. Schmalhofer & C. Perfetti (Eds.), *Higher level language processes in the brain: Inference and comprehension processes* (pp. 53–102). Mahwah, NJ: Lawrence Erlbaum Associates.

Francis, D. J., Fletcher, J. M., Catts, H. W., & Tomblin, J. B. (2005). Dimensions affecting the assessment of reading comprehension. In S. A. Stahl & S. G. Paris (Eds.), *Children's reading comprehension and assessment* (pp. 369–394). Mahwah, NJ: Lawrence Erlbaum Associates.

Francis, D. J., Snow, C. E., August, D., Carlson, C. D., Miller, J., & Iglesias, A. (2006). Measures of reading comprehension: A latent variable analysis of the diagnostic assessment of reading comprehension. *Scientific Studies of Reading, 10,* 301–322.

Gates, A. I. (1949). Character and purposes of the yearbook. In N. B. Henry & A. I. Gates (Eds.), *The forty-eighth yearbook of the National Society for the Study of Education.* Chicago: University of Chicago Press.

Goff, D. A., Pratt, C., & Ong, B. (2005). The relations between children's reading comprehension, working memory, language skills and components of reading decoding in a normal sample. *Reading and Writing: An Interdisciplinary Journal, 18,* 583–616.

Hoover, W. A., & Gough, P. B. (1990). The simple view of reading. *Reading and Writing: An Interdisciplinary Journal, 2,* 127–160.

Joshi, R. M., Williams, K. A., & Wood, J. R. (1998). Predicting reading comprehension from listening comprehension: Is this the answer to the IQ debate? In C. Hulme, & R. M. Joshi (Eds.), *Reading and spelling: Development and disorders* (pp. 319–327). Mahwah, NJ: Lawrence Erlbaum Associates.

Juel, C. (1988). Learning to read and write: A longitudinal study of 54 children from first through fourth grades. *Journal of Educational Psychology, 80,* 437–447.

Kaplan, E., Fein, D., Kramer, J., Delis, D. C., & Morris, R. D. (1999). *Wechsler Individual Intelligence Scale, Third Edition: Process instrument.* San Antonio, TX: The Psychological Corporation.

Keenan, J. M., Betjemann, R. S., & Olson, R. K. (2008). Reading comprehension tests vary in the skills they assess: Differential dependence on decoding and oral comprehension. *Scientific Studies of Reading, 12,* 281–300.

Keenan, J. M., Betjemann, R. S., Wadsworth, S. J., DeFries, J. C., & Olson, R.K. (2006). Genetic and environmental influences on reading and listening comprehension. *Journal of Research in Reading, 29,* 79–91.

Kroger, J. K., Sabb, F. W., Fales, C. L., Bookheimer, S. Y., Cohen, M. S., & Holyoak, K. J. (2002). Recruitment of anterior dorsolateral prefrontal cortex in human reasoning: A parametric study of relational complexity. *Cerebral Cortex, 12,* 477–485.

Lazerson, R. H. C., Rombouts, S. A. R. B., Machielsen, W. C. M., Scheltens, P., Witter, M. P., Uylings, H. B. M., & Barkhof, F. (2000). Visualizing brain activation during planning: The Tower of London Test adapted for functional MR imaging. *American Journal of Neuroradiology, 21,* 1407–1414.

Leach, J. M., Scarborough, H. S., & Rescorla, L. (2003). Late-emerging reading disabilities. *Journal of Educational Psychology, 95,* 211–224.

Locascio, G., Mahone, E. M., Eason, S. H., & Cutting, L. E. (2010). Executive dysfunction among children with reading comprehension deficits. *Journal of Learning Disabilities, 43,* 441–454.

MacGinitie, W. H., MacGinitie, R. K., Maria, K., & Dreyer, L. G. (2000). *Gates MacGinitie Reading Tests—Fourth Edition.* Itasca, IL: Riverside Publishers.

Mason, R. A., & Just, M. A. (2004). How the brain processes causal inferences in text: A theoretical account of generation and integration component processes utilizing both cerebral hemispheres, *Psychological Science, 15,* 1–7.

McCloskey, G., Perkins, L. A., & Van Divner, B. R. (2009). *Assessment and intervention for executive function difficulties.* New York, NY, US: Routledge/Taylor & Francis Group.

Nation, K., Adams, J. W., Bowyer-Crane, C. A., & Snowling, M. J. (1999). Working memory deficits in poor comprehenders reflect underlying language impairments. *Journal of Experimental Child Psychology, 73,* 139–158.

Nation, K., & Snowling, M. J. (1998). Semantic processing and the development of word-recognition skills: Evidence from children with reading comprehension difficulties. *Journal of Memory and Language, 39,* 85–101.

———. (1999). Developmental differences in sensitivity to semantic relations among good and poor comprehenders: Evidence from semantic priming. *Cognition, 70,* B1–13.

National Reading Panel (2000). *Report of the National Reading Panel: Teaching children to read: An evidence-based assessment of the scientific research literature on reading and its implications for reading instruction: Reports of the subgroups.* Rockville, MD: NICHD Clearinghouse.

Oakhill, J. (1993). Children's difficulties in reading comprehension, *Educational Psychology Review, 5,* 223–237.

Oakhill, J., & Garnham, A. (1988). *Becoming a skilled reader.* Oxford: Blackwell.

Oakhill, J., & Yuill, N. (1996). Higher order factors in comprehension disability: Processes and remediation. In C. Cornaldi and J. Oakhill (Eds.), *Reading comprehension difficulties: Processes and intervention* (pp. 69–92). Mahwah, NJ: Lawrence Erlbaum Associates.

Perfetti, C. A., Marron, M. A., & Foltz, P. W. (1996) Sources of comprehension failure: Theoretical perspectives and case studies. In C. Cornoldi & J. Oakhill (Eds.), *Reading comprehension difficulties: Processes and intervention* (pp. 137–166). Mahwah, NJ: Lawrence Erlbaum Associates.

Ricketts, J., Nation, K., & Bishop, D. V. (2007). Vocabulary is important for some, but not all reading skills. *Scientific Studies of Reading, 11,* 235–257.

Rimrodt, S., Lightman, A., Roberts, L., Denckla, M. B., & Cutting, L. E. (2005, February). *Are all tests of reading comprehension the same?* Poster presented at the Annual Meeting of the International Neuropsychological Society, St. Louis, MO.

Sabatini, J. P., Sawaki, Y., Shore, J. R., & Scarborough, H. S. (2010). Relationships among reading skills of adults with low literacy. *Journal of Learning Disabilities, 43,* 122–138.

Samuelstuen, M. S., & Braten, I. (2005). Decoding, knowledge, and strategies in comprehension of expository text. *Scandinavian Journal of Psychology, 46,* 107–117.

Scarborough, H. S. (1990). Very early language deficits in dyslexic children. *Child Development, 61*, 1728–1743.

Sesma, H. W., Mahone, E. M., Levine, T., Eason, S. H., & Cutting, L. E. (2008). The contribution of executive skills to reading comprehension. *Child Neuropsychology, 15*, 1–15.

Shankweiler, D., Lundquist, E., Katz, L., Stuebing, K. K., Fletcher, J. M., Brady, S., & Shaywitz, B. A. (1999). Comprehension and decoding: Patterns of association in children with reading difficulties. *Scientific Studies of Reading, 3*, 69–94.

Snow, C. (2002). *Reading for understanding: Toward an R&D program in reading comprehension*. Santa Monica, CA: RAND Corporation.

Stahl, S. A., & Nagy, W. E. (2005). *Teaching word meanings*. Mahwah, NJ: Lawrence Erlbaum Associates.

Swanson, H. L. (1999). Reading comprehension and working memory in learning-disabled readers: Is the phonological loop more important than the executive system? *Journal of Experimental Child Psychology, 72*, 1–31.

Swanson, H. L., & Alexander, J. E. (1997). Cognitive processes as predictors of word recognition and reading comprehension in learning-disabled and skilled readers: Revisiting the specificity hypothesis. *Journal of Educational Psychology, 89*, 128–158.

Swanson, H. L., & Trahan, M. (1996). Learning disabled and average readers' working memory and comprehension: Does metacognition play a role? *The British Journal of Educational Psychology, 66*, 333–355.

Taboada, A., Tonks, S. M., Wigfield, A., & Guthrie, J. T. (2009). Effects of motivational and cognitive variables on reading comprehension. *Reading and Writing: An Interdisciplinary Journal, 22*, 85-106.

Torppa, M., Tolvanen, A., Poikkeus, A.-M., Eklund, K., Lerkkanen, M.-K., Leskinen, E., & Lyytinen, H. (2007). Reading development subtypes and their early characteristics. *Annals of Dyslexia, 57*, 3–32.

van den Broek, P. (2010). Using texts in science education: Cognitive processes and knowledge representation. *Science, 328*, 453–456.

Vellutino, F. R., Tunmer, W. E., Jaccard, J. J., & Chen, R. (2007). Components of reading ability: Multivariate evidence for a convergent skills model. *Scientific Studies of Reading, 11*, 3–32.

Wechsler, D. L. (1992). *Wechsler Individual Achievement Test*. San Antonio, TX: Psychological Corporation.

Wiederholt, J. I., & Bryant, B. R. (2001). *Gray Oral Reading Tests—Fourth Edition: Examiner's Manual*. Austin, TX: PRO-ED.

Woodcock, R. W. (1998). *Woodcock Reading Mastery Test–Revised/Normative Update (WRMT-R/NU)*. Circle Pines, MN: American Guidance Service.

NOTE

1. The set we have pictured for is for illustrative purposes and is not exhaustive.

Chapter Seven

NLP Methods for Supporting Vocabulary Analysis

Paul Deane[1]

INTRODUCTION

What is vocabulary knowledge? How can we characterize it? How is it acquired?

These are questions that are of critical importance to reading, because successful reading presupposes a mastery of the language to be read. Vocabulary is well recognized as an essential component of reading proficiency (Beck & McKeown, 1991; Carroll, 1993; Cunningham & Stanovich, 1997; Daneman, 1988; Hirsch, 2003; Perfetti, Landi, & Oakhill, 2005), with correlations between vocabulary and reading comprehension assessments ranging from .6 to .7 (Anderson & Freebody, 1981).

This is not surprising, as it has been estimated that adequate reading comprehension depends on a person knowing between 90% and 95% of the words in a text (Hsueh-Chao & Nation, 2000). Students who will become proficient readers typically have larger vocabularies than struggling readers as early as preschool, and this advantage tends to grow over time (Graves, Brunetti, & Slater, 1982; Graves & Slater, 1987; Hart & Risley, 1995).

Vocabulary development is a critical part of learning to read well and appears to be a significant aspect of the gap between competent and struggling readers. It is thus important to develop a clear picture of how vocabulary develops and what students need to learn to acquire advanced or specialized vocabularies, because growth in vocabulary knowledge is a primary determinant of reading comprehension.

The chief concern of this chapter will be how natural language processing (NLP) techniques can contribute to the study of vocabulary development and word learning. We will discuss a number of techniques, including latent semantic analysis (Deerwester, Dumais, Furnas, Landauer, & Harshman, 1990;

Landauer & Dumais, 1997; Landauer, Laham, & Foltz, 1998; Landauer & Ross, 2002), topic modeling (Blei, Griffiths, Jordan, & Tenenbaum, 2004; Blei & Lafferty, 2006, 2007; Griffiths & Steyvers, 2007; Griffiths, Steyvers, Blei, & Tenenbaum, 2005; Li & Yamanishi, 2003; Newman, Smyth, & Steyvers, 2006; Steyvers & Griffiths, 2007; Steyvers, Smyth, Rosen-Zvi, & Griffiths, 2004), and related methods.

In particular, this chapter will argue that a significant portion of vocabulary learning—particularly for relatively rare domain-specific vocabulary—consists first in learning what domain a word is associated with, and second in learning to distinguish among words assigned to the same domain, and that much of the domain structure of vocabulary can be modeled in a statistically useful way, especially if combined with explicit semantic knowledge.

NLP methods therefore provide a way of mapping what children must acquire as they develop domain-specific vocabularies and can be used to measure progress toward adult-like levels of performance.

WHAT WE KNOW ABOUT THE
GROWTH OF VOCABULARY KNOWLEDGE

Before we consider applications of NLP techniques, it will be useful to consider what we know about the growth of vocabulary knowledge and what that implies. Natural language processing is a method for capturing information from corpus data. Its usefulness depends on whether those techniques capture information that will be useful either to model how students learn vocabulary, or provide structures that can support vocabulary teaching.

Teaching vocabulary directly can help enhance vocabulary learning and reading comprehension (Beck & McKeown, 1991; Stahl & Fairbanks, 1986). However, Beck, McKeown, and McCaslin (2002) estimate that students can only be explicitly taught some 400 words per year in school. These 400 words can be of immense importance to those children who are behind and need to be brought to the point of understanding key words as fast as possible.

But if we want all of our children to comprehend well, they must learn many more words each year. A twelfth-grade student who scores well enough on the verbal portion of the SAT to get into a selective college knows between 60,000 and 100,000 words (Hirsch, 2003). That suggests that the high-achieving twelfth-grader has learned over 5,000 words a year, a rate of some 15 words a day since age 2.

However, even high-performing twelfth-graders do not learn 15 words all at once per day but rather by accruing bits of word knowledge for each of the thousands of words encountered daily (Nagy & Scott, 2000). While significant knowledge can be acquired from just a few exposures through so-called "fast mapping" strategies (Carey, 1978; Heibeck & Markman, 1987; Oetting, Rice, & Swank, 1995; Rice, Buhr, & Nemeth, 1990), one does not just learn a word's meaning and then have the word. More likely, he or she knows these words with varying degrees of complexity and precision.

One gradually learns the word's denotations and connotations and its modes of use little by little over a variety of language experiences (Nagy & Scott, 2000). That is, growth of word knowledge appears to be slow and incremental, with most vocabulary growth resulting from massive immersion in the world of language and knowledge.

As word learning proceeds, meanings of words grow richer over time. Perfetti and Hart (2001) describe word knowledge as a complex assemblage of representations that vary both in the information they contain and the degree to which they have been fully specified (i.e., in terms of orthographic, phonemic, syntactic, and semantic quality), which they refer to as the Lexical Quality Hypothesis (Perfetti & Hart, 2002).

Consistent with the Lexical Quality Hypothesis, we expect that the normal course of development is one in which the meaning of a word is initially totally unknown and then gradually becomes more fully specified with continued experience.

Durso and Shore (1991) present evidence that word knowledge varies from total lack of knowledge, to varying degrees of partial knowledge, to complete knowledge. They point out that after the first few exposures to a word in context, people may have only implicit rather than explicit knowledge about those words, yet may demonstrate clear evidence of comprehension, such as knowing whether a word was used in a grammatically or semantically appropriate way.

A number of theorists have outlined stages of word meaning that similarly postulate differing degrees of depth of word knowledge. Dale and O'Rourke (1986) postulate four stages of word learning, ranging from stage I, where the word is completely unknown, through stage II (implicit word knowledge), stage III (partial knowledge but mastery in some contexts), and stage IV (full mastery across a range of uses).

Stahl and Fairbanks (1986) outline a similar (three-stage) theory, which is applied in Brown, Frishkoff, and Eskenazi (2005) to the task of automatically generating questions designed to probe different aspects of vocabulary depth. Brown, Frishkoff, and Eskenazi primarily use WordNet semantic relationships generating definition, synonym, antonym, hypernym, hyponym, and cloze questions. In their discussion, they characterize these tasks as primarily providing evidence for the middle level of Stahl's hierarchy.

The literature suggests that children rely on many skills to learn new words, including association (Merriman, 1999; Plunkett, Sinha, Moeller, &

Strandsby, 1992), social awareness of reference (Baldwin et al., 1996), inference about events that are not present (Gleitman, 1990), knowledge of syntax (Fisher, Gleitman, & Gleitman, 1991), and pragmatic inference (Clark, 2003), among others (Bloom, 2000).

There are a number of existing models of word learning (Cottrell & Plunkett, 1994; Elman, Bates, Johnson, & Karmiloff Smith, 1996; Farkas et al., 2001; Gasser & Smith, 1998; Gupta & MacWhinney, 1997; Landauer & Dumais, 1997; Li & Farkas, 2002; MacWhinney, 1987; Merriman, 1999; Miikkulainen, 1997; Niyogi, 2002; Plaut, 1999; Regier, 1996; Roy & Pentland, 2002; Schafer & Mareschal, 2001; Siskind, 1992, 1996; Tenenbaum & Xu, 2000; Thompson & Mooney, 2003; Yu, Ballard, & Aslin, 2005), but many of these studies focus on word learning in the early years.

They do not focus on vocabulary development in the period from fourth through twelfth grades when students acquire much of the vocabulary necessary to long-term success in academic and career settings. Biemiller (2003a; 2003b; 2003c; 2005; 2006) and Biemiller and Slonim (2001) present considerable evidence that core vocabulary is acquired in a predictable sequence, that students are responsive to vocabulary instruction, and thus that systematic instruction in vocabulary is both practicable and effective.

However, the explosion of vocabulary that happens in the later grades after students begin to read widely goes well beyond the critical vocabulary set most easily targeted for instruction, involving not only so-called Tier II words, but also large sets of topic- and subject-specific words, and word meanings that integrate closely with the acquisition of specialized knowledge within each domain (Beck et al., 2002).

The ability to learn the meanings of words through reading is thus arguably a critical vocabulary development skill (Beck et al., 2002; Nagy & Scott, 2000; Sternberg & Powell, 1983), though one more likely to help first- than second-language students (Laufer & Hulstijn, 2001). Moreover, differences between written and spoken language indicate that inference from written texts might be important for vocabulary development. Written language is lexically richer than spoken language and may, therefore, provide a greater number of learning opportunities than available in spoken contexts (Cunningham & Stanovich, 1997).

Avid readers encounter considerably more words each year than their less well-read peers (Anderson, Wilson, & Fielding, 1988), and measures of 9- to 11-year-olds' exposure to print predicts significant growth in vocabulary (Echols, West, Stanovich, & Zehr, 1996). Practice at reading is likely to lead to more efficient access to word meaning.

Regular reading can also provide repeated opportunities to acquire, refine, and consolidate vocabulary knowledge through inference from written texts

(Beck, McKeown, & McCaslin, 1983; Carroll & White, 1973; Fukkink, Henk, & De Glopper, 2001; Graves, 1986; Nagy, Anderson, & Herman, 1987; Schatz & Baldwin, 1986), though such processes of inference may not be particularly straightforward. In fact, programs of instruction in learning word meanings by inference from written texts meet with relative success (Fukkink & De Glopper, 1998) and can benefit even poor readers (Stahl & Fairbanks, 1986).

However, we do not yet have as good an understanding as we would like of the conditions under which word learning takes place most efficiently or of the factors that make some students more efficient at inferring the meanings of unknown words from textual cues. In (Swanborn & De Glopper, 1999) meta-analysis of the literature on incidental word learning as a result of reading, there was only one significant automatically measurable text feature that predicted incidental word learning, namely density of unknown words surrounding target words.

This effect is used as one basis for automatic selection of reading materials for students in the REAP project (Collins-Thompson & Callan, 2004), where it is termed *vocabulary stretch* (Brown & Eskenazi, 2004) and operationalized as the percentage of words in a text believed to be unknown for a specific student. However, it is obvious that students do absorb other forms of information, such as the syntactic patterns a word appears in or the topical connections of words with which it is associated, as knowledge of such patterns can be measured even when people do not yet fully know the meaning of a word.

In many ways, vocabulary stretch is a boundary condition. It makes sense to assume that it is hard to learn word meanings if a document is hard to understand, but where surrounding portions of a document are comprehensible, students with good word-learning skills must be able to exploit this context in order to learn something about the target word.

Thus, it is important to determine what other aspects of text provide favorable conditions for vocabulary learning. The surrounding context can provide information by which people may make inferences about the meaning and use of unknown words, though this hypothesized ability depends partly on the actual cues provided in the text and partly on having necessary background knowledge (Goldman et al., 2000). Schwanenflugel, Stahl, and McFalls (1997) report far greater learning effects for individual word characteristics such as part of speech and concreteness than they do when context support is varied.

While Rappaport and Kibby (2002) present a theory of how vocabulary inferencing could be taught as a skill through direct instruction, it is far from established how often or effectively students make use of contextual information in this fashion.

We have a significant combination of circumstances. There is general agreement that people have partial word knowledge that matures into deeper knowledge over time, as well as a wide range of hypotheses about how it occurs, but limited understanding of the actual processes by which word meanings are learned. These circumstances rather strongly suggest that we need a capability that provides more nuanced information about how much students actually know about words.

We also need more detailed information about when they learn it, which in turn requires a richer understanding of the structure of the vocabulary knowledge that they ultimately acquire. One aspect of this structure—and an important one for our purposes—is what is sometimes referred to as breadth of vocabulary knowledge, which may roughly be viewed as the general richness of a person's vocabulary knowledge. It may not be meaningful to speak of a person's knowledge of any one word in isolation; what really matters is his or her grasp of entire groups of words that are needed to address specific topics in a meaningful way.

The usual conception of vocabulary breadth is a simple estimate of the size of someone's vocabulary. For this purpose, a variety of word frequency indices have been developed (Breland, Jones, & Jenkins, 1994; Carroll, 1970, 1971, 1976; Carroll & White, 1973; Zeno et al., 1995). However, this assumption runs into serious difficulties for estimating breadth in general.

The flaw in this strategy is that the use of unmodified word frequencies presupposes that words are used uniformly, without variations in frequency due to topic, genre, or social variables. While the standard frequency index originated in Carroll (Carroll, 1971) makes an effort to measure word dispersion across genres and uses that measure to correct the frequency index, it still treats equal difficulty for equally frequent words as the norm, not the exception.

But words are not, in fact, distributed evenly across texts, and there are strong interdependencies among sets of correlated words. While there are important sets of words that are widely distributed across a broad range of topics (so-called "Tier One" and "Tier Two" words), cf. Beck et al. (2002), a very large part of the vocabulary required by an educated adult has strong topical connections (so-called "Tier Three" words). This fact has major implications for measuring vocabulary knowledge, and for the ways in which vocabulary is learned or taught.

The vocabulary to which students are exposed has implicit prerequisites, in that students need to know other words if they are to integrate the new vocabulary into their existing stock of words. Such prerequisite relationships logically explain many word frequency differences (for instance, we may reasonably expect *hunt* to be more frequent than *predator*), but if two words have disjoint prerequisites, their relative frequencies may vary across corpora (cf. Gernsbacher [1984], Zevin & Seidenberg [2002]).

For instance, one must know what a dinosaur is to know the meaning of *tyrannosaurus*, and one must know what a bridge is to know the meaning of *abutment*, but the relative frequency of *tyrannosaurus* and *abutment* in a corpus is a function of how many texts in the corpus concern themselves with ancient animals or civil engineering.

Similarly, there are interdependencies between words that form natural (but nonhierarchical) sets; for instance, the words *mean, median,* and *mode* fall into a natural group without one clearly being prior to either of the others (in a mathematics or statistics topical context), though the word *mean* will in fact have a different base frequency because of its other meanings.

What such dependencies mean is that breadth of vocabulary may be better understood not in terms of the raw size of vocabulary, but in terms of coverage of different kinds and groups of words, because there is limited generalizability across words that happen to have similar, low overall frequency in the language. In fact, frequency estimates highly underestimate the likelihood of knowing sets of words, because the conditional probability of seeing a low frequency word (and its topical neighbors) is much higher once one sees it in any given text than one might presuppose given its rate of occurrence in an entire corpus.

These considerations imply that the statistical interdependencies among domain-specific words, and the structure of the domains in which such vocabulary appears, is of critical importance in students' ability to learn more specialized vocabularies. On the one hand, it is relatively easy to see how it can be learned by reading, by inferring statistical and meaning-based associations among words as a result of reading a large collection of documents. On the other hand, it is also likely that such word groupings can be taught explicitly, if the patterns of word groupings are accessible for study.

While other aspects of vocabulary can also be studied using NLP techniques, the focus of the discussion that follows will be on these kinds of dependencies and natural language processing (NLP) techniques that can help identify them.

NLP TECHNIQUES FOR
MODELING TOPICAL DEPENDENCIES

Latent Semantic Analysis, or LSA, is probably the best known automated method for analyzing vocabulary usage. Viewed from a purely technical standpoint, LSA is a method for capturing generalizations about patterns of co-occurrence among words in a corpus (Deerwester et al., 1990).

An LSA semantic space suppresses relatively infrequent patterns of co-occurrence and identifies dimensions of covariance using Singular Value Decomposition, a mathematical method loosely related to factor analysis. The result is a set of vectors that can be used (i) to identify which words show up in the same sorts of documents, or (ii) to identify which documents tend to use the same sorts of words.

Since LSA captures the tendency of documents to contain the same words, and conversely the tendency of words to appear in the same documents, there is a strong connection between similarity of LSA vectors and similarity of topical content.

To the extent that two documents discuss the same topics, they will tend to contain the same or semantically related words, a fact that supports not only the use of "bag of words" methods in information retrieval (Baker & McCallum, 1998), but also the use of vocabulary patterns to identify topical segments within a document (Hearst, 1994). LSA has been shown to be useful for similar purposes without some of the fragility of methods that require exact lexical matches (Brants, Chen, & Tsochantaridis, 2002; Foltz, Kintsch, & Landauer, 1998).

The literature on LSA tends to make rather stronger claims. Landauer and Dumais (1997) and Landauer, Laham, Rehder, and Schreiner (1997) argue that LSA actually corresponds fairly directly to how the brain represents meaning, as do Landauer & Ross (2002) and Landauer (2007).

There are issues with these claims, insofar as word meanings and word usage are arguably more structured than LSA allows, both in supporting specific relationships such as part/whole hierarchies, agent/action associations, and the like, and in having specific properties such as polysemy that are not well-represented by LSA vectors. We will not concern ourselves with such issues here. Rather of more interest to us is the use of LSA to capture topical similarities.

Even here LSA is problematic in important ways. LSA represents words as vectors, where the dimensions of the vector are uninterpreted, which makes it in many ways like a factor analysis that makes use of unrotated dimensions. It is impossible to examine the weightings of an LSA vector and conclude anything from it; that is why LSA is termed a latent representation. Words or documents are similar if they have similar LSA vectors, but the dimensions are not directly interpreted.

At most, proponents of LSA have proposed partial visualization of some dimensions to reveal interesting connections and contrasts among sets of words or documents (Landauer, Laham, & Derr, 2004). Thus if there is any specific structure underlying the LSA space, it is not visible to the analyst, who might for instance wish to identify recurrent topics shared across documents, or specific domains shared by pairs of words.[2] Intuitively, for instance, it would be useful to be able to note that *strike* shares a topic in one sense with *foul* and *ball*, and in another sense with *union* and *picket*.

A second issue worth mentioning is a technical consequence of the way that LSA is calculated. Singular value decomposition proceeds by extracting the dimension that accounts for the most variance, then applying recursively to extract from the remainder the dimension that accounts for the next largest degree of variance.

An LSA space is created by selecting the first N dimensions, where N is typically set to a relatively small number such as 300 to eliminate noise. But there is no guarantee that a co-occurrence pattern that holds between a relatively small set of relatively rare words will make it into the first N dimensions, where N is a relatively small number like 300, particularly since word frequencies follow a Zipfian distribution (Powers, 1998).

And yet such a co-occurrence pattern may be quite important for a small class of words or documents. We have observed (on examining a database of word-word conditional probabilities) that some of the strongest conditional probability relationships among words can be lost in a space created by applying singular value decomposition, just in case the relationship does not participate in the strongest dimensions extracted by the underlying algorithm.

Thus, if our purpose is to understand specific topical groupings, to be able ultimately to state what words should be learned together (to maximize probability of understanding certain classes of domain-specific documents), and to be able ultimately to state what words are likely to be prerequisites to acquiring more specialized domain vocabulary, then LSA may not be the best choice, as LSA does not provide an explicit representation of vocabulary groupings and focuses on those distinctions that matter for very large or very general vocabulary groupings.

The point of these observations is not to denigrate the use of LSA for purposes for which it is appropriate, but to point out that for certain purposes, such as modeling finer-grained topical relationships among vocabulary words, LSA may not be the best choice. That is why, in fact, other algorithms have been advanced.

Foremost among these are various topic modeling methods that create an explicit, Bayesian graphical model of word co-occurrence within a corpus, typically by assigning words a probability distribution that is conditioned by topic, treating documents as containing a mixture of topics, and predicting word distributions within documents in terms of a mixture. Blei, Ng, Jordan, and Lafferty (2003) propose a model in which topics are induced using Latent Dirichlet Allocation (LDA)—of which a good example application is Blei and Lafferty (2007)—and extend that model in Blei et al. (2004) to generate a hierarchical array of topics.

Somewhat different methods have been proposed as authors attempt to improve the statistical modeling methods underlying this approach (Griffiths & Steyvers, 2004; Griffiths et al., 2005; Li & Yamanishi, 2003; Newman, Chemudugunta, Smyth, & Steyvers, 2006; Rosen-Zvi, Chemudugunta, Griffiths, Smyth, & Steyvers, 2010; Steyvers & Griffiths, 2007; Steyvers et al., 2004).

What topic modeling approaches have in common is the fact that they explicitly assign words a probability by topic (which LSA does not do) and can therefore model polysemy and other situations in which the same word has higher-than-expected probabilities in multiple topics. It is important to note, however, that topic modeling approaches such as LDA are unsupervised statistical methods that depend on sampling. The quality of topics (that is, their interpretability from a human perspective) can vary considerably depending on training parameters and the structure of the underlying corpus.

Perhaps more importantly from our perspective, the size of the sample needed to get an accurate picture of word co-occurrence relationships varies considerably depending where those words are in Zipfian word frequency distributions. The topics extracted by topic modeling approaches will tend to be the most robust, and the most dominant, for the most frequent words, and least stable for the rarer words, within each topic.

An alternative to unsupervised methods is to predefine topics using human judgment, and then to assess documents by the extent to which particular topics are represented in them. Deane, Sheehan, Sabatini, Futagi, & Kostin (2006) experimented with a technique of this sort by defining an array of word lists, each exemplifying a semantic category, and classifying documents according to the presence or absence of words from each list. The advantage of this kind of approach is that it can benefit from human judgment, making it possible to eliminate noise from the model.

The next section of this chapter will discuss a somewhat similar approach, which combines human judgment with automated methods to produce a kind of topic map in which all topics are directly interpretable.

What all of these methods do is create a formal representation of the underlying conditional probabilities that words will co-occur in the same document. Documents can be classified as similar (to the extent that they exemplify the same latent classes of words), and words can be classified as similar (to the extent that they exemplify the same latent classes of documents). If the latent classes correspond to types of words (or topical groupings of documents) that make sense from a human point of view, they can be used to support various kinds of analysis.

Our particular interest is in using models of this kind to represent word knowledge, in particular, the kinds of dependencies among words that are characteristic of Tier III vocabulary. When people learn domain-specific vocabulary, they need to acquire sets of frequently co-occurring terms, understand how they relate to more common vocabulary, and finally, learn how to distinguish them from one another.

A HYBRID METHOD FOR
CONSTRUCTING A HIERARCHICAL TOPIC MAP

Given that we are specifically concerned with Tier III vocabulary—vocabulary that needs to be learned as part of building up specific domain knowledge—we need a method that is not biased toward the most frequent vocabulary and that provides direct and interpretable representations of rarer words and rarer topics. In this section we will discuss one such method, which combines statistical and linguistic techniques to build a detailed map of domain-specific vocabulary.

We start with an initial database of word associations, use this database to induce a hierarchical clustering, and then modify that clustering manually following linguistic analysis to produce a hierarchical topic map that identifies words strongly associated with particular topics. We then compute statistics for each word in the corpus indicating how strongly it is associated with each topic in the map.

We can then determine the extent to which documents are associated with particular topics and examine which words differentially associate with some topic over another. Since the topics are hierarchically arranged, one of the effects is to produce models that indicate more general versus more specialized vocabulary within the same subject domain.

Corpus and Underlying Statistics

We analyzed a large corpus (in excess of 1 billion words of running text) containing primarily stories, articles, informational books, and journal articles ranging from first-grade reading level to postgraduate. This corpus was assembled at Educational Testing Service as part of a research effort intended to support selection of stimulus materials for tests (Passonneau, Hemat, Plante, & Sheehan, 2002; Sheehan et al., 2006; Sheehan, Kostin, & Futagi, 2007). Documents in the corpus were broken into paragraphs.

We collected frequency statistics for the co-occurrence of word pairs within the same paragraph and calculated a number of statistics based upon this, most critically, the true and pointwise mutual information between each pair of terms. Since the selection of materials was driven by the need of ETS testing programs to sample reading materials appropriate for K-12, college-ready, and postgraduate populations, a broad sampling of domains and topics was represented, including the physical sciences, social sciences, and humanities.

Clustering within the Association Space Defined by a Single Word

Given a single word, and the existing database of word associations, we can search for associates. For example, if we start with the word *mitosis*, the 100 strongest associates are:

> *cells cell chromosomes meiosis mitotic spindle interphase during chromosome anaphase nucleus division metaphase dna microtubules cycle protein proteins fig centromere microtubule telophase chromatin centrosomes prophase phase replication checkpoint yeast cytokinesis nuclear kinetochores g is gene required nucleolus chromomere kinase chromatids diakinesis codominance cellular assembly genes segregation autosome progression centrosome nuclei transduction nucleosome observed cytogenetics zygote phenotype process exonuclease segregate cyclin chromosomal kinetochore mammalian mutants endonuclease centromeres xenopus polyploidy onset replicon mutant s bacteriophage localization 3 cytoplasm plasmid divide centrioles components genome recessive function wild-type polymerase phosphorylation daughter mendelian allele thus activation two activity extracts this sub.2 drosophila chromatid 4 defects poles phage sequence 2 normal formation sub.1 absence egg*

For each word in this list, we can, similarly, retrieve the strongest words associated with each. For instance, for the word *interphase*, the 30 strongest associates are:

> *mitosis nucleus polymer metaphase mitotic anaphase prophase chromosome telophase cells fig chromosomes phase diakinesis chromomere autosome adhesion matrix cell codominance nucleolus interfacial exonuclease nucleosome meiosis centromere endonuclease bacteriophage polyploidy during*

If we collect the set of words that are strongly associated with the seed word, or with its associates, we get a set of words that includes (though it extends beyond) the immediate topical neighborhood of the target word. By extracting all the associations among words in this set, we obtain a graph, which can then be subjected to graph clustering techniques.

In particular, we experimented with using the MCL (Markov Cluster) algorithm (van Dorn, 2000).[3] The MCL algorithm works by dynamically simulating flow patterns through the network of interconnections in a graph, iteratively strengthening those that participate most strongly in connecting parts of the graph, and pruning those that have the least impact. This tends to preserve the strongest associations and delete the weakest, modified by the general strength of interconnections between the two nodes by less direct routes.

One advantage of this method is that it does not require the number of clusters to be specified in advance; clusters emerge as islands of strongly interconnected nodes as the MCL algorithm simplifies the graph.

When we apply this technique to the set of words retrieved in one or two steps of association from the word *mitosis*, we end up with 37 clusters. The largest cluster, which contains the target word, is shown later in this chapter. It largely contains cell biology vocabulary. Some of the other clusters extracted are part of the immediate topical neighborhood of the target word, such as this cluster:

> *bateson botstein e.s. factors heredity inheritance lander mendel mendelian quantitative*

Other clusters contain words completely unrelated to the target but that are related to one another (and that happened to have tangential associations with words connected with the target), such as this cluster:

> *amount further given law necessary needed number order provide require required*

Overall the MCL algorithm appears to work very well. The advantage of this technique, from our point of view, is that it tends to capture strong clusters among relatively rare words that might be missed by other techniques.

> *acid acids activate activated activation amino amplified analysis anaphase apc arabidopsis arm attachment autosome backcross bacteria bind binding biology blood body brain bread budding camkii cancer celera cell cells cellular centrin centriole centrioles centromere centromeres centromeric centrosomal centrosome centrosome-associated centrosomes cerevisiae chl4 chromatid chromatids chromomere chromosomal chromosome chromosomes cleavage cms codominance cohesin cohesion colleagues com compared concluded conserved contractile contrast crossover cytogenetics cytokinesis cytoplasm cytoplasmic deletion diakinesis disease dna domain domains doxsey duplicated duplication embryonic endonuclease enzymes events exonuclease expressed expression factor fertility fitness formation functional furrow gene genes genet genetic geneticist genetics genome genomes genomic genomics growth helix heterochromatic homologs human identified iml3 immune induced inhibition inhibitor intracellular involved karyoplasts kinase kinases kinetochore kinetochores known linear linkage localization localize localized located location male malesterile mammalian mammals mapk mapping markers mechanism mechanisms membrane metaphase mice midzone mitochondrial mitogen-activated mitosis*

*mitotic molecular molecules mouse mrna mts mutant mutants mutation muta-
tions narrative nerve net neurons newsrx nonempty normal nucleolus nucleotide
oligonucleotide opposite organelles pathway pathways phenotype phenotypes
phenotypic phone phones phosphorylated phosphorylation plasma progression
project prophase protein proteins rappaport rearrangements receptor receptors
recombination reduced region regions researchers residues resistance response
restoration restorer restriction ring rna saccharomyces samples scientists selection separation sequence sequenced sequences sequencing showed signal
signaling sister species specific spindle spindles spinning stem stimulation
strain subcellular swi6 telomeres telophase therapy thread tissue tissues trait
traits transcription transduction transgenic translocation treatment tumor tu-
mors two-hybrid tyrosine venter vivo wheat wild-type wool yeast 2004*

REPEATED CLUSTERING; HIERARCHICAL CLUSTERING
BASED UPON REPEATED CLUSTERING DECISIONS

The major limitation of the method we have just described is that it produces
a single one-level clustering of a small part of the vocabulary. In order to get
richer and more complete information (without the computational costs that
make MCL prohibitive to cluster a graph containing hundreds of thousands
of words), we selected more than 10,000 words as targets, extracted the surrounding vocabulary for each target, and ran the MCL algorithm for each
vocabulary set.

The result was a large number of categorization decisions: pairs of words
were either assigned to the same clusters and connected to the same target
words, or not. We devised a simple hierarchical clustering algorithm that
grouped words together preferentially the more often they were assigned to
the same cluster across all target word clusterings.

The choice of target words was driven by our desire to study particular
subject domains, e.g., history and biology. We selected words that were significantly more frequent in corpora of Wikipedia articles on biological and
historical subjects than would have been expected given their general pattern
of frequency in our billion-word general-purpose corpus. Given the broad
scope of the word selection algorithm (selecting words strongly associated
with words strongly associated with the target word), the actual clusters included a broad selection of words from many other domains.

The hierarchical clustering algorithm was a greedy algorithm that weighted
word pairs by combining the strength of their original association with the
number of times they were assigned to the same cluster in the MCL clustering. The resulting hierarchical clustering roughly arranged words into sets
with similar topical properties. There was, however, significant noise in the

clusterings because some words had ambiguous topical relationships, and because some rarer words were assigned to a cluster one, or a very few times even over all 10,000 MCL clusterings.

However, the result of this stage of the analysis imposed sufficient order upon the data that we were able to move to the next step of the development process, which imposed human judgments on the initial clusters, based upon linguistic analysis.

Manual Modification of the Topic Hierarchy

The next step in our analysis was to subject the entire hierarchy to a manual linguistic analysis. Words that were obviously unrelated to other words in a cluster were deleted. Alternate morphological forms of words were added where appropriate. Some clusters were split or merged to reflect obvious semantic and topical similarities, or to eliminate confounds where polysemy of a key word had resulted in other words being grouped together inappropriately Clusters were rearranged to associate clusters that had strong semantic connections. Rearrangements were checked in the underlying association database, so as to avoid grouping together clusters without some reasonable degree of association in the underlying data.

This step took some months of work, as the goal was to produce a topic hierarchy that could be consulted as a linguistic resource without obvious errors due to its underlying statistical basis.

The resulting hierarchy was encoded as an XML file, with topics grouped hierarchically. Labels were assigned manually to primary and superordinate topics, roughly reflecting the lists of words assigned to each topic. To illustrate the kinds of decisions that were made, the word *mitosis* was ultimately assigned to the following cluster, to which we assigned the topic label MEIOSIS:

> *centromeric centromeres meiosis meiotic kinetochore kinetochores spindle mitotic spindles centromere mitosis telomere telomeres telomeric telomerase cell-cycle anaphase metaphase interphase prophase telophase chromatid chromatids autosome diakinesis chromomere codominance*

The clusters derived in this fashion are not necessarily completely cleaned up (in the sense that not every word can be shown to fit the topic perfectly), but obvious errors have been eliminated, and neighboring topics fit hierarchically into a reasonable framework. For instance, the MEIOSIS topic belongs to a cell structure topic under biology that includes topics dealing with cytoplasm in general, nucleosomes, lysosomes, centrosomes, vesicles, cell membranes, cytoskeleton, mitochondria, ATP, and enzymatic processes.

At the highest level, the topic hierarchy has nodes corresponding to logical and mathematical inquiry, human sciences (sociology, anthropology, psychology, philosophy), the physical sciences (earth sciences, astronomy, physics, chemistry, biology and medicine), general social domains (language, civilization, history, politics and government, economics, art, recreation, religion and education), and various general vocabulary topics. While it may not be a complete lexical resource on all possible topics, it provides a detailed map of a variety of focused vocabularies.

Mapping Associations between Words and Topics

A key advantage of the manually produced topic hierarchy is that it can be used as a key to access summary information about word associations. For each word in our corpus, we calculated the average and maximum pointwise mutual information between that word and every cluster in the hierarchy. We also calculated the average co-occurrence frequency between words and topics. The result is a very detailed map showing connections between words and topics (or between topics and words). For instance, the topics most strongly associated with the word *meiosis* are shown in table 7.1:

Conversely, the words most strongly associated with the meiosis topic are those shown in table 7.2, which includes most of the words in the manually edited topic in the XML file, but also includes other words. (Table 7.2 shows the first 60 words, for convenience.) Other words, even closely associated ones, may display different profiles of association with topics, and thus reveal themselves as being relatively more or less important in association with particular topical views of the lexicon.

Table 7.1. Topics most strongly associated with the word *meiosis*.

Topic Name	Average Pointwise Mutual Information
Cytoplasm_General	1.18
Ploidy	1.17
Cytology_General	1.03
Reproduction_General	0.75
Meiosis	0.71
Nucleosomes	0.70
Fertility	0.60
Genetics_General	0.44
Chromosomes	0.41
Eggs_And_Sperm	0.37
Mutations	0.37
Natural_Selection	0.35

Table 7.2.   Words with the highest average pointwise mutual information with the meiosis topic.

Word	Avg PMI	Word	Avg PMI	Word	Avg PMI
metaphase	0.86	centromeric	0.53	endonuclease	0.46
centromere	0.85	spindle	0.53	mutation	0.46
anaphase	0.84	segregate	0.53	translocation	0.46
mitosis	0.79	kinetochores	0.53	recombination	0.45
prophase	0.78	exonuclease	0.52	sgo1	0.45
meiosis	0.71	chromomere	0.51	iml3	0.45
mitotic	0.68	polyploidy	0.51	chl4	0.45
chromosome	0.68	microtubules	0.51	homologs	0.45
centromeres	0.64	phenotype	0.51	genome	0.45
interphase	0.61	nucleus	0.50	zygote	0.45
chromosomes	0.61	codominance	0.50	plasmid	0.45
meiotic	0.60	homologous	0.49	cerevisiae	0.44
chromatids	0.59	autosome	0.48	oligonucleotide	0.44
kinetochore	0.58	mutants	0.48	bacteriophage	0.44
chromatin	0.57	replicon	0.48	heterochromatin	0.44
nucleosome	0.56	chromosomal	0.48	homolog	0.44
chromatid	0.56	cytogenetics	0.47	crossover	0.43
cohesin	0.56	yeast	0.47	checkpoint	0.43
telophase	0.55	polymerase	0.47	replication	0.43
diakinesis	0.54	nucleolus	0.47	wild-type	0.43

An important feature of the hierarchical arrangement of topics is that superordinate topics contain all the words contained in every subordinate topic. As a result, the average pointwise mutual information (PMI) will be low unless a word co-occurs with most words in the list. That has the effect of giving high average PMI only to relatively general vocabulary. The nature of the effect can be seen by considering the top words for the topic superordinate to the meiosis topic: cell structure (see table 7.3).

Table 7.3.   Words with the highest average pointwise mutual information with the cell structure topic.

Word	Avg PMI	Word	Avg PMI	Word	Avg PMI
proteins	0.50	Yeast	0.42	cytoplasm	0.38
protein	0.47	Vitro	0.39	wild-type	0.38
cell	0.44	Mutant	0.39	cellular	0.37
binding	0.44	Complexes	0.39	binds	0.37
membrane	0.44	Mammalian	0.39	activation	0.37
cells	0.43	Dna	0.39	phosphorylation	0.37
Fig	0.42	Kinase	0.38	localization	0.36

The implication is that certain words—such as *protein, cell, binding, membrane, DNA,* or *cytoplasm*—are important across the entire cell structure topic, and thus more likely to function as basic vocabulary students need to learn before they are likely to understand the more complex vocabulary that is important to one of the subtopics.

In effect, the hierarchical topic map, when combined with frequency and association data, provides a way to make informed decisions about which words may need to be learned together (because they tend to co-occur in many of the same documents and deal with similar conceptual content), or which words may need to be learned when a more general subject is introduced (because they represent concepts needed to discuss any of the more specific topics).

Evaluation

There are various ways we could evaluate the resulting topics. In a separate study (Deane, Ramineni, & Wang, 2010), we have examined the contribution that topic map features make to the prediction of essay scores on standardized tests. That study, which examined data from more than 80,000 essays in two major testing programs, demonstrated that the topic map features contribute to the prediction of human rater judgments about essay quality, and contribute even when they are placed in direct competition with literal word overlap.

In this study, we focus on the quality of the information provided by individual topics. We expect that raters will reliably identify words that are associated with the topic, and reliably distinguish them from words that have no association with the topic at all. We also expect that rater consensus will help distinguish words that have a stronger statistical association with the topic from words whose associations are somewhat weaker.

Selection of Stimuli

1. We selected two subsets of topics from the larger topic map. One subset consisted of 101 topics focused on biology. The second consisted of 168 topics focused on the domains of history and geography. In each topic, we selected 75 words, selected as follows:
2. In each topic, the software was used to extract the 100 words most strongly associated with the topic. Fifty target words were selected from this set of 100. Where possible, the top 50 were selected, but morphological variants of the same word were excluded, as were certain other categories, primarily abbreviations or meaningless components of larger phrases, such as *de* or *los*. Some of these 50 words belonged to the manually selected word sets that had been used to define the topic when the topic map was constructed, but

others did not, although they too were showed strong statistical associations with the selected topic in our corpus data.
3. In each topic, 50 words were selected as potential foils. Each foil had to have low associations with the topic as measured by the software, and was matched in frequency with one of the 50 target words. Half of this set was selected at random to produce a list of 25 foils.

Selection of Participants

We recruited 50 raters for history/geography, and 50 for biology. Raters were recruited from the pool of content experts (scorers used to score AP examinations in history and biology). Raters were paid a flat sum for their participation in the experiment, and classified all words in several topics.

Procedure

Five to 10 raters rated each topic (more in biology, where there were fewer topics, but at least five in each history topic). Stimulus materials were presented and responses were collected online. Each rater rated the stimulus words from their assigned topics, judging whether the words were "related," "somewhat related," or "unrelated" to the topic. They had access to all the words they had rated in a topic while they were rating new words, and had the opportunity to change classifications if they changed their mind before the classification procedure was finished

Results. A total of 13,450 target words were tested over 269 topics. Of these, 9,066 had been manually selected during the preparation of the topic hierarchy and assessed as prototypical examples of that topic. We expected high agreement between the manual classification and the human raters, with most manually selected words being classified as "related." Table 7.4 shows that this expectation was satisfied.

The other target words were selected because they scored highly on a combined association measure that ranked words (a) directly for strength of topic associations; and (b) indirectly by examining similarity of overall association patterns.[4] Depending on the distribution of association strengths, this set might contain a mix of strong and medium associates: weaker, if the number

Table 7.4. **Overall distribution of rater judgments for words drawn from the seed sets for each topic.**

	Related		*Somewhat Related*		*Not Related*	
Biology	88%	(10216)	9%	(1035)	3%	(332)
History	86%	(10662)	11%	(1394)	3%	(375)

Table 7.5. Overall distribution of rater judgments for other target words for each topic.

	Related	Somewhat Related	Not Related
Biology	61% (13981)	28% (6244)	11% (2653)
History	62% (17063)	29% (7871)	9% (2552)

of strong associates for a topic is small; stronger, if there are more than 50 to 100 words strongly associated with any particular topic.

Given the way that this set of words was selected, we expected that they would predominantly consist of strongly related words (with some more weakly related words thrown in). This expectation was met. As table 7.5 illustrates, slightly over 60% of rater judgments identified these words as related. Just under 30% of judgments classified these words as somewhat related, and around 10% of judgments classified these words as unrelated.

More generally, we expected that raters would classify target words as related, and foil words as not related. Once again, these expectations were satisfied. On average, at least 71% of rater judgments about foil words fell into the "unrelated" category, and at least 69% of rater judgments about target words fell into the "'related" category (see tables 7.6 and 7.7).

At the time of writing, we are still analyzing this dataset, examining rater behavior and the statistical properties of individual topics in detail, but the overall trends are clear: The clusterings embodied by the topic map are confirmed by human judgments about whether words are related to individual topics. While these results must be viewed as preliminary, they indicate that the strategy we have adopted—of defining explicit topical clusters and rating words statistically by their relationship to each cluster—is performing as intended.

CONCLUSION

It should be noted that the technology we have described here potentially has many other applications, roughly comparable to the potential applications

Table 7.6. Overall distribution of rater judgments for target words (high topic associations).

	Related	Somewhat Related	Not Related
Biology	70% (24,197)	21% (7,279)	9% (2,985)
History	69% (27,725)	23% (9,265)	7% (2,927)

Table 7.7. Overall distribution of rater judgments for foil words (low topic associations).

	Related		*Somewhat Related*		*Not Related*	
Biology	6%	(1,004)	17%	(3,048)	77%	(13,696)
History	8%	(1,618)	21%	(4,394)	71%	(14,487)

of LSA or topic modeling. Our central concern, however, is how we would go about modeling student learning of Tier III vocabulary. The hierarchical topic map we have constructed represents a kind of target, based as it is upon a large, varied corpus of (mostly adult-focused) writing: It reflects the way people actually deploy words and provides a structure with which to view that usage that is roughly compatible with the knowledge structures that underlie that vocabulary.

In principle, we would expect that the association patterns that can be observed using this tool should correspond to the judgments of people who know the vocabulary. We know that the patterns of co-occurrence reflected in the map reflect actual communicative behavior, and therefore expect that adult vocabulary knowledge should be roughly aligned with the information provided by the map. Similar results have already been reported for LSA (Landauer & Ross, 2002), and we have every reason to expect that the current model, which is more detailed and interpretable, but based upon the same underlying associative patterns, will behave similarly.

But perhaps even more importantly, the hierarchical topic map we have developed provides a principled way to sample vocabulary, and thus raises the possibility of profiling the growth in vocabulary knowledge by observing when people begin using words in particular portions of the map, and how that knowledge changes over time. Much depends upon further research and analysis, but by providing a highly structured, interpretable picture of vocabulary, the method we have described opens a wide range of possibilities, including possible practical applications for assessment and instruction.

REFERENCES

Anderson, R. C., & Freebody, P. (1981). Vocabulary knowledge. In J. T. Guthrie (Ed.), *Comprehension and teaching* (pp. 77–117). Newark, DE: International Reading Association.

Anderson, R. C., Wilson, P. T., & Fielding, L. G. (1988). Growth in reading and how children spend their time outside of school. *Reading Research Quarterly, 23*, 285–303.

Baker, L. D., & McCallum, A. K. (1998, August). *Distributional clustering of words for text classification.* Paper presented at the 21st Annual International ACM SIGIR Conference on Research and Development in Information Retrieval, Melbourne, Australia.

Baldwin, D. A., Markman, E. M., Bill, B., Desjardins, R. N., Irwin, J. M., & Tidbill, G. (1996). Infants' reliance on a social criterion for establishing word-object relations. *Child Development, 67,* 3135–3153.

Beck, I. L., & McKeown, M. G. (1991). Conditions of vocabulary acquisition. In R. Barr, M. L. Karmil, P. Mosenthal, & D. D. Pearson (Eds.), *Handbook of reading research* (pp. 749–814). New York: Longman Publishing Group.

Beck, I. L., McKeown, M. G., & Kucan, L. (2002). *Bringing words to life.* New York: Guilford Press.

Beck, I. L., McKeown, M. G., & McCaslin, E. C. (1983). Vocabulary development: Not all contexts are created equal. *Elementary School Journal, 83,* 177–181.

Biemiller, A. (2003a). Oral comprehension sets the ceiling on reading comprehension. *American Educator, 27,* 23–44.

———. (2003b). Teaching vocabulary in the primary grades: Vocabulary instruction needed. In J. Baumann & E. Kame'enui (Eds.), *Reading vocabulary: Research to practice* (pp. 28–40). New York: Guilford Press.

———. (2003c). Vocabulary: Needed if more children are to read well. *Reading Psychology, 24,* 323–335.

———. (2005). Size and sequence in vocabulary development: Implications for choosing words for primary grade vocabulary instruction. In A. Hiebert & M. Kamil (Eds.), *Teaching and learning vocabulary: Bringing research to practice* (pp. 223–242). Mahwah, NJ: Lawrence Erlbaum Associates.

———. (2006). Vocabulary development and instruction: A prerequisite for school learning. In S. Neuman & D. Dickinson (Eds.), *Handbook of early literacy research* (Vol. 2, pp. 41–51). New York: Guilford Press.

Biemiller, A., & Slonim, N. (2001). Estimating root word vocabulary growth in normative and advantaged populations: Evidence for a common sequence of vocabulary acquisition. *Journal of Educational Psychology, 93,* 498–520.

Blei, D. M., Griffiths, T. L., Jordan, M. I., & Tenenbaum, J. B. (2004). Hierarchical topic models and the nested Chinese restaurant process. *Advances in Neural Information Processing Systems, 16.*

Blei, D. M., & Lafferty, J. D. (2006, June). *Dynamic topic models.* Paper presented at the Proceedings of the 23rd International Conference on Machine Learning, Pittsburgh, PA.

———. (2007). A correlated topic model of science. *Annals of Applied Statistics, 1,* 17–35.

Blei, D. M., Ng, A. Y., Jordan, M. I., & Lafferty, J. (2003). Latent Dirichlet allocation. *Journal of Machine Learning Research, 3,* 993–1022.

Bloom, P. (2000). *How children learn the meanings of words.* Cambridge, MA: MIT Press.

Brants, T., Chen, F., & Tsochantaridis, I. (2002, November). *Topic-based document segmentation with probabilistic latent semantic analysis.* Paper presented at the

Eleventh International Conference on Information and Knowledge Management (CIKM 2002), McLean, VA.

Breland, H. M., Jones, R. J., & Jenkins, L. (1994). *The College Board vocabulary study* (No. RR-94-26). Princeton, NJ: Educational Testing Service.

Brown, J., & Eskenazi, M. (2004, June). *Retrieval of authentic documents for reader-specific lexical practice.* Paper presented at the InSTIL/ICALL Symposium, Venice, Italy.

Brown, J., Frishkoff, G. A., & Eskenazi, M. (2005, October). *Automatic question generation for vocabulary assessment.* Paper presented at the Conference on Human Language Technology and Empirical Methods in Natural Language Processing, Vancouver, Canada.

Carey, S. (1978). The child as word learner. In M. Halle, J. Bresnan, & G. A. Miller (Eds.), *Linguistic theory and psychological reality* (pp. 264–293). Cambridge, MA: MIT Press.

Carroll, J. B. (1970). An alternative to Juilland's usage coefficient for lexical frequencies, and a proposal for a standard frequency index (SFI). *Computer Studies in the Humanities and Verbal Behavior, 3*, 61–65.

———. (1971). Measurement properties of subjective magnitude estimates of word frequency. *Journal of Verbal Learning and Verbal Behavior, 10*, 722–729.

———. (1976). *Word retrieval latencies as a function of frequency and age-of-priming, repeated trials, and individual differences.* Princeton, NJ: Educational Testing Service.

———. (1993). *Human cognitive abilities: A survey of factor-analytic studies.* New York: Cambridge University Press.

Carroll, J. B., & White, M. N. (1973). Word frequency and age of acquisition as determiners of picture-naming latency. *Quarterly Journal of Experimental Psychology, 25*, 85–95.

Clark, E. V. (2003). *First language acquisition.* Cambridge: Cambridge University Press.

Collins-Thompson, K., & Callan, J. (2004). Information retrieval for language tutoring: An overview of the REAP project. *SIGIR Forum*, 544–545.

Cottrell, G. W., & Plunkett, J. K. (1994). Acquiring the mapping from meaning to sounds. *Connection Science, 6*, 379–412.

Cunningham, A. E., & Stanovich, K. E. (1997). Early reading acquisition and its relation to reading experience and ability 10 years later. *Developmental Psychology, 33*, 934–945.

Dale, E., & O'Rourke, J. (1986). *Vocabulary building.* Columbus, Ohio: Zaner-Bloser.

Daneman, M. (1988). Word knowledge and reading skill. In M. Daneman & T. G. Waller (Eds.), *Reading research: Advances in theory and practice* (Vol. 6, pp. 145–175). San Diego, CA: Academic Press.

Deane, P., Ramineni, C., & Wang, V. (2010). *An exploration of methods for improving E-rater essay content scoring.* Princeton, NJ: Educational Testing Service.

Deane, P., Sheehan, K., Sabatini, J., Futagi, Y., & Kostin, I. (2006). Differences in text structure and its implications for assessment of struggling readers. *Scientific Studies of Reading, 10*, 257–275.

Deerwester, S., Dumais, S. T., Furnas, G. W., Landauer, T. K., & Harshman, R. (1990). Indexing by latent semantic analysis. *Journal of the American Society for Information Science, 41*, 391–407.

Durso, F. T., & Shore, W. J. (1991). Partial knowledge of word meanings. *Journal of Experimental Psychology: General, 120*, 190–202.

Echols, L. D., West, R. F., Stanovich, K. E., & Zehr, K. S. (1996). Using children's literacy activities to predict growth in verbal cognitive skills: A longitudinal investigation. *Journal of Educational Psychology, 88*, 296–304.

Elman, J. L., Bates, E. A., Johnson, M. H., & Karmiloff Smith, A. (1996). *Rethinking innateness: A connectionist perspective on development*. Cambridge, MA: MIT Press.

Farkas, I., Li, P., Altmann, E. M., Cleeremans, A., Schunn, C. D., & Gray, W. D. (2001). A self-organizing neural network model of the acquisition of word meaning. In *Proceedings of the 2001 Fourth International Conference on Cognitive Modeling* (pp. 67–72). Mahwah, NJ: Lawrence Erlbaum Associates.

Fisher, C., Gleitman, H., & Gleitman, L. (1991). On the semantic content of subcategorization frames. *Cognitive Psychology, 23*, 331–392.

Foltz, P. W., Kintsch, W., & Landauer, T. K. (1998). The measurement of textual coherence with latent semantic analysis. *Discourse Processes, 25*, 285–307.

Fukkink, R. G., & De Glopper, K. (1998). Effects of instruction in deriving word meaning from context: A meta-analysis. *Review of Educational Research, 68*, 450–469.

Fukkink, R. G., Henk, B., & De Glopper, K. (2001). Deriving word meaning from written context: A multicomponential skill. *Language Learning, 51*, 477–496.

Gasser, M., & Smith, L. B. (1998). Learning nouns and adjectives: A connectionist account. *Language and Cognitive Processes, 13*, 269–306.

Gernsbacher, M. A. (1984). Resolving 20 years of inconsistent interactions between lexical familiarity and orthography, concreteness, and polysemy. *Journal of Experimental Psychology: General, 113*, 256–281.

Gleitman, L. (1990). The structural sources of verb meanings. *Language Acquisition 1*, 1–55.

Goldman, S. R., Rakestraw, J. A., Jr., Kamil, M. L., Mosenthal, P. B., Pearson, P. D., & Barr, R. (2000). Structural aspects of constructing meaning from text. In *Handbook of reading research*, (Vol. III, pp. 311–335). Mahwah, NJ: Lawrence Erlbaum Associates.

Graves, M. F. (1986). Vocabulary learning and instruction. *Review of Research in Education, 13*, 49–89.

Graves, M. F., Brunetti, G. J., & Slater, W. H. (1982). The reading vocabularies of primary-grade children of varying geographic and social backgrounds. In J. A. Niles & L. A. Harris (Eds.), *New inquiries in reading research and instruction: Thirty-first yearbook of the National Reading Conference* (pp. 99–104). Rochester, NY: National Reading Conference.

Graves, M. F., & Slater, W. H. (1987). *The development of reading vocabularies in rural disadvantaged students, inner-city disadvantaged and middle-class suburban students*. Paper presented at the Annual Conference of the American Educational Research Association, Washington, DC.

Griffiths, T. L., & Steyvers, M. (2004). *Finding scientific topics.* In *Proceedings of the National Academy of Sciences of the United States of America, 101,* 5228–5235.

———. (2007). Topics in semantic representation. *Psychological Review, 114,* 211–244.

Griffiths, T. L., Steyvers, M., Blei, D. M., & Tenenbaum, J. B. (2005). Integrating topics and syntax. *Advances in Neural Information Processing Systems, 17,* 537–544.

Gupta, P., & MacWhinney, B. (1997). Vocabulary acquisition and verbal short-term memory: Computational and neural bases. *Brain and Language, 59,* 267–333.

Hart, B., & Risley, T. R. (1995). *Meaningful differences in the everyday experience of young American children.* Baltimore, MD: Paul H. Brookes Publishing Co.

Hearst, M. A. (1994, June). *Multi-paragraph segmentation of expository text.* Paper presented at the 32nd Annual Meeting of the Association for Computational Linguistics, ACL-94, Las Cruces, NM.

Heibeck, T. H., & Markman, E. M. (1987). Word learning in children: An examination of fast mapping. *Child Development, 58,* 1021–1034.

Hirsch, E. D., Jr. (2003). Reading comprehension requires knowledge of words and the world. *American Educator, 27,* 10–48.

Hsueh-Chao, M., & Nation, P. (2000). Unknown vocabulary density and reading comprehension. *Reading in a Foreign Language, 13,* 403–430.

Landauer, T. K. (2007). LSA as a theory of learning. In T. K. Landauer, D. S. McNamara, S. Dennis, & W. Kintsch (Eds.), *Handbook of latent semantic analysis.* Mahwah, NJ: Lawrence Erlbaum Associates.

Landauer, T. K., & Dumais, S. T. (1997). A solution to Plato's problem: The latent semantic analysis theory of acquisition, induction, and representation of knowledge. *Psychological Review, 104,* 211–240.

Landauer, T. K., Laham, D., & Derr, M. (2004). From paragraph to graph: Latent semantic analysis for information visualization. In *Proceedings of the National Academy of Sciences of the United States of America, 101,* 5214–5219.

Landauer, T. K., Laham, D., & Foltz, P. (1998). Learning human-like knowledge by singular value decomposition: A progress report. In M. I. Jordan, M. J. Kearns & S. A. Solla (Eds.), *Advances in neural information processing systems* (Vol. 10, pp. 45–51). Cambridge, MA: MIT Press.

Landauer, T. K., Laham, D., Rehder, B., & Schreiner, M. E. (1997, August). *How well can passage meaning be derived without using word order? A comparison of latent semantic analysis and humans.* Paper presented at the Nineteenth Annual Conference of the Cognitive Science Society, Stanford University, Stanford, CA.

Landauer, T. K., & Ross, B. H. (2002). On the computational basis of learning and cognition: Arguments from LSA. In *The psychology of learning and motivation: Advances in research and theory* (Vol. 41, pp. 43–84). San Diego, CA: Academic Press.

Laufer, B., & Hulstijn, J. (2001). Incidental vocabulary acquisition in a second language: the construct of task-induced involvement. *Applied Linguistics, 22,* 1–26.

Li, H., & Yamanishi, K. (2003). Topic analysis using a finite mixture model. *Information Processing and Management, 39,* 521–541.

Li, P., & Farkas, I. (2002). A self-organizing connectionist model of bilingual processing. In R. Heredia & J. Altarriba (Eds.), *Bilingual sentence processing* (pp. 59–85). North-Holland: Elsevier Science.

MacWhinney, B. (1987). *Mechanisms of language acquisition*. Mahwah, NJ: Lawrence Erlbaum Associates.

Merriman, W. E. (1999). Competition, attention, and young children's lexical processing. In B. MacWhinney (Ed.), *The emergence of language* (pp. 331–358). Mahwah, NJ: Lawrence Erlbaum Associates.

Miikkulainen, R. (1997). Dyslexic and category-specific aphasic impairments in a self-organizing feature map model of the lexicon. *Brain and Language, 59*, 334–366.

Nagy, W. E., Anderson, R. C., & Herman, P. A. (1987). Learning word meanings from context during normal reading. *American Educational Research Journal, 24*, 237.

Nagy, W. E., & Scott, J. A. (2000). Vocabulary processes. In M. L. Kamil, P. B. Mosenthal, P. D. Pearson, & R. Barr (Eds.), *Handbook of reading research* (Vol. III, pp. 269–284). Mahwah, NJ: Lawrence Erlbaum Associates.

Newman, D., Chemudugunta, C., Smyth, P., & Steyvers, M. (2006, August). *Statistical entity-topic models*. Paper presented at the 12th ACM SIGKDD International Conference on Knowledge Discovery and Data Mining, Philadelphia.

Newman, D., Smyth, P., & Steyvers, M. (2006). Scalable parallel topic models. *Journal of Intelligence Community Research and Development*.

Niyogi, S. (2002). *Bayesian learning at the syntax-semantics interface*. In *Proceedings of the 24th Annual Conference of the Cognitive Science Society* (pp. 697-702). Mahwah, NJ: Lawrence Erlbaum Associates.

Oetting, J. B., Rice, M. L., & Swank, L. K. (1995). Quick incidental learning (QUIL) of words by school-age children with and without SLI. *Journal of Speech and Hearing Research, 38*, 434–445.

Passonneau, R., Hemat, L., Plante, J., & Sheehan, K. (2002). *Electronic sources as input to GRE reading comprehension item development: Source finder prototype evaluation* (No. RR-02-12; GREB-99-18P). Princeton, NJ: Educational Testing Service.

Perfetti, C. A., & Hart, L. (2001). The lexical basis of comprehension skill. In D. S. Gorfien (Ed.), *On the consequences of meaning selection: Perspectives on resolving lexical ambiguity* (pp. 67–86). Washington, DC: American Psychological Association.

———. (2002). The lexical quality hypothesis. In L. Verhoeven, C. Elbro, & P. Reitsma (Eds.), *Precursors of functional literacy* (pp. 189–213). Amsterdam, Philadelphia: John Benjamins.

Perfetti, C. A., Landi, N., & Oakhill, J. (2005). The acquisition of reading comprehension skill. In M. J. Snowling & C. Hulme (Eds.), *The science of reading: A handbook* (pp. 227–247). Malden, MA: Blackwell Publishing.

Plaut, D. C. (1999). A connectionist approach to word reading and acquired dyslexia: extension to sequential processing. *Cognitive Science, 23*, 543–568.

Plunkett, K., Sinha, C., Moeller, M. F., & Strandsby, O. (1992). Symbol grounding or the emergence of symbols? Vocabulary growth in children and a connectionist net. *Connection Science, 4,* 293–312.

Powers, D. M. W. (1998). Applications and explanations of Zipf's law. In *NeMLaP3/ CoNLL98: Proceedings of the Joint Conferences in New Methods in Language Processing and Computational Natural Language Learning* (pp. 151–160). Stroudsburg, PA: Association for Computational Linguistics.

Rappaport, W. J., & Kibby, M. W. (2002). Contextual vocabulary acquisition: A computational theory and educational curriculum. In N. Callaos & A. Breda (Eds.), *Proceedings of the 6th World Multiconference on Systemics, Cybernetics and Informatics* (Vol. 2: Concepts and Applications of Systemics, Cybernetics, and Informatics I, pp. 261–266). Orlando, FL: International Institute of Informatics and Systemics.

Regier, T. (1996). *The Human semantic potential.* Cambridge, MA: MIT Press.

Rice, M. L., Buhr, J. C., & Nemeth, M. (1990). Fast mapping word-learning abilities of language-delayed preschoolers. *Journal of Speech and Hearing Disorders, 55,* 33–42.

Rosen-Zvi, M., Chemudugunta, C., Griffiths, T., Smyth, P., & Steyvers, M. (2010). Learning author-topic models from text corpora. *ACM Transactions on Information Systems, 28,* 1–38.

Roy, D. K., & Pentland, A. P. (2002). Learning words from sights and sounds: a computational model. *Cognitive Science, 26,* 113–146.

Schafer, G., & Mareschal, D. (2001). Modeling infant speech sound discrimination using simple associative networks. *Infancy, 2,* 7–28.

Schatz, E. K., & Baldwin, R. S. (1986). Contextual clues are unreliable predictors of word meanings. *Reading Research Quarterly, 21,* 439–453.

Schwanenflugel, P. J., Stahl, S. A., & McFalls, E. L. (1997). Partial word knowledge and vocabulary growth during reading comprehension. *Journal of Literacy Research, 29,* 531–553.

Sheehan, K. M., Kostin, I., Deane, P., Hemat, R., Zuckerman, D., & Futagi, Y. (2006). *Inside sourcefinder: Predicting the acceptability status of candidate reading comprehension source documents* (No. RR-06-24). Princeton, NJ: Education Testing Service.

Sheehan, K. M., Kostin, I., & Futagi, Y. (2007, October). *SourceFinder: A construct-driven approach for locating appropriately targeted reading comprehension source texts.* Paper presented at the SLaTE Workshop on Speech and Language Technology in Education ISCA Tutorial and Research Workshop, Farmington, PA.

Siskind, J. M. (1992). *Naïve physics, event perception, lexical semantics and language acquisition.* (unpublished doctoral dissertation). Massachusetts Institute of Technology, Cambridge, MA.

———. (1996). A computational study of cross-situational techniques for learning word-to-meaning mappings. *Cognition, 6,* 39–91.

Stahl, S. A., & Fairbanks, M. M. (1986). The effects of vocabulary instruction: A model-based meta-analysis. *Review of Educational Research, 56,* 72–110.

Sternberg, R. J., & Powell, J. S. (1983). Comprehending verbal comprehension. *American Psychologist, 38*, 878–893.

Steyvers, M., & Griffiths, T. (2007). Probabilistic topic models. In T. K. Landauer, D. S. McNamara, S. Dennis, & W. Kintsch (Eds.), *Handbook of latent semantic analysis*. Hillsdale, NJ: Lawrence Erlbaum Associates.

Steyvers, M., Smyth, P., Rosen-Zvi, M., & Griffiths, T. L. (2004, August). *Probabilistic author-topic models for information discovery.* Paper presented at the 2004 ACM SIGKDD International Conference on Knowledge Discovery and Data Mining, Seattle, WA.

Swanborn, M. S. L., & De Glopper, K. (1999). Incidental word learning while reading: A meta-analysis. *Review of Educational Research, 69*, 261–285.

Tenenbaum, J. B., & Xu, F. (2000, August). *Word learning as Bayesian inference.* Paper presented at the 22nd Annual Conference of the Cognitive Science Society, Philadelphia.

Thompson, C. A., & Mooney, R. J. (2003). Acquiring word-meaning mappings for natural language interfaces. *Journal of Artificial Intelligence Research, 18*, 1–44.

van Dorn, S. (2000). *Graph clustering by flow simulation* (unpublished doctoral dissertation). Universiteit Utrecht, Utrecht, The Netherlands.

Yu, C., Ballard, D. H., & Aslin, R. N. (2005). The role of embodied intention in early lexical acquisition. *Cognitive Science, 29,* 961-1005.

Zeno, S., Ivens, S., Millard, R., & Duvarri, R. (1995). *The educator's word frequency guide.* Brewster, NY: Touchstone Applied Science Associates (TASA), Inc.

Zevin, J. D., & Seidenberg, M. S. (2002). Age of acquisition effects in word reading and other tasks. *Journal of Memory and Language, 47*, 1-29.

NOTES

1. The work reported in this study was supported under a grant from the Institute of Educational Science (IES), PR/Award Number R305A080647.

2. We have experimented with rotating semantic spaces of the sort associated with SVD following methods typically used in factor analysis, such as Promax rotation. Such rotations typically do identify clusters of words with high LSA cosine similarity, making for a more interpretable semantic space. It is not clear whether such rotations, which end up assigning one cluster of words to a dimension, fully capture what is going on in the vocabulary, even in an LSA space, but they do suggest that LSA analyses could be made more interpretable than they currently tend to be.

3. Accessible on the web at http://igitur-archive.library.uu.nl/dissertations/1895620/inhoud.htm. MCL resources are available at www.micans.org/mcl.

4. Technically, the first measure is based upon a combination of the average and maximum pointwise mutual information between the target word and the defining words for the topic. The second measure requires that we establish an association measure between topics, taking the centroid association strength between the target word and the set of words that define each topic. We then compare the centroid topic associations with the target words by calculating cosine similarity.

Section II

HOW TO BUILD FOR THE FUTURE

Chapter Eight

An Explanative Modeling Approach to Measurement of Reading Comprehension

Mark Wilson and Stephen Moore[1]

The primary aim of this chapter is to illustrate how to use *explanatory* item response models in the context of the measurement of reading competency. The typical purpose of using measurement models is to measure certain outcome variables related to persons, so that the persons are *described* in terms of these variables. To accomplish this, standard measurement models typically estimate a parameter for each of the persons as well as a parameter (or several parameters) for each of the items that persons encounter during the assessment.

The broader approach we illustrate builds upon and complements this typical "descriptive" measurement approach by modeling how responses to items are affected by a range of additional item properties (e.g., item format, a specific type of item content, etc.) and person properties beyond those of location (e.g., a particular type of training the person has had, the person's learning style, etc.) We call this approach "explanatory" (De Boeck & Wilson, 2004).

If we can explain responses of persons to items in terms of person and item properties, then we are explaining how those responses are generated, and hence, broadening our understanding of what we are doing when we are measuring.

Parameters in explanatory models are estimates of the effects that the modeled item and person properties have on the process of generating responses to items. The interpretation of explanatory model parameters is akin to regression weights. In descriptive models, one fixed measurement scale location is estimated for each item and person. In explanatory models, the location for each person and item is computed by applying the combination of effects for the particular set of properties that the person or item may have.

The explanatory approach accommodates between-persons designs—based, for example, on groups to which people belong: gender, ethnicity, school, or a treatment category, and so on. And because the item properties vary within the test that each person takes, these properties can be viewed from the perspective of explanatory models as within-persons design factors, akin to those that are manipulated in standard experiments.

When the outcome variable is a student's reading competency, the person properties might include demographics such as the gender and the type of education program that he or she is in. The item properties might include different *aspects* of reading, different text *types*, and different text *formats* (note that we will expand upon this example context in later sections).

THE INTERNATIONAL SCHOOLS' ASSESSMENT

To show how the models we will deal with in this chapter can be used for reading comprehension, we will use an example data set based on the International Schools' Assessment (ISA; ACER, 2007), developed by the Australian Council for Educational Research. The data are from the 2004 administration of the test given to students in 23 countries, across grades from 3 to 10, but we used responses only from the 3,097 students in grade 7 in these example analyses. The test was developed under the same general guidelines as the reading test developed by the Organization for Economic Cooperation and Development (OECD) for its international testing program called PISA.[2]

In this program, reading competency is a "described variable" with five successive levels of sophistication in performing reading tasks. These levels are shown in table 8.1 (OECD, 2002).

The test data are based on 31 dichotomous items. An example of an item is shown in figure 8.1. Each item was constructed according to three item properties:

- Reading aspect
- Text format
- Text type

The three reading aspects represent types of informational tasks that the reader is called upon to do in the item: (i) retrieving information from the text, (ii) interpreting it, and (iii) reflecting on and evaluating it.

- *Retrieving* " . . . tasks can range from locating details required by an employer from a job advertisement to finding a telephone number with several prefixes" (OECD, 2002).
- *Interpreting* tasks involves making internal sense of the information. An example of an *interpreting* task "may involve connecting two parts of a

Table 8.1.   The PISA combined reading literacy scale.

	Distinguishing features of tasks at each level ...
5	The reader must: sequence or combine several pieces of deeply embedded information, possibly drawing on information from outside the main body of the text; construe the meaning of linguistic nuances in a section of text; or make evaluative judgments or hypotheses, drawing on specialized knowledge. The reader is generally required to demonstrate a full, detailed understanding of a dense, complex or unfamiliar text, in content or form, or one that involves concepts that are contrary to expectations. The reader will often have to make inferences to determine which information in the text is relevant, and to deal with prominent or extensive competing information.
4	The reader must: locate, sequence or combine several pieces of embedded information; infer the meaning of a section of text by considering the text as a whole; understand and apply categories in an unfamiliar context; or hypothesize about or critically evaluate a text, using formal or public knowledge. The reader must draw on an accurate understanding of long or complex texts in which competing information may take the form of ideas that are ambiguous, contrary to expectation, or negatively worded.
3	The reader must: recognize the links between pieces of information that have to meet multiple criteria; integrate several parts of a text to identify a main idea, understand a relationship or construe the meaning of a word or phrase; make connections and comparisons; or explain or evaluate a textual feature. The reader must take into account many features when comparing, contrasting or categorizing. Often the required information is not prominent but implicit in the text or obscured by similar information.
2	The reader must: locate one or more pieces of information that may be needed to meet multiple criteria; identify the main idea, understand relationships or construe meaning within a limited part of the text by making low-level inferences; form or apply simple categories to explain something in a text by drawing on personal experience and attitudes; or make connections or comparisons between the text and everyday outside knowledge. The reader must often deal with competing information.
1	The reader must: locate one or more independent pieces of explicitly stated information according to a single criterion; identify the main theme or author's purpose in a text about a familiar topic; or make a simple connection between information in the text and common, everyday knowledge. Typically, the requisite information is prominent and there is little, if any, competing information. The reader is explicitly directed to consider relevant factors in the task and in the text.

text, processing the text to summarize the main ideas, or finding a specific instance of something described earlier in general terms" (OECD, 2002).
- *Reflecting and evaluating* tasks includes reflecting on both form and content and using information from outside the text to answer the question.

The two text formats are (i) continuous and (ii) noncontinuous. *Continuous* text is standard prose; *noncontinuous* text is composed of distinct parts,

Pushcart Endurance Relay

THE ENERGY BREAKTHROUGH PUSHCART WEEKEND
PUSHCART ENDURANCE RELAY

Venue: Track 1

The Endurance Relay will take place on a circular street track – a section of the Main Energy Breakthrough track.

Time: Friday between 10:00 am and 12:30 pm.

Teams have been allocated heats.

What is Required of Teams:

- The Endurance Relay will require the teams of eight to split into pairs named Pairs 1, 2, 3 and 4.
- Each pair must have at least one girl.
- Each team member must have a turn at pushing and steering during the relay.
- Each team member will be required to push approximately 210 metres and drive 210 metres.
- Pairs 1 and 3 will start at the Start/Finish line and Pairs 2 and 4 will start at the back of the circuit, near the Tennis Courts. (See Diagram 1 below.)
- The relay will run in a clockwise direction.
- Each pair is required to:
  - Take the pushcart from their starting point to a changeover point 210 metres from their starting point (a quarter of the circuit).
  - Change positions (i.e. the driver becomes the pusher and vice versa) and take the pushcart to the next hand-over point.
  - Hand the pushcart over to the next pair who will follow the same format.
  - Pairs will hand over the cart either halfway around the track or at the Start/Finish line.
- Every team will be expected to participate in the heats.
- Teams are allocated points on the basis of the times recorded in their heats, taking into account any penalties given.

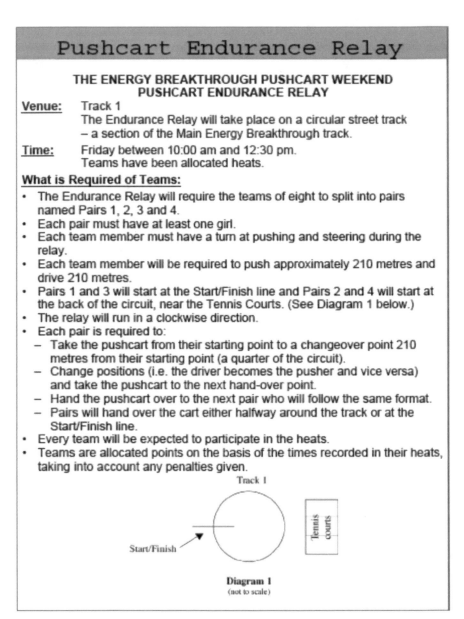

Track I

Start/Finish

Tennis courts

Diagram 1
(not to scale)

Figure 8.1. A sample ISA reading item

Pushcart Endurance Relay

The piece of writing opposite provides information about the Pushcart Endurance Relay. A pushcart is a small four-wheeled vehicle that can seat a driver and is pushed by another person.

A typical pushcart

Use the information about the Pushcart Endurance Relay to answer the questions below and on the next page.

1 Diagram 1 at the bottom of the opposite page shows the Pushcart Endurance Relay track.

Write the numbers 1, 2, 3 and 4 on Diagram 1 to indicate the positions of the pairs at the start of a race.

2 Describe one way that the Pushcart Endurance Relay is fair for all participants.

_____

_____

3 Explain one way that the Pushcart Endurance Relay might **not** be fair for all participants.

_____

_____

usually not involving grammatical sentences, in many places, such as one might see in a television program guide.

The seven *text types* are: (i) narrative, (ii) poem, (iii) injunction, (iv) expository, (v) diagram, (vi) graph, and (vii) argument. These categories are self-explanatory.

These categories are illustrated by the questions in figure 8.1. The first question is classified as a retrieving information item, which is noncontinuous in its format and is a diagram in terms of text type. The second and third questions are both classified the same: reflecting and interpreting, using a continuous text form, and an expository format.

Seen as an experimental design, our item properties (reading aspect, text format, and text type) are the three design factors in a 3 x 2 x 7 design, thus resulting in 42 possible different classes of items. In fact, however, fewer classes are available in this data set, as some classes were sparsely populated or not present at all in the item set.

We illustrate this classification of the items in table 8.2. Note that, in this item set, there were not enough items to populate all of the text type classes, so we combined narrative with poem (NP), injunction with expository (IE), and diagram with graph (DG). Including argument (A), there are four classes in all. The text format classification is labeled C for continuous and N for noncontinuous. Only the first two students and the last student are shown in table 8.2.

In addition to the design factors described above for the item side of the model, we have two factors on the person side of the model. The two person properties (i.e., background variables on the students) are gender (coded 0 for girls and 1 for boys), and ESL, or English as a Second Language status (coded 0 for no-ESL and 1 for ESL).

STRUCTURE OF DATA: PERSON SIDE, ITEM SIDE, OR BOTH?

The structure of the data matrix, illustrated in table 8.2, has two sides: a person and an item side. The information for the person side is in the *rows*. The information for the item side is in the *columns*. The sum scores for the items across students (a.k.a., raw item difficulties) are shown in table 8.2 at the bottom, and the sum scores for the students across items are shown on the far right.

Naturally, some students have relatively higher sum scores across the items, while the sum scores of others are relatively lower (e.g., persons 1, 2, and 3097 have sum scores of 13, 4, and 10, respectively). The most likely reason for the difference in the sum scores is that some students tend to have

Table 8.2. The structure of the ISA data.

	Person Properties			Item Properties																			Student Sum Score
				Retrieving								Interpreting	Reflecting and evaluating										
				Continuous				Non-Continuous					Continuous				Non-Continuous				
ID	Gender	ESL		NP	IE	DG	A	NP	IE	DG	A		NP	IE	DG	A	NP	IE	DG	A	
1	1	1		1	0	0	1	1	1	0	1		0	1	1	1	1	1	1	0	13
2	0	X		0	1	0	0	0	0	0	0		0	1	0	0	0	1	0	0	4
.	.	.		.	.	.	.	.	.	.	.		.	.	.	.	.	.	.	.	.
3097	1	0		0	1	0	0	0	1	0	0		0	1	0	0	0	0	0	1	10
Raw item difficulty				.85	.65	.87	.34	.86	.20	.73	.71		.29	.77	.54	.55	.75	.35	.65	.29	

Notes. NP = narrative & poem, IE = injunction & expository, DG = diagram & graph, A = argument. The raw item difficulty is the proportion of correct responses to the item across all examinees.

more ability than others in reading literacy. Therefore, it seems reasonable to use this test as a measurement tool for reading literacy, with the sum score derived from the test as an indication of that ability.

The analysis of the data matrix can be thought of in a totally different way than described above, where it was done in terms of student ability.

With this second view, we want to find out what the effect is of three item properties (reading aspect, text format, and text type) and our two person properties (gender and ESL), rather than having much interest in the measurement of individuals, *per se*. Thus, data that would traditionally serve the purpose of measuring the reading ability of the persons in our study can be used for this additional purpose. (Note that although the measurement concerns are not the main focus of this approach, that kind of information is still obtained.)

As stated above, the covariates of the repeated observations are the properties of the items in the test. In general, item properties are either manipulated within-subject design factors, such as in our example, or relate to an unplanned variation of the items (which is more common). When the test is intentionally constructed on the basis of these item properties, they, and the way they are combined in items, might be considered the elements of the "test blueprint." An example of unplanned variation might be properties derived from a post-hoc content analysis of the items in an extant test.

In table 8.2, we note some patterns that can be observed on the item side of the matrix. Looking at the data, we might derive the mean score per item over persons so that 31 item means are obtained. These 31 item means might be seen as the dependent variable in a linear regression, with the test properties as the predictors. But this is too simplistic because it assumes that there are no individual differences in the regression slopes and/or in the intercept.

Using an explanatory item response model is a more appropriate way of approaching the data that would capture the individual differences among the persons while still estimating and testing the effects of the item properties.

DESCRIPTIVE VERSUS EXPLANATORY ITEM RESPONSE MODELS

To illustrate the distinction between a *descriptive* approach and an *explanatory* approach in the context of the measurement of reading competency, we will discuss four item response models that differ in whether they are descriptive or explanatory on the person and the item side. The models we have selected as examples represent only tiny subsets of all possible models of the four model types. All four are logistic item response models and belong to the Rasch tradition, but this does not imply any restrictions on the approaches we illustrate.

The four types of models are shown in table 8.3 in a 2 x 2 structure, deriving from the presence or absence of properties for person and for items.

In the upper left cell of table 8.3 is the standard Rasch model, for which no item or person properties are modeled beyond each person's and item's location on the outcome variable. This model is descriptive for both persons and items. Therefore we call this "doubly descriptive."

In the lower left cell is the linear logistic test model (LLTM), which includes only item properties (Fischer, 1973). We call this model "item explanatory."

In the upper right cell is the latent regression Rasch model, which includes only person properties. We call this model "person explanatory."

Finally, in the lower right cell is the latent regression LLTM, which includes both item properties and person properties. We call this model "doubly explanatory."

In the sample data set, we have information on person as well as item properties so the two types of explanatory models (person and item) can be illustrated. See Zwinderman (1997) and Adams, Wilson, and Wu (1997) for alternate taxonomies and short descriptions of these and similar models. Also see De Boeck and Wilson (2004) for more formal definitions and complete descriptions of the models shown in this chapter.

Models are hierarchical if one is nested in the other. Two models are nested if they are identical except that one of the two fixes or restricts model parameter(s) that the other one leaves unrestricted. The restricted or nested model is a special case of the more general model, in which one or more of the parameters of the more general model are restricted to be equal to some fixed value (often zero). The models described in table 8.3 are hierarchical.

The most general of these four models is the doubly explanatory latent regression LLTM. In that model, both persons and items may have modeled properties. The person explanatory latent regression model is the same as the doubly explanatory model, except that all item property effects are restricted to be equal to zero. The item explanatory LLTM is the same as the doubly explanatory model, except that all person property effects are restricted to be equal to zero. The doubly descriptive Rasch model is the same as the doubly explanatory model, except that all properties of both persons and items are restricted to be equal to zero.

In a later section, we will compare the models in terms of what can be learned from each about persons, items, and factors affecting responses of persons to items. We will also compare models in terms of "relative model fit." We will not test models with respect to their absolute goodness of fit, that is, the extent to which a particular model is able to reproduce the data as a function of the parameters it has estimated from the data. Instead we will compare the relative fit within hierarchical pairs of models. See Bozdogan

Table 8.3.   **Models as a function of the absence or inclusion of properties.**

	Person Properties	
Item Properties	Absence of Properties	Inclusion of Properties
Absence of properties	Doubly descriptive: Standard Rasch Model	Person explanatory: Latent Regression Rasch Model
Inclusion of properties	Item explanatory: Linear Logistic Test Model (LLTM)	Doubly explanatory: Latent Regression LLTM

(1987) and Akaike (1974) for an explanation of criteria used to assess absolute and relative fit for item response models.

In terms of the ISA example, the two different perspectives, descriptive and explanatory, can be summarized as being the difference between the "standard" use of the test for measuring student reading competency and other uses such as (a) to understand effects that specific person properties (such as gender and ESL status in our example) may be having on persons' responses, and (b) to understand effects that specific item properties (such as reading aspect, text format, and text type in our examples) may be having on persons' responses.

The capability of investigating phenomena that go beyond the standard use of test data to measure persons on some ability, proficiency, or progress variable invites a number of additional research and test design purposes. Some of these additional purposes are discussed here. See De Boeck and Wilson (2004) for discussions of a broad range of purposes served by explanatory item response models.

The four models described in table 8.3 are relatively simple within the full range that are possible within the families of item response models, but some of them are more complex than the common range of item response models.

On one hand, all four models provide for measurement of individual differences, ranging in measurement from purely descriptive to fully explanatory. On the other hand, as discussed above, one may see the explanatory models also as models for repeated observation data used to test the effect of person and item properties, as in a psychological experiment. Specifically for the example data, the person properties are gender and ESL status, while the properties of the item are reading aspect, text type, and text format.

A DOUBLY DESCRIPTIVE MODEL: THE RASCH MODEL

We begin by estimating the Rasch model (Rasch, 1960). The sample data set was analyzed with *ACERConquest* software (Wu, Adams, Wilson, &

Haldane, 2007). The Rasch model is descriptive for both the person and the item side of the data matrix. It describes variation in the persons through a person ability parameter θ_p, which is considered a random effect, and variation in items through an item difficulty parameter d_i, which is considered a fixed effect. See De Boeck and Wilson (2004) for an explanation of random and fixed effects in item response models.

Think of a representation where the person abilities are represented as points along a line that correspond to the measurement scale for some outcome variable, and the item difficulties are shown as points along the same line. The probability of a given person responding correctly to a given item is proportional to the difference between the respective locations on the Rasch scale—$(\theta_p - d_i)$. (Note that this chapter will use the term "Rasch scale" for purposes of our discussion. The reader is referred to Wilson 2005 for a full definition and discussion of the Rasch model and the logit scale.)

For our example data, the estimated *item parameters* vary from -1.88 to $+3.18$ on the Rasch scale. By convention, the item parameters have an average value of 0.0 for the full set of items. Also by convention, lower values of the item parameters imply higher probabilities that test takers will respond correctly (i.e., are "easier" to get right). Higher values of item parameters imply the items are more difficult. Hence, the item estimates are often referred to as "item difficulty" parameters.

In the data we use for our example, the average item value happens to be slightly lower than the mean of the persons, so that the average person in the example has a probability of about .6 to get an average item correct. In terms of standard Rasch scale units, the variance of the scale is 0.95, (SD = .97).

Traditionally, effect size is reported as a mean-centered value, scaled in standard deviation units (e.g., Cohen, 1992). We will follow a similar logic as applied to examining the Rasch scale computed for our example scale.

In item response modeling, effect size can be seen as the effect (i.e., change) on a person's probability of responding correctly to an item that would be associated with a one standard deviation increase on the ability scale (q).

By convention, a person's probability of responding correctly to an item with difficulty (δ) at the same point on the measurement scale as the person's ability (q) is p = 0.50, assuming this is a generic person, and that increasing that generic person's ability by one standard deviation on the Rasch scale computed for our example data increases a person's probability of responding correctly to such an item from the conventional p = 0.50 to p = 0.80. That is, an increase of one standard deviation in the ability captured in this Rasch scale is associated with a 0.30 (0.80 − 0.50) increase in the probability of succeeding at a task that requires this ability.

For later models, we will examine how this increase in probability changes compared to the 0.30 effect size for the Rasch model.

Another way to understand the information obtained from a Rasch analysis is to create a Wright map, named in honor of American Rasch model pioneer Benjamin Wright (Wilson, 2005). A Wright map plots person ability estimates and item difficulty estimates on either side of a line representing the scale for the outcome variable being measured, running from lower values of the scale at the bottom of the figure to higher values at the top.

The Wright map resulting from fitting the Rasch model to our data is provided in figure 8.2, where the person parameters are plotted as a histogram of the estimated student ability distribution on the left-hand side of the measurement scale and the difficulty parameters for the individually numbered items are plotted on the right-hand side.

In this way, it is easy to see how specific items relate both to the scale itself and to the persons whose abilities are measured on the scale. The placement of persons and items in this kind of direct linear relationship has been the genesis of an extensive methodology for interpreting measures (Masters, Adams, & Wilson, 1990; Wilson, 2005; Wright, 1968; Wright, 1977).

For example, segments of the line representing the measurement scale can be defined in terms of particular item content and person proficiencies, in order to make specific descriptions of the progress of students or other test takers whose ability estimates place them in a given segment. The set of such segments can be interpreted as qualitatively distinct regions that characterize the successive levels of development on the outcome variable. Defining the boundaries of these "criterion zones" is often referred to as standard setting.

Wright maps have proven extremely valuable in supporting and informing the decisions of content experts in the standard-setting process. See Draney and Wilson (2009) and Wilson and Draney (2002) for descriptions of standard setting techniques and sessions conducted with Wright maps in a broad range of testing contexts.

Now we can ask what we have learned from this doubly descriptive analysis. We note that when we use the Rasch model, effectively we are measuring the tendency of individual students to answer the items correctly. We found that, when used for this purpose, the 31 items are a rather narrow basis for a reliable measurement. The reliability estimate for the Rasch scale is .82. However, because we want to concentrate more on the model and less on its application to measurement, we will not follow up on the reliability of the person measurement. Instead, we will switch to models that can explain the person and item parameters.

```
-------------------------------------
                    |
                 X|18
                    |
    3               |
                    |
               XX|
                    |
                    |
              XXX|
                    |
    2       XXXXX|24
                X|
            XXXXX|
               X|23
         XXXXXXXX|31
          XXXXXXX|
               XX|5 17 21
       XXXXXXXXXX|
    1   XXXXXXXXX|4
              XXX|8 30
         XXXXXXXX|7
         XXXXXXXX|19
              XXX|27
         XXXXXXXX|
         XXXXXXXX|16
         XXXXXXXX|
    0          XX|
         XXXXXXXX|22
         XXXXXXXX|2 10
           XXXXXX|
              XXX|26 29
           XXXXXX|6 14 25
             XXXX|11 20
   -1        XXXX|
                X|15
              XXX|
               XX|
               XX|9 13
               XX|1
                X|12
                X|3 28
   -2           X|
                    |
                    |
=====================================
Each 'X' represents approximately 19 cases
```

Figure 8.2. The Wright map estimated by the Rasch model

A PERSON EXPLANATORY MODEL:
THE LATENT REGRESSION RASCH MODEL

The person explanatory model we will describe is the *latent regression Rasch model,* which models person properties in order to explain differences in reading literacy between persons in our example data set. In a person-explanatory model such as this, the item side is left unexplained. The person-explanatory model treats it as descriptive.

Fitting the *latent regression Rasch model* to our data, the estimated *person variance* is 0.87 on the Rasch scale, and the mean of the person distribution is 0.28. The reliability is .81 (almost the same as for the Rasch model). The estimated *item parameters* vary from −1.87 to +3.17 on the logit scale, very close to the values for the Rasch model. As above, the size of the person effects can be examined by considering the effect of a change of one standard deviation on the ability scale as it is captured by this person-explanatory model.

For the *latent regression Rasch model,* the equivalent change in probability is 0.22 (i.e., 0.72-0.50). Note that this is the change we would predict, given a 1.00 standard deviation change in the person ability, if the item has not changed and the only change in the person is in ability. Again, we assume this is a generic person in this analysis, but this person here is effectively a female non-ESL student, as that is the default case where both ESL and gender are coded as zero.

Why is the probability increase associated with one standard deviation increase in ability as measured by the scale for the person-explanatory model less than the corresponding probability increase for the purely descriptive standard Rasch model? The reason lies with the two modeled person effects. The estimated *effect of gender* is 0.19 units on the Rasch scale in favor of females, with a standard error for that model parameter equal to .03. This effect is highly statistically significant (at an $\alpha = .01$ level of significance). This parameter value translates to a relative probability for the average male in our sample of $p = .45$ for responding correctly to an item for which the average female's probability of success is equal to the standard $p = .50$.

The estimated *effect of ESL status* is 0.48 Rasch scale units in favor of non-ESL students, with a standard error of .03, which again is highly statistically significant. This parameter value translates to a relative probability for the average ESL student in our sample of $p = .38$ for responding correctly to an item for which the average non-ESL student's probability of success is equal to the standard $p = .50$. See Wilson (2005) for an explanation of how values of model parameters estimated on the Rasch scale are related to the scale of probabilities.

Gender and ESL status are expected to explain part of the original variation observed for person ability, and the *latent regression Rasch model* confirms this hypothesis for both of these factors. Because these factors are specifically modeled, the variation in ability associated with them is "partialed out" of the resulting Rasch scale, and the probabilities of success associated with them are estimated separately in their respective parameter estimates.

In fact, the variance for this scale is .87 (SD = .93), compared to .95 (SD = .97) for the standard Rasch model scale for these data. This is why the item success probability advantage associated with one standard deviation increase in ability is less on this scale. The scale necessarily leaves out part of the variation associated with gender and ESL. But when information about gender and ESL is included for a given person, that person's item success probability goes up or down according to his or her modeled characteristics.

For example, using the *latent regression Rasch model,* the probability advantage relative to the generic person at the conventional p = .50 value, associated with one standard deviation increase in ability, is p = .83 for a person where the individual is known to be ESL and male. Compared, the probability change is now 0.33. Compare this to the 0.30 probability change obtained using the standard Rasch model that estimates probabilities for all persons in the same way, regardless of their characteristics. This is not a very large change, but then we only have two dichotomous pieces of information about each person—his or her gender and ESL status.

Every item response model is associated with a "deviance" value that is proportional to the amount of variation in the data that remains unmodeled or unaccounted for after the model is fit to the data. The difference between the deviance values associated with two hierarchically related models is a chi-square test statistic with degrees of freedom equal to the difference in the number of parameters estimated by the two models.

It tests the null hypothesis that the fit of the model with additional parameters is not significantly better than the fit of the model without those parameters. A significant chi-square test rejects the null and supports the hypothesis that the additional parameters do improve model fit (Bozdogan, 1987, and Akaike, 1974).

The fit of the *latent regression Rasch model* to the fit of the Rasch model is compared by subtracting the deviance values of the latter from the former. The difference is highly statistically significant at standard levels of significance, and hence one can interpret that the latent regression Rasch model has better fit than the Rasch model, at least in the conventional sense that, if the data had been generated by the latent regression Rasch model, then one would expect to get a better fit from a Rasch model less than 5 percent of the time (at the standard α = 5 percent level of significance).

The problem with this interpretation is that, where there are large numbers of cases, even small effects can be statistically significant. Thus, one needs to look beyond statistical significance and examine the size of effects in terms of relative probabilities of responding correctly to an item and parameter values as proportions of scale standard deviations.

Now we can ask what we have learned from this person explanatory analysis. We have found that, as far as the estimation of persons is concerned, the results are pretty much as they were for the simpler Rasch model, and the item estimation also is similar. What has been added is a way to explain a certain amount of the variation in the person estimates.

Both gender and ESL status have statistically significant effects on person location, with the effect of gender ($.19/.93 = .20$ of a standard deviation of the scale) being classified as a "small" effect according to Cohen's (1992) labels for effect size, and the effect of ESL ($.48/.93 = .52$ of a standard deviation) as a "medium" effect. Overall, the person explanatory model fits better than the Rasch model, which is consistent with the identification of the two person-effects as statistically significant.

Thus, we can contrast the descriptive and explanatory ways to interpret the results: (a) in a practical sense, where we just wanted to measure persons, then the descriptive Rasch model would suffice, but (b) in an explanative sense, if we want to understand better the pattern of results, then the person explanatory model is a better option. Of course, from a purely technical perspective, if we want to use the best fitting model, then the person explanatory model is better. Note this will not always be the case (see the next model).

AN ITEM EXPLANATORY MODEL: THE LLTM

In the third model, the *linear logistic test model* (LLTM), item properties are used to explain the differences between items in terms of the effect they have on the probability of responses (Fischer, 1973). The LLTM differs from the Rasch model in that, instead of estimating individual item parameters, the effects of item *properties* are estimated. The LLTM also allows interaction between item property variables. If one is interested in the interaction between two item property variables, the product of both can be added as an additional item property variable.

The difference between the Rasch model and the LLTM is that the contribution of each item is explained through the item properties. The model implies it is reasonable to expect that the item's location on the scale can be explained entirely from its properties. This is a strong assumption and makes the model highly restrictive. The fit of LLTM will depend greatly on how well the item properties reproduce the Rasch parameters.

Consistent with the usual finding, the LLTM does not fit very well compared to the Rasch model (Wilson & De Boeck, 2004). The estimated Rasch scale variance is 0.52. Note that the variance is considerably smaller than for the Rasch model (where it was 0.95). This illustrates how the estimates on the person side of the model are affected by this different approach on the item side (explanatory instead of descriptive).

This phenomenon can be explained as a scaling effect (Snijders & Bosker, 1999). In the context of our application, this effect follows from the different estimation of the scale of reconstructed item parameters in comparison to the scale of freely estimated item parameters, and is due to the less-than-perfect explanation of these item parameters on the basis of the item properties. We no longer have estimates of individual *item parameters*: Instead we arrive at item estimates that are constructed from information about item properties.

The LLTM effects were reduced to 6 in the process of estimating the model due to the small number of items in several of the text type categories (the combination of narrative and poem, injunction and expository, diagram and graph). The resulting predictions for item difficulty parameters (labeled as "SynthDelt") are plotted against the Rasch parameter estimates (labeled as "RaschDelt") in figure 8.3. Clearly, they are a poor match—the correlation is 0.34.

The distribution of items across the reading aspects [retrieving information (RI), interpreting (I) and reflecting and evaluating (RE)], and the text formats [continuous (c) and noncontinuous (N)] are shown in figure 8.4. This repeats the information in figure 8.3—there are no strong patterns among the loca-

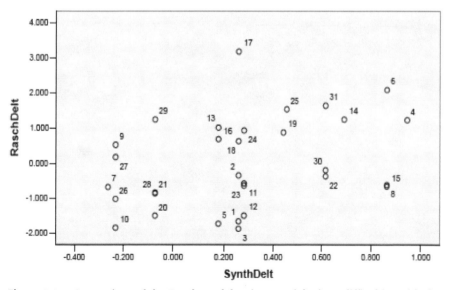

Figure 8.3. Comparison of the Rasch model estimates of the item difficulties with the LLTM estimates

```
          ------------------------------------
                             RI      I      RE
                          --------------------
                    X |            C
         3            |
                   XX |
                      |
                  XXX |
                      |
         2        XXXXX | N
                      X |
                  XXXXX |
                      X | N
                XXXXXXX |                    C
                XXXXXXX |
                     XX |       C C C
             XXXXXXXXXX |
         1    XXXXXXXXX |                    C
                    XXX |                  C C
              XXXXXXXXX |       N
              XXXXXXXXX | C
                    XXX |       N
              XXXXXXXXX |
              XXXXXXXXX |       C
              XXXXXXXXX |
         0           XX |
              XXXXXXXXX |                    C
              XXXXXXXXX |     C N
                 XXXXXX |
                    XXX |     N C
                 XXXXXX | C              C N
                   XXXX | N     C
        -1         XXXX |
                      X |                    C
                    XXX |
                     XX |
                     XX |     N C
                     XX |       C
                      X | N
                      X |     C C
        -2            X |
                      |
          ====================================
          Each 'X' represents approximately 19 cases
```

Figure 8.4. The ISA Wright map, showing the distribution of items by reading aspect and text format

tions of the item design factors, which is reflected in the poor prediction of the item difficulties from the item characteristics.

Now we can ask what we have learned from this item explanatory analysis. We found that, as far as the estimation of persons is concerned, the results show that we have not spread out the persons as well as the more complex Rasch model did, nor were the item results similar. We found that the three item characteristics—reading aspects and text format and type—did not well explain the variation in the item estimates. Overall, the item explanatory model fits less well than the Rasch model.

Again, there are two ways to interpret the results: (a) in a descriptive and practical sense, where we just wanted to measure persons, the Rasch model would be preferable; and (b) in an explanative sense, if we want to better understand the pattern of item results, then the item explanatory model is the one that will more likely lead to better explanations. However, in this case, the characteristics that we have available to explain the results have not been very adequate to capture the variation in this data set, and the technical perspective (i.e., the overall fit) indicates that the descriptive model is the better fit.

Presumably, however, examination of item properties in general, and the use of explanatory item response models in particular, may be quite useful in explaining item variation in other data sets. For example, Kostin (2004) analyzed Test of English as a Foreign Language (TOEFL) data using correlation and regression to assess the relationship between item difficulty and 49 item properties, falling into five categories: *word-level, sentence-level, discourse-level, lexical overlap,* and *task complexity.*

Among Kostin's findings were that the following properties all were significantly related to item difficulty: (a) the number of negatives in a passage, (b) requiring inference beyond what is explicitly given in the passage, and (c) the pattern in which facts and questions about facts are presented in the passage.

And in a study of the cognitive processes underlying literacy proficiency in young adults assessed in OECD countries, Kirsch and Mosenthal (1990) identified item properties of two types that are related to item difficulty: *task characteristics*, (e.g., task complexity, plausibility of distractors), and *materials characteristics*, (e.g., number of syllables, sentences, and labels within the passage).

Test data structured to include item-property covariates such as these would be ideal for exploration using explanatory item response models. (The reader is also referred to *Adult Literacy in OECD Countries: Technical Report on the First International Adult Literacy Survey* for additional information on models and constructs underlying literacy and items assessing literacy.)

Finally, we can combine the two models above, yielding a doubly explanatory model, the latent regression LLTM. In this combined model, the person contribution is explained in terms of person properties, while the item contribution is explained in terms of item properties. Looking over the results, we can conclude that the combination of the person with the item explanation has given results that are simply the summation of the two separate models that are combined into this model.

Note that this need not be the case—where there are important interactions of effects between persons and items, we would expect to see some interestingly different results here. To model them, we would need to add another level of complexity to our story—item-person interaction effects—but that is beyond the scope of this chapter [see Wilson and De Boeck (2004) for examples and discussion of this possibility].

CONCLUSION

Looking over the results for the ISA example, we can see that the explanatory perspective can provide a way to go beyond the usual descriptive sorts of analysis and results provided by regular item response theory approaches. Sometimes, it provides interesting and potentially important results, as was the case for the person explanatory model we investigated. Sometimes it does not result in an interesting or useful perspective, as was the case for the item explanatory model we investigated.

In the long run, both sorts of finding are needed: positive ones to tell us when we are improving our understanding of the measurement situation, and negative ones that tell us that we have not yet mastered the situation. Negatives ones make us think of possible alternatives—in this case, it may be that the item characteristics are in need of augmentation, or it may be that the items we are using are not good representatives of those characteristics.

The four models we have presented here serve as an introductory selection to illustrate the contrast between descriptive and explanatory models, specifically; the parameters can either be descriptive or explanatory. Explanatory parameters are effects of properties or, in other words, of external variables. Descriptive parameters are simply the person and item locations.

This distinction, which is at the basis of the presentation of the four models in this chapter, can be extrapolated to include situations such as multilevel models (van den Noortgate & Paek, 2004); random (or hierarchical) item models (Janssen, Schepers, & Peres, 2004); person-by-item interaction models (including differential item function, or DIF, models) (Meulders & Xie, 2004); multidimensional and 2PL models (Rijmen & Briggs, 2004); and mixture models (Fieuws, Spiessens, & Draney, 2004).

These model extensions can be easily incorporated by adopting the non-linear mixed model framework for item response theory models as described in Rijmen, Tuerlinckx, De Boeck, and Kuppens (2003), and in De Boeck and Wilson (2004).

REFERENCES

Adams, R. J., Wilson, M., & Wu, M. (1997). Multilevel item response models: An approach to errors in variables regression. *Journal of Educational and Behavioral Statistics, 22,* 47–76.

Akaike, H. (1974). A new look at the statistical model identification. *IEEE Transactions on Automatic Control, 19,* 716–723.

Australian Council for Educational Research (2007). International Schools' Assessment Brochure. Retrieved June 26, 2007, from www.acer.edu.au/documents/ISA_Brochure.pdf.

Bozdogan, H. (1987). Model selection for Akaike's information criterion (AIC). *Psychometrika, 53,* 345–370.

Cohen, J. (1992). A power primer. *Psychological Bulletin, 112,* 155–159.

De Boeck, P., & Wilson, M. (Eds.) (2004). *Explanatory item response models: A generalized linear and nonlinear approach.* New York: Springer-Verlag.

Draney, K., & Wilson, M. (2009). Selecting cut scores with a composite of item types: The Construct Mapping procedure. In Smith, E. V., & Stone, G. E. (Eds), *Applications of Rasch measurement in criterion-reference testing: Practice analysis to score reporting.* Chicago: JAM Press.

Fieuws, S., Spiessens, B., & Draney, K. (2004) Mixture models. In P. De Boeck & M. Wilson (Eds.), *Explanatory item response models: A generalized linear and nonlinear approach* (pp. 317–342). New York: Springer-Verlag.

Fischer, G. H. (1973). The linear logistic test model as an instrument in educational research. *Acta Psychologica, 3,* 359–374.

Janssen, R., Schepers, J., & Peres, D. (2004). Models with item and item group predictors. In P. De Boeck & M. Wilson (Eds.), *Explanatory item response models: A generalized linear and nonlinear approach* (pp. 189–212). New York: Springer-Verlag.

Kirsch, I. S., & Mosenthal, P. B. (1990). Exploring document literacy: Variables underlying the performance of young adults. *Reading Research Quarterly,* 25, 5–30.

Kostin, I. (2004). *Exploring item characteristics that are related to the difficulty of TOEFL dialog items* (No. RR-04-11). Princeton, NJ: Educational Testing Service.

Masters, G. N., Adams, R. A., & Wilson, M. (1990). Charting of student progress. In T. Husen & T. N. Postlethwaite (Eds.), *International encyclopedia of education: Research and studies* (Supp. Vol. 2, pp. 628–634). Oxford: Pergamon Press.

Meulders, M., & Xie, Y. (2004). Person-by-item predictors. In P. De Boeck & M. Wilson (Eds.), *Explanatory item response models: A generalized linear and nonlinear approach* (pp. 213–240). New York: Springer-Verlag.

Organisation for Economic Cooperation and Development (OECD). (2002). *PISA 2000 Technical Report*. Paris: Author.

Rasch, G. (1960). *Probabilistic models for some intelligence and attainment tests.* Copenhagen, Denmark: Danish Institute for Educational Research.

Rijmen, F., & Briggs, D. (2004). Multiple person dimensions and latent item predictors. In P. De Boeck & M. Wilson (Eds.), *Explanatory item response models: A generalized linear and nonlinear approach* (pp. 247–266). New York: Springer-Verlag.

Rijmen, F., Tuerlinckx, F., De Boeck, P., & Kuppens, P. (2003). A nonlinear mixed model framework for item response theory. *Psychological Methods, 8,* 185–205.

Snijders, T., & Bosker, R. (1999). *Multilevel analysis.* London: Sage.

van den Noortgate, W., & Paek, I. (2004). Person regression models. In P. De Boeck & M. Wilson (Eds.), *Explanatory item response models: A generalized linear and nonlinear approach* (pp. 167–188). New York: Springer-Verlag.

Wilson, M. (2005). *Constructing measures: An item response modeling approach.* Mahwah, NJ: Lawrence Erlbaum Associates.

Wilson, M., & De Boeck, P. (2004). Descriptive and explanatory item response models. In P. De Boeck & M. Wilson (Eds.), *Explanatory item response models: A generalized linear and nonlinear approach* (pp. 43–74). New York: Springer-Verlag.

Wilson, M. & Draney, K. (2002). A technique for setting standards and maintaining them over time. In S. Nishisato, Y. Baba, H. Bozdogan, & K. Kanefuji (Eds.), *Measurement and multivariate analysis*. New York: Springer-Verlag.

Wright, B. (1968). Sample-free test calibration and person measurement. In *Proceedings of the 1967 Invitational Conference on Testing* (pp. 85–101). Princeton, NJ: Educational Testing Service.

——. (1977). Solving measurement problems with the Rasch model. *Journal of Educational Measurement, 14,* 97–116.

Wu, M., Adams, R.J., Wilson, M., Haldane, S. (2007). *ACERConQuest 2.0* [computer program]. Hawthorn, Australia: Australian Council for Educational Research.

Zwinderman, A. H. (1997). Response models with manifest predictors. In W. J. van der Linden & R. K. Hambleton (Eds.). *Handbook of modern item response theory* (pp. 245–256). New York: Springer.

NOTES

1. We wish to thank the Australian Council for Educational Research, who generously provided the data set used in the example. A longer version of this chapter was first presented as the Samuel J. Messick Memorial Lecture, Language Testing Research Colloquium, University of Melbourne, Australia, June 2006. Many thanks to Professor Tim McNamara of the University of Melbourne, for valuable support in envisioning this chapter, and helpful criticism of earlier versions.

2. PISA stands for "Programme for International Student Assessment." The test administration occurs every three years, and is given in over 50 countries, in at least three areas: reading, mathematics and science.

Chapter Nine

Cognitive Psychometric Models as a Tool for Reading Assessment Engineering

Joanna S. Gorin and Dubravka Svetina

One of the most notable challenges for reading comprehension assessment design in the twenty-first century is the increasingly varied use and purpose of assessment. Whereas test scores have historically been used to order students in terms of ability, place them in appropriate classes, or select them for admission to special programs, test uses in the twenty-first century focus more on diagnostic score interpretations that are substantively meaningful and instructionally relevant (Huff & Goodman, 2007).

For example, whereas reading assessments were once used to identify "poor" versus "good" readers, tests that identify the source of reading difficulties in terms of encoding, decoding, and other cognitively based processes are now of more interest. The premise is that test scores supporting interpretations at a finer grained cognitive level are more useful than traditional normative scores when selecting interventions for individual students.

However, in order to justify the validity of such score interpretations and uses, items on these tests must be designed appropriately. That is, items must be written to elicit behaviors that allow for differentiations among cognitive skills. Moreover, empirical evidence demonstrating the validity of these differentiations and of the subsequent score interpretations is paramount.

Items on current large-scale reading assessments are not understood at this level of cognitive specificity. More problematic is that the existing test items were not designed at the outset to yield diagnostically meaningful behaviors. Thus, even if attempts were made to interpret scores from existing tests at a process-specific level, the validity of such interpretations would be suspect.

Recent assessment design frameworks that emphasize principled item construction at the outset offer considerable promise for the development of instructionally relevant reading assessment. Such frameworks include Mislevy's evidence-centered design (ECD; Mislevy, 1994, 1995), Embretson's cognitive design system (CDS; Embretson, 1998), and Wilson's construct modeling approach (Wilson, 2005).

Though each approach is distinct in several ways, three hallmark features are in common. First, each approach begins with a comprehensive definition of the construct to be measured and the inferences to be made about students. For assessment of reading, the rich cognitive and educational literatures provide strong models of student proficiency in reading from which to draw.

Second, item development proceeds from this model in a principled fashion by incorporating design components of the items to the hypothesized cognitive processes comprising the construct. Specific attention to a student proficiency (i.e., cognitive) model during item design is critical if the final test scores are to support the desired inferences at a cognitive level. To the extent that psychometric item analysis can provide an index not only of the overall statistical quality of the item, but also of the correspondence between the item and the targeted cognitive processes, the strength of any diagnostic score interpretation is improved.

As a final step in the test design process, the relationships among cognitive skills/processes, item design features, and student responses can be evaluated via psychometric models. The same model could be used in this final step as that applied during item development, only as a summative rather than a formative indicator of score meaning and utility.

The current chapter focuses on cognitively based psychometric modeling as a critical component of item design for twenty-first-century reading comprehension assessments. We summarize how psychometric models that include parameters for item design features linked to cognitive processes may inform test development. Further, we emphasize that the use of these psychometric models throughout the item design process, as opposed to the culminating event in assessment design, is most likely to generate a reading test useful for twenty-first-century testing purposes.

COGNITIVE PSYCHOMETRIC MODELS

Psychometric modeling of reading assessment data typically occurs after large sets of data are collected. The sole purpose for the modeling is to examine the scalability. Scaling typically includes examination of dimensionality, reliability estimation, and parameter estimation focusing on item difficulty and discrimination indices. Little, if any, information is provided regarding construct meaning and representativeness of the scores as they relate to reading processes (Embretson, 1983; Messick, 1989). Nor is the relationship between the specific design of a test question and examinee response processes assessed.

Thus, at the end of the psychometric analysis, one is left with numerical indices of the statistical quality of items that are in place on one's assessment. Should the items look problematic, neither the opportunity to alter the items, nor a suggested approach to improve the test questions, is provided.

Alternatively, applying psychometric models to assessment data that scale both the overall item responses as well as the substantive meaning of item scores throughout the test development process may solve both issues. The majority of measurement models, either classical true score theory (CTST) models or item response theory (IRT) models, are not well suited for this purpose. However, an emerging category of models called *cognitive psychometric models,* which include parameters associated with individual cognitive processes, offers a promising alternative.

Cognitive psychometric models (CPMs) can be thought of generally as statistical models appropriate for the analysis of student response data that include parameters associated with cognitive subskills and processes.[1] The model parameters are not "cognitive" in that they do not estimate student proficiency on cognitive processes. However, the parameters are "cognitive" in that they represent characteristics of the test questions designed to elicit specific cognitive processes.

For example, a parameter could be included to represent the length of the sentences in a reading passage. This parameter is considered "cognitive" because the length of the sentence is presumed to affect students' cognitive processing in terms of encoding, coherence, and integration. By using CPMs as opposed to traditional psychometric models, the impact of the cognitively based item characteristics, sometimes called *item design features,* can be evaluated.

In CPMs, the item design features are represented mathematically in an incidence matrix, also called a *q*-matrix. In a dichotomous *q*-matrix, originally introduced by Fischer (1973) as part of an explanatory item response model called the Linear Logistic Latent Trait Model (LLTM), the relationship between the items and their design features is expressed by assigning 1s to those features present on a particular item and 0s to those not present (Fisher, 1973; Tatsuoka, 2005).

The structure of the *q*-matrix need not (and in many cases should not) be dichotomous. The traditional *q*-matrix using 1s and 0s to represent the presence or absence of item features is a useful tool when the construct of interest and the items allow for such a structure.

However, for reading assessment, it is unlikely that any reading subprocess (e.g., encoding, coherence, etc.) would be absent completely from an item. Rather, it is more likely that the degree of complexity of the various processes would vary. Accordingly, design features of items related to the processes (e.g., vocabulary level, sentence length) might exist on a more continuous scale. In such situations, psychometric models that allow for design features scored on continuous and polytomous scales in the q-matrix are appropriate.

To construct the q-matrix, researchers, cognitive psychologists, and/or experts in the domain of interest compile a list of cognitive processes believed to describe the student interaction and problem solving with the item. This information can be augmented with process-tracing data while students solve test questions, including data from verbal protocols, digital eye-tracking, and cognitive labs (Gorin, 2006; Leighton, 2004). Sound identification of the cognitive attributes is essential for accuracy and appropriateness of parameter and score interpretations.

Reading assessments are well positioned for applications of CPMs due to the extensive literature that exists on the reading process and associated cognitive processes. This literature could provide a foundation to construct a q-matrix that accurately and completely captures the requisite skills to correctly solve test questions.

When item features and cognitive processes are represented explicitly in models through statistical parameters, psychometric scaling becomes an integral part of the item development process. The item design parameter estimates can provide feedback to item developers regarding their success in designing items to measure specific skills.

The results from scaling and model parameterization inform item development by suggesting how items might be modified to better assess specific subsets of skills to greater or lesser extents in individual items. By designing items with an intentional structure, student responses can be interpreted in terms of predetermined processes. That is, the sources of item complexity can be more carefully controlled.

For example, sets of reading items could be written to reduce the effect of encoding on response processes while emphasizing the role of coherence, or vice versa. Scores from distinct sets of items, each of which emphasizes different reading processes, could then be compared to provide a diagnostic "profile" regarding students' specific weaknesses that could be targeted with interventions.

Latent Trait CPMs

The hallmark of any CPM is the inclusion of model parameters associated with theoretical cognitive processes. One mathematical approach to CPMs is via nonlinear latent trait models, such as those used in IRT (see De Boeck & Wilson, 2004, and Embretson & Reise, 2000, for a full review).

Latent trait models characterize individual differences among persons in terms of a continuous unobservable latent variable(s) that accounts for the response behavior for an item or test. However, unlike more traditional IRT models, CPM latent-trait models include component parameters to link the examinees' item responses to hypothesized cognitive processes comprising the latent trait.

An example of a CPM that incorporates information at the item level is the LLTM (Fischer, 1973), an extension of the Rasch IRT model. The Rasch model (Rasch, 1966) expresses the probability of correctly answering item i, given the examinee's ability (θ_v) and difficulty parameter for item, β_i, as:

$$P(+ \mid \theta_v, \beta_i) = \frac{e^{\theta_v - \beta_i}}{1 + e^{\theta_v - \beta_i}} \qquad (1)$$

The LLTM extends the Rasch model by decomposing the difficulty parameter, β_i in the form of:

$$\beta_i = \sum_{j=1}^{p} q_{ij}\eta_j \; ; p < k \qquad (2)$$

where,

k is the total number of items,

p is the total number of cognitive processes (attributes),

η_{ij} is a linear combination of the basic parameters that measure the contribution of cognitive processes to the difficulty of the item, and

q_{ij} are some fixed weights with respect to the item difficulty.[2]

As can be seen from equation (2), rather than estimating a traditional item difficulty for each item, the LLTM model decomposes item difficulty into a linear combination of item design features and weights. The item design features for the set of items on a test are specified via a q-matrix, and the weights indicate the degree to which the item design features affect the students' response process.

It is expected that the design features used to create the items will have significant relationships with item difficulty. The decomposition of item difficulty into parameters associated with individual skills allows for formal hypothesis testing of the substantive meaning of item scores.[3]

Applications of the LLTM model to reading assessment have shown significant promise for improved item design, score interpretation, and validity argumentation. Much of this work is based on Kintsch's coherence-integration (C-I) theory (Kintsch, 1988, 1994; Kintsch & Keenan, 1973; Kintsch & van Dijk, 1978), including processes associated with encoding, coherence, and integration.

The theoretical model specifies that certain features of text, including propositional density, have predictable effects on the cognitive complexity of comprehension. These hypothesized relationships have implications for item design on standardized tests of reading comprehension that can be tested via LLTM modeling of student responses.

In one of the earliest applications of the LLTM model to reading assessment data, Embretson and Wetzel (1987) combined aspects of C-I with an information-processing model to represent student cognition when solving passage-based multiple-choice reading comprehension items (see figure 9.1).

When the LLTM model was fitted to item responses from the Armed Services Vocational Aptitude Battery Paragraph Comprehension test (ASVAB-PC), significant model parameters indicated that item processing could be characterized in terms of both text representation (i.e., encoding and coherence processes) and decision processes.

Encoding involves translating the printed text into known word meaning. Coherence processes, on the other hand, involve linking words and propositions into a meaningful representation of the text.

Response decision contains three major subprocesses: encoding and coherence processing; text mapping; and evaluating the truth status of response alternatives. Encoding and coherence processes are the same as for text representation except that the response alternatives are represented.

Text mapping involves linking the propositions in the alternative to relevant propositions in the text. Evaluating the truth status is a two-stage process involving first an attempt to falsify the alternative by material in the text and then attempting to confirm the alternative. Items may be described on the difficulty of these processes by scoring their stimulus features. For example, the difficulty of encoding is influenced by word frequency or word reading-grade level.

Coherence processes, in turn, are influenced by the density and type of propositions, as well as the density of arguments and content words. Response decision processes, such as text mapping, are influenced by variables such as the proportion of relevant text and the amount of inference and paraphrasing required to compare propositions. The analysis indicated that numerous design features, such as vocabulary difficulty, propositional density, lexical similarity of response options and text, and level of reasoning impacted item difficulty.

The results of the ASVAB LLTM analysis provide guidance for principled item design and test assembly for reading comprehension assessment. The scatterplot in figure 9.2 shows a bivariate distribution of predicted item difficulties analogous to those presented in Embretson and Wetzel (1987). Each point on the plot represents one test item in terms of its predicted difficulty based on its relevance to (a) text representation processes and (b) decision processes. By plotting both indices simultaneously, the location of an item within the scatterplot indicates the primary source of item difficulty.

Text Representation   Response Decision

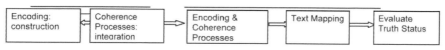

Figure 9.1. **Cognitive processing model for ASVAB reading comprehension items**

For example, items in the upper left quadrant of the scatterplot were difficult primarily due to text representation processes, as opposed to decision processes. Embretson and Gorin (2001) argue that these would be the most desirable items on a test of reading comprehension as they measure primarily construct-relevant processes.

Items in the lower right quadrant measure primarily decision processes. For purposes of score interpretations based on students' reading ability (not reasoning ability), these items are less desirable. Depending on the purpose of the assessment, item developers could study the format and structure of items emphasizing each of the various cognitive processes and generate larger numbers of the desired sort. One can envision a similar analysis of items

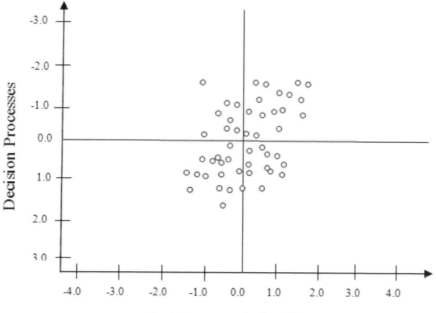

Figure 9.2. **Illustration of item difficulties predicted by cognitive components of item design**

measuring multiple construct-relevant reading processes in order to generate subsets of items, each targeting different skills.

Following Embretson and Wetzel's analysis, numerous studies have examined the item features of reading comprehension assessment with cognitively based latent trait models, including the LLTM. Table 9.1 provides a list of relevant studies, including the names of the assessments analyzed, the psychometric model applied to the data, and the item features and/or cognitive processes that contributed most strongly to the difficulty of the items.

Interestingly, though the general structure of the items for all studies was virtually identical (i.e., passages followed by multiple-choice questions with four or five response options), the relevant cognitive processes identified for each assessment are similar but not identical. For example, Gorin and Embretson (2006) found that reading comprehension items from the Graduate Record Examination's (GRE) verbal subtest, unlike the ASVAB items, were primarily driven by response decision processes, as opposed to text representation. A review of the studies presented in table 9.1 suggests that less obvious differences across items from unique tests (e.g., length of the passage, level of vocabulary) may result in difference in score meaning.

This table serves primarily as a selected guide and not an exhaustive list of research involving reading assessments. Rather, we hope to emphasize the growing number of empirical studies of reading assessment applying CPMs to a variety of item types and assessments, and the diversity in the existing findings regarding the meaning of scores from reading comprehension assessments. If future reading tests are to be interpreted in terms of specific skill strengths and weaknesses, then more attention should be paid to the design features of the items and the cognitive skills that they are likely to evoke in student responses.

To this end, few studies on reading comprehension assessment design have explored the process of writing or modifying items to emphasize specific skills. Gorin (2005) experimentally manipulated reading comprehension items from the GRE based on the significant LLTM features identified in Embretson and Wetzel's (1987) study. Her purpose was to examine the extent to which items could be engineered to emphasize select cognitive processes in some items over others. Significance tests of the LLTM weights were used to examine the effect of changing propositional density, use of passive voice, increased use of negation, and changes in semantic overlap on item processing.

Surprisingly, though previous research has suggested that these features predict item difficulty in correlational studies, their explicit manipulation did not affect the difficulty of items. Less surprising was the fact that the use of negative wording, even in the relevant sections of the passage as opposed to the stem of the question, increased item difficulty. More research in this vein

Table 9.1. Selected studies utilizing models with design/cognitive components.

Study	Assessment	Model	Main (Significant) Processes
Buck, Tatsuoka, & Kostin (1997)	TOEFL[a]	RSM[f]	Attributes related to understanding the questions, locating the necessary information, understanding the necessary information, selecting the correct response
Embretson & Wetzel (1987)	ASVAB[b]	LLTM[g]	Propositional density of the text and percent content words (text model variables); percent relevant text, falsification, word frequency for distractors, reasoning level of correct response, confirmation (decision processing)
Freedle & Kostin (1993)	TOEFL	IDM[h]	Vocabulary difficulty level in the response options and the key
Gorin (2005)	GRE[c]	LLTM	Passive voice and negative word change (item difficulty), information order change and response alternative change (time response)
Gorin & Embretson (2006)	GRE	IDM	Decision processing processes (vocabulary level of correct response, reasoning level of correct response), special item format, length of passage
Gorin & Svetina (2008)	SAT[d]	LLTM	KDL, KDR, PSR, NI, LSAk
Sheehan & Ginther (2001)	TOEFL	TBR[i]	Location effects, correspondence effects, elaboration of information
Sheehan, Kostin, & Persky (2006)	NAEP[e]	TBR	Type of search variable, relevant information variable, semantic similarity between text and key
VanderVeen, et al. (2007)	SAT	IDM	Word meaning, sentence meaning, global text meaning, pragmatic meaning
Wang & Gierl (2007)	SAT	AHM[j]	A3, A3a, A4, A4a, A9l

Notes:

[a] Test of English as a Foreign Language
[b] Armed Services Vocational Aptitude Battery
[c] Graduate Record Examination
[d] Scholastic Aptitude Test
[e] National Assessment of Educational Progress
[f] Rule-space methodology
[g] Latent logistic test model (Fischer, 1973)
[h] Item difficulty modeling (regression-type analysis, including linear, stepwise, and hierarchical regression)
[i] Tree-based regression (Sheehan, 1997)
[j] Attribute hierarchy model (Leighton, Gierl, & Hunka, 2004)
[k] KDL: Key and Distractor – Linguistic (attributes associated with the length of a vocabulary level of the keyed response and the four distractors for each item), KDR: Key and Distractor —Reasoning (attributes associated with confirmation of the correct response, falsifiability of the distractors, level of transformation of the key relative to the text, reasoning level of the key, and plausibility of the distractors), PSR: Primary Skill Rating (attributes based on primary skills generated by VanderVeen et al. (2007)), NI: Necessary Information (attributes related to linguistic measures of relevant portions of the text for each question), and LSA: Latent Semantic Analysis (attributes related to lexical correspondence between the keyed response and the distractors with the relevant portions of text for each question (i.e., NI))
[l] A3: Understanding the content, form and function of sentences, A3a: Literal understanding of sentences with minimal amount of inferences, A4: Understanding the content, form and function of larger sections of text, A4a: Literal understanding of larger sections of text with minimal amount of inferences, and A9: Using rhetorical knowledge

is currently lacking, but initial studies, such as that on the GRE items, suggest promise for this approach to principled reading assessment design.

An Alternative Approach

In addition to the latent trait models just described, a latent class approach to modeling item design features and students' cognitive skills has recently gained momentum. This second type of model called *diagnostic classification models* (DCMs; Rupp and Templin, 2008) provides diagnostic score interpretations, based on the knowledge of the cognitive requirements of the test items. These models have been most popular in testing situations for which diagnostic score reports are desired and/or complex item types are used.

Several DCMs that estimate cognitive parameters for persons rather than items have been particularly popular in recent assessment literature (see Rupp, Templin, & Henson, 2010, for a complete review). These models have primarily been touted for their utility in diagnostic score reporting rather than examinations of validity and item design.

Applications to tests of mathematics, reading comprehension, and listening (Buck & Tatsuoka, 1998; Buck, Tatsuoka, & Kostin, 1997; Tatsuoka, Corter, & Tatsuoka, 2004) have generated cognitive score reports for individual examinees and groups of examinees. To the extent that the desired outcome of any diagnostic assessment system is the generation of "diagnostic" scores, DCMs offer great promise.

In DCMs, though the cognitive information regarding skill requirements is initially specified at the item level, it is ultimately translated into person parameters. That is, a q-matrix specifying item features is entered into the analysis and a description of students' cognitive abilities associated with those features is yielded.

This is potentially a distinct advantage of the DCMs over the latent trait models like the LLTM. Rather than a summed score or a single unidimensional latent trait estimate, a DCM's purpose is to classify students into a diagnostic state associated with one of several patterns of skill mastery and nonmastery. The student's skill level is diagnosed based on responses to items and the association between the items and skills.

Like the latent trait models, the DCMs begin with positing a structure of construct of interest, identification of the item characteristics, and psychometric modeling. Once the construct is identified (i.e., one has defined what ought to be measured and what inferences ought to be made), an evaluation of skills needed to solve a problem correctly is specified again through a q-matrix.

However, unlike the LLTM, the DCM q-matrix requires item design features to be coded dichotomously. That is, a feature is either present or absent, meaning the cognitive skill associated with the item feature is either required to solve the item or is unnecessary.

Further, regarding reading assessment specifically, the strong assumption of DCMs that the q-matrix be dichotomously scored may be inconsistent with the cognitive nature of the reading construct. Recall from the previous discussion of q-matrices that a dichotomously score q-matrix is interpreted to mean that the skill associated with a design feature to indicated that a skill is either (a) required to correctly solve the item, or (b) completely unnecessary.

For content domains such as mathematics and science where discrete skills can be tested in isolation or combined explicitly in writing a test item, this assumption is plausible. However, reading comprehension is quite distinct. It is more likely that all processes associated with reading (e.g., encoding, coherence, etc.) are needed to one extent or another on any given test question. It is the degree of influence of these processes based on the design of the test question that can vary. Thus, the permissible q-matrix for the LLTM and other latent trait models that include item design features on continuous scales are likely more appropriate than the DCMs.

CONCLUSION AND A CAVEAT

Though we have focused this chapter on describing the unique characteristics of CPMs, their ultimate role in assessment development is uncertain. CPMs may prove to be a transitional phase in assessment design that primarily serves to increase our attention to the impact that item design can have on the substantive meaning of test scores and the inferences we would like to make.

Though in this chapter and elsewhere a distinction had been made among CPMs and other CTST and IRT models, as well as distinctions among categories of CPMs, it is not clear that such delineations are needed—or useful (Gorin, 2009).

Work by Wilson and his colleagues with the BEAR (Berkeley Evaluation & Assessment Research Center) assessment system have shown that when items are constructed appropriately, the unidimensional Rasch model can provide diagnostically meaningful score interpretations (Briggs, Alonzo, Schwab, & Wilson, 2006).

This diagnostic information is yielded from structuring items as ordered multiple-choice questions (OMCs; Briggs et al., 2006) for which each response distractor is associated with a developmental level of understanding of the science concept being measured. Students do not receive diagnostic classifications. However, as a result of the careful design of items, each point on the continuous latent trait continuum is associated with a description of students' cognition, possibly including their strengths and weaknesses.

When designing items or examining existing tests, CPM parameterization could be an initial step toward understanding the nature of the construct and how items, item responses, and score interpretations are connected. In the end, however, reporting a unidimensional ability estimate that is understood at the cognitive level versus reporting a diagnostic state based on a CPM system may be instructionally and substantively indistinguishable.

The approach most likely to yield instructionally relevant reading assessments will require a combination of analytic approaches such as those as previously discussed. Early applications of CPMs in the item design process can lead to careful construction of items that generate cognitively interpretable scores. The nature of the construct, specifically regarding the extent to which subprocesses can be distinguished and measured in isolation in a test item, may determine whether a traditional psychometric model or complex CPMs make more sense for final scaling and score reporting.

The models described in this chapter are merely two of a large number of existing models that function much in the same way. Many of the models are relatively new to the psychometric literature and have yet to be examined fully in terms of their statistical properties and potential limitations. Further, few studies have compared the quality of these models to one another, either in simulations or when applied to operational test data.

One of the largest reasons for this apparent oversight is the lack of appropriate assessments. While the psychometric literature on diagnostic assessment and modeling continues to grow, the number of available assessments to which the models can be applied is stagnant. Once such assessments are built, further research can be conducted to determine which modeling approach will be most useful for reading assessment. Most likely, it will depend on the nature of the task included on the assessment as well as the specific interpretations and uses of the test scores.

REFERENCES

Briggs, D. C., Alonzo, A. C., Schwab, C., & Wilson, M. (2006). Diagnostic assessment with ordered multiple-choice items. *Educational Assessment*, *11*, 33–63.

Buck, G., & Tatsuoka, K. K. (1998). Application of the rule-space procedure to language testing: examining attributes of a free response listening test. *Language Testing, 15,* 119–157.

Buck, G., Tatsuoka, K. K., & Kostin, I. (1997). The skills of reading: Rule-space analysis of a multiple-choice test of second language reading comprehension. *Language Learning, 47*, 423–466.

De Boeck, P., & Wilson, M. (Eds.) (2004). *Explanatory item response models: A generalized linear and nonlinear approach.* New York: Springer.

Embretson, S. E. (1983). Construct validity: Construct validity vs. nomothetic span. *Psychological Bulletin, 93,* 179–197.

———. (1998). A cognitive design system approach to generating valid tests: Application to abstract reasoning. *Psychological Methods, 3,* 380–396.

Embretson, S. E., & Gorin, J. S. (2001). Improving construct validity with cognitive psychology principles. *Journal of Educational Measurement, 38,* 343–368.

Embretson, S. E., & Reise, S. P. (2000). *Item response theory for psychologists.* Mahwah, NJ: Lawrence Erlbaum Associates.

Embretson, S. E., & Wetzel, C. D. (1987). Component latent trait models for paragraph comprehension. *Applied Psychological Measurement, 11,* 175–193.

Fischer, G. H. (1973). Linear logistic test model as an instrument in educational research. *Acta Psychologica, 37,* 359–374.

Freedle, R., & Kostin, I. (1993). *The prediction of TOEFL reading comprehension item difficulty for expository prose passages for three item types: Main idea, inference, and supporting idea items* (No. RR-93-13). Princeton, NJ: Educational Testing Service.

Gorin, J. S. (2005). Manipulation of processing difficulty on reading comprehension test questions: The feasibility of verbal item generation. *Journal of Educational Measurement, 42,* 351–373.

———. (2006). Test design with cognition in mind. *Educational Measurement: Issues and Practice, 25,* 21–35.

———. (2009). Diagnostic classification models: Are they necessary? Commentary on Rupp and Templin. *Measurement: Interdisciplinary Research and Perspectives, 7,* 30–33.

Gorin, J. S., & Embretson, S. E. (2006). Item difficulty modeling of paragraph comprehension items. *Applied Psychological Measurement, 30,* 394–411.

Gorin, J. S., & Svetina, D. (2008). *SAT Critical Reading Q-Matrix Study: LLTM analysis of Q-matrix attributes.* Technical report submitted to the College Board.

Huff, K., & Goodman, D. P. (2007). The demand for cognitive diagnostic assessment. In J. P. Leighton and M. J. Gierl (Eds.), *Cognitive diagnostic assessment for education: Theory and Applications* (pp. 19–60). Cambridge, UK: Cambridge University Press.

Kintsch, W. (1988). The role of knowledge in discourse comprehension: A construction-integration model. *Psychological Review, 95,* 163–182.

———. (1994). Text comprehension, memory, and learning. *American Psychologist. 49,* 294–303.

Kintsch, W., & Keenan, J. (1973). Reading rate and retention as a function of the number of propositions in the base structure of sentences. *Cognitive Psychology, 5,* 257–274.

Kintsch, W., & van Dijk, A. (1978). Toward a model of text comprehension and production. *Psychological Review, 85*, 363–394.

Leighton, J. P. (2004). Avoiding misconception, misuse, and missed opportunities: The collection of verbal reports in educational achievement testing. *Educational Measurement: Issues and Practice, 23*, 6–15.

Messick, S. (1989). Validity. In R. L. Linn (Ed.), *Educational measurement* (3rd ed., pp. 13–103). New York: American Council on Education/Macmillan.

Mislevy, R. J. (1994). Evidence and inference in educational assessment. *Psychometrika, 59*, 439–468.

———. (1995). Probability-based inference in cognitive diagnosis. In P. D. Nichols, S. F. Chipman, and R. L. Brennan (Eds.) *Cognitively diagnostic assessment* (pp. 42–71). Hillsdale, NJ: Lawrence Erlbaum Associates.

Rasch, G. (1966). An item analysis which takes individual differences into account. *British Journal of Mathematical and Statistical Psychology, 4*, 49–57.

Rupp, A. A., & Templin, J. L. (2008). Unique characteristics of diagnostic classification models: A comprehensive review of the current state-of-the-art. *Measurement: Interdisciplinary Research and Perspectives, 6*, 219–262.

Rupp, A., Templin, J., & Henson, R. (2010). *Diagnostic measurement: Theory, methods, and applications*. New York: Guilford Press.

Sheehan, K. M., & Ginther, A. (2001, April). *What do passage-based multiple-choice verbal reasoning items really measure? An analysis of the cognitive skills underlying performance on the current TOEFL reading section*. Paper presented at the Annual Meeting of the National Council on Measurement in Education, Seattle, WA.

Sheehan, K. M., Kostin, I., & Persky, H. (2006, April). *Predicting item difficulty as a function of inferential processing requirements: An examination of the reading skills underlying performance on the NAEP grade 8 reading assessment*. Paper presented at the Annual Meeting of the National Council on Measurement in Education, San Francisco.

Tatsuoka, K. K. (2005, April). *Rule space method: Cognitively diagnostic statistical tool*. Paper presented at the Annual Meeting of the National Council of Measurement in Education, Montreal, QC.

Tatsuoka, K. K., Corter, J. E., & Tatsuoka, C. (2004). Patterns of diagnosed mathematical content and process skills in TIMSS-R across a sample of 20 countries. *American Educational Research Journal, 41*, 901–926.

VanderVeen, A., Huff, K., Gierl, M. J., McNamara, D. S., Louwerse, M., & Graesser, A. (2007). Developing and validating instructionally relevant reading competency profiles measured by the critical reading section of the SAT reasoning test. In D. S. McNamara (Ed.), *Reading comprehension strategies: Theories, interventions, and technologies* (pp. 137–172). Mahwah, NJ: Lawrence Erlbaum Associates.

Wang, C., & Gierl, M. J. (2007, April). *Investigating the cognitive attributes underlying student performance on the SAT Critical Reading subtest: An application of the attribute hierarchy method*. Poster presented at the Annual Meeting of the National Council on Measurement in Education, Chicago.

Wilson, M. (2005). *Constructing measures: An item response modeling approach*. Mahwah, NJ: Lawrence Erlbaum Associates.

NOTES

1. *Subskills* and *processes* are used to refer to any aspect or component of student ability or knowledge that could be subsumed by a more global ability that is often characterized as the construct measured by a test.

2. In addition to between-item specific characteristics, De Boeck and Wilson (2004) discuss between-person characteristics, as part of the psychometric modeling.

3. There is also an arbitrary normalization constant, omitted from equation (2).

Conclusion

John P. Sabatini and Tenaha O'Reilly

The authors of this volume can be considered pioneers in new but strikingly familiar territory. As advances in technology push the boundaries of what was seemingly impossible at one point in time, the vestiges of our core roots are still alive and visible. Smartphones, tablets, e-mail, and the Internet have drastically changed the vehicle of human interaction, but the fundamentals of discourse, communication, and what it means to comprehend have a long and familiar history. To neglect this history is to ignore proven methods that have withstood the test of time.

At the same time, as educational reforms such as the Race to the Top initiative, the Common Core Standards, and the Partnership for 21st Century Skills movement align and ripen simultaneously, the call for change has never been louder. To neglect this opportunity for advancing science and education is to deny innovative and potentially fruitful possibilities for the next generation. The crux of this dilemma of course is the challenge of how to promote a reform that is feasible, implementable, and sustainable in an environment that has seen so many promising solutions that had not so many promising endings.

The authors of this book and its companion piece have taken steps in the right direction by breaking down former barriers. Traditionally measurement specialists, cognitive scientists, and learning specialists have worked at arm's length of each other. The cross-fertilization of ideas and advances in the various disciplines was not communicated efficiently because of differences in taxonomy, practice, and end goals. By forging a line of communication, the authors have blazed a path for encouraging cross-fertilization and unity among researchers. Through their example, advances can be catalyzed by fueling communication with practitioners and policy makers to ensure that potential advances in science are realized as successes in practice. We need to avoid the pitfalls of the past by implementing innovations that are feasible and practical in the classroom.

Updating the construct of reading comprehension and utilizing the latest techniques in measurement are key steps for moving forward, but the ultimate judge of the next generation of reading assessments will be their added value for instruction. This challenge is no less daunting, but pioneers are explorers who are willing to take risks, stake claims, and pave the way for future generations.

Reaching an Understanding: Innovations in How We View Reading Assessment

Editor Biographies

John Sabatini is a senior research scientist in the Center for Global Assessment, Research and Development Division at Educational Testing Service in Princeton, New Jersey. His research interests and expertise are in reading literacy development and disabilities, assessment, cognitive psychology, and educational technology, with a primary focus on adults and adolescents. Currently, he is the principal investigator of an Institute for Education Sciences–funded grant to develop pre-K to 12 comprehension assessments as part of the Reading for Understanding initiative. He is also principal investigator in an NICHD-funded Learning Disabilities Research Center project studying subtypes of reading disabilities in adolescents and recently completed a NICHD/Department of Education/National Institute for Literacy grant studying the relative effectiveness of reading programs for adults. He also serves as a co-investigator on projects exploring the reading processes of adolescents, English language learners, and students with reading-based disabilities. He provides technical and research advice to national and international surveys including the National Assessments of Adult Literacy (NAAL), Programme for the International Assessment of Adult Competencies (PIAAC), and Progress in International Reading Literacy Study (PISA).

Dr. Sabatini was formerly an educational researcher at the National Center on Adult Literacy (NCAL) at the University of Pennsylvania. He received his doctorate at the University of Delaware in cognition and instruction with a focus on literacy and his bachelor's at the University of Chicago in behavioral science with a focus on neuropsychology.

Elizabeth Albro is currently the associate commissioner of the Teaching and Learning Division of the National Center for Education Research at the Institute of Education Sciences, U.S. Department of Education. Dr. Albro joined IES as an SRCD/AAAS Executive Branch Policy Fellow in 2002. Her responsibilities at IES have included serving as program officer for the Cognition and Student Learning, Reading and Writing Education, and Intervention for Struggling Adolescent and Adult Readers and Writers Research Programs. Throughout her research career, Dr. Albro has sought to build bridges across disciplines and looked for ways to learn from both basic and applied research agendas. Exploring the development of children's ability to tell and understand stories as a window into comprehension processes was one line of research she pursued. In other research, she has used children's ability to narrate about goal-directed events to examine young children's memories of events with liked and disliked peers in early childhood, their understanding of the process of conflict resolution, and the role of teachers in fostering solutions to conflicts in the classrooms.

Prior to coming to the institute, Dr. Albro was a member of the faculty in the Department of Psychology at Wheaton College in Norton, Massachusetts, and in the Department of Education and Child Development at Whittier College in Whittier, California. She received a B.A. in behavioral sciences, an M.A. in the social sciences, and a Ph.D. in psychology from the University of Chicago.

Tenaha O'Reilly is currently a research scientist in the Center for Global Assessment, Research and Development Division, at Educational Testing Service. His research interests are broadly concerned with improving the validity of reading and writing assessments. In particular, he is interested in developing ways to measure and control for variables that may impact the interpretation of reading and writing scores. These variables include background knowledge, student interest and motivation, and print skill efficiency. Dr. O'Reilly is also interested in developing ways to use assessment as a tool for modeling students' learning, memory, and transfer of ideas to novel situations. By blending the lessons learned from the domain of strategy instruction with assessment, assessments can be designed to both measure and support effective learning. To this aim, he has been a principal investigator and co-investigator on a number of projects geared toward developing cognitively based assessments of reading comprehension.

Dr. O'Reilly was formerly a researcher at the Institute for Intelligent Systems Literacy (IIS) at the University of Memphis. He received his doctorate at the University of Alberta in cognitive science with a focus on the application of prior knowledge and his bachelor's at Acadia University in psychology with a focus on reading strategy interventions.

Author Affiliations

Chapter	Title	Author(s)	Affiliation(s)
1	Assessing Multiple Source Comprehension through Evidence-Centered Design	Kimberly A. Lawless Susan R. Goldman Kimberly Gomez Flori Manning Jason Braasch	University of Illinois at Chicago University of Illinois at Chicago University of Pittsburgh University of Illinois at Chicago University of Poitiers, France
2	The Case for Scenario-Based Assessments of Reading Competency	Kathleen M. Sheehan Tenaha O'Reilly	Educational Testing Service Educational Testing Service
3	Assessing Comprehension Processes during Reading	Keith Millis Joseph Magliano	Northern Illinois University Northern Illinois University
4	Searching for Supplementary Screening Measures to Identify Children at High Risk for Developing Later Reading Problems	Donald L. Compton Amy M. Elleman Hugh W. Catts	Vanderbilt University Vanderbilt University University of Kansas
5	Assessment and Instruction Connections: The Impact of Teachers' Access and Use of Assessment-to-Instruction Software	Carol McDonald Connor Frederick J. Morrison Barry Fishman Christopher Schatschneider	Florida State University & the Florida Center for Reading Research University of Michigan University of Michigan Florida State University & the Florida Center for Reading Research
6	Multiple Bases for Comprehension Difficulties: The Potential of Cognitive and Neurobiological Profiling for Validation of Subtypes and Development of Assessments	Laurie E. Cutting Hollis S. Scarborough	Vanderbilt University Haskins Laboratories
7	NLP Methods for Supporting Vocabulary Analysis	Paul Deane	Educational Testing Service
8	An Explanative Modeling Approach to Measurement of Reading Comprehension	Mark Wilson Stephen Moore	University of California, Berkeley University of California, Berkeley
9	Cognitive Psychometric Models as a Tool for Reading Assessment Engineering	Joanna S. Gorin Dubravka Svetina	Arizona State University Arizona State University